Opening Education

We live in a society with ever-changing needs and expectations. Education practitioners and policy-makers need therefore to face the challenges of new economic, social and technological conditions in their work.

There is a global concern to develop forms of education and training which are open to the demands and needs of learners, and which are accessible at times and places suitable to those learners. Governments, institutions and practitioners are developing and implementing policies which reflect these ends.

The overall theme of this book is the relationships between government and organisational policies and the work of practitioners in open and distance learning. The book does this by exploring a selection of international examples.

The authors, many of them recognised experts, write from a wide range of international and organisational perspectives. Each one draws on significant experience within his or her field.

Terry Evans is Director of Research and Head of the Graduate School, Faculty of Education at Deakin University. He was the foundation director of the Master of Distance Education course there and has extensive experience teaching undergraduate and postgraduate students.

Daryl Nation is Deputy Head of the School of Humanities and Social Sciences at Monash University. He is Associate Professor in the School and divides his time between policy development, research and teaching.

Routledge studies in distance education
Series editor: Desmond Keegan

Opening Education

Policies and practices from open and
distance education

Edited by Terry Evans and Daryl Nation

ROUTLEDGE

London and New York

First published 1996
by Routledge
11 New Fetter Lane, London EC4P 4EE

Simultaneously published in the USA and Canada
by Routledge
29 West 35th Street, New York, NY 10001

Selection and editorial material © 1996 Terry Evans and Daryl Nation; individual
chapters © their contributors

Typeset in Times by Datix International Limited, Bungay, Suffolk
Printed and bound in Great Britain by T J Press (Padstow) Ltd, Padstow, Cornwall

British Library Cataloguing in Publication Data
A catalogue record for this book is available from the British Library

Library of Congress Cataloguing in Publication Data
Opening education / policies and practices from open and distance education / edited
by Terry Evans and Daryl Nation.
p.   cm.
Includes bibliographical references (p.   ) and index.
1. Distance education.   2. Non-formal education.   3. Education and state.
4. Open learning.   5. University extension.   I. Evans, Terry D. (Terry Denis)
II. Nation, Daryl.
LC5800.0676   1996   96–7571
                                                              CIP

ISBN   0–415–14182–6 (hbk)
ISBN   0–415–14183–4 (pbk)

Contents

Contributors

Ole Aabenhus is Head of Radio Production at DaniCom, Denmark, where he is a specialist in media development and the planning, management and organisation of communications systems. He is currently a consultant with DaniCom (Danish Development Communication Consultants), which is a division of the Danish Broadcasting Corporation. Since 1984 Ole has been actively involved in the design of communication strategies for rural development for a number of countries in Africa and Asia. He has also worked for many years as a journalist and editor in broadcasting and the print media in both Denmark and Japan.

Mick Campion is a senior lecturer in sociology at Murdoch University in Western Australia. He has published journal articles and book chapters analysing distance education and open learning theory and policy from a sociological perspective. Previously he has held a number of distance education related roles at Murdoch University and at the United Kingdom Open University in Scotland.
Email: campion@cleo.murdoch.edu.au

Angela Castro is Resources Officer at the Social Sciences Research Centre, The University of Hong Kong, where she assists in the University's teaching and learning quality process audit, teaches qualitative research methods, conducts workshops on computer-mediated communications for government departments and other educational institutions and freelances as a distance education and information design consultant. She has previously worked for Hong Kong University of Science and Technology, Hong Kong Baptist University and Deakin University (Australia). She has published widely on aspects of technology in open and distance education.
Email: acastro@hkucc.hku.hk

Terry Evans is Director of Research and Head of the Graduate School, Faculty of Education, Deakin University, Australia. He is a past vice president (Australasia and Oceania) of the International Council of Distance Education and was a member of the Executive of the Open and Distance Learning Association of Australia. He is on the editorial boards of the journals: *Open*

Learning; *Distance Education*; and *Media & Technology for Human Resource Development*. He was the foundation Director of the Master of Distance Education course at Deakin University. Terry has co-edited *Critical Reflections on Distance Education* (London, Falmer Press, 1989), *Reforming Open and Distance Education* (London, Kogan Page, 1993) and three *Research in Distance Education* collections (Geelong, Deakin University Press, 1990, 1992, 1994). He has also written *Understanding Learners in Open and Distance Education* (London, Kogan Page, 1994).
Email: tevans@deakin.edu.au

James Hall is the founding President of Empire State College, State University of New York (SUNY) and is also Vice Chancellor for Technology of the SUNY system. Holding a Ph.D. in American Civilisation from the University of Pennsylvania, he has served on the faculties of SUNY at Albany and Cedar Crest College. He is the author of *Access Through Innovation: New Colleges for New Students* (New York, Macmillan, 1991).
Email: jhall@sescva.esc.edu

Margaret Haughey is a Professor in the Department of Educational Policy Studies at the University of Alberta, Edmonton, Alberta, Canada. She was involved in a variety of distance education projects at the University of Victoria as a distance education instructor, course designer, media producer and university coordinator of distance education. Margaret is a past president of the Canadian Association of Distance Education. She has published widely on matters of distance education theory, practice and policy.
Email: Margaret.Haughey@UAlberta.ca

Viktor Jakupec is Director of the Masters of Distance Education and Training Management Programmes, in the Faculty of Education at Deakin University, Australia. He has substantial research and consultancy experience in open and distance education. He has published widely in the area of open and distance education policy.
Email: viktorj@deakin.edu.au

Richard Johnson was Professor of Classics at The Australian National University from 1962 to 1984, when he was appointed Secretary of the Department of Education and Youth Affairs of the Australian Government. From 1985 to 1987 he worked on distance education policy in the Commonwealth Tertiary Education Commission and the Department of Employment, Education and Training until his retirement in 1989. He is now a visiting fellow in the Centre for Continuing Education, ANU.
Email: richard.johnson@anu.edu.au

Brian Kenworthy is a senior lecturer in the Flexible Learning Centre at the University of South Australia. Previously he established and was Head of the Centre for Applied Learning Systems at Adelaide Institute of TAFE. He has also worked as a primary school teacher and teacher librarian within

Australia and Canada. He has carried out consultancies for aid agencies in Mongolia, the Philippines and Indonesia as well as being a consultant to the Commonwealth of Learning.
Email: kenworthyb@under.underdale.unisa.edu.au

Andrea McIlroy is a senior lecturer in the Department of Management Systems at Massey University in New Zealand. She teaches in the extramural programme and has research interests in distance education and also in quality management in service and manufacturing organisations. Andrea is currently completing her Ph.D. which examines aspects of quality in university business studies off-campus courses. Andrea is a member of the Executive and the immediate past President of the Distance Education Association of New Zealand. She chairs the editorial board of the *Journal of Distance Learning*.
Email: A.McIlroy@massey.ac.nz

Roland Meighan is a founding co-director of Education Now Ltd and director and owner of Educational Heretics Press. He was appointed Special Professor at the University of Nottingham in recognition of his research and writing relating to alternative education, home-based education and flexible forms of learning. He has considerable experience as a teacher, university lecturer and educational consultant. Until recently, he was a longstanding editor of *Educational Review*. He is the author of many books including *A Sociology of Educating* (London, Holt, Rinehart & Winston, 2nd edn, 1986), *Flexischooling* (Ticknall, Education Now, 1988), *Learning from Home-Based Education* (Ticknall, Education Now, 1992) and *Theory and Practice of Regressive Education* (Nottingham, Educational Heretics Press, 1993).

Daryl Nation is Deputy Head of the School of Humanities and Social Sciences at Monash University in Australia. He holds a position as Associate Professor in the School and divides his time between policy development, research and teaching. He has over twenty years' experience in teaching at a distance and extensive experience of integrating a variety of media into teaching. He was involved in the creation of an Open Learning Australia foundation course introducing students to university studies at a distance. Daryl has co-edited: *Critical Reflections on Distance Education* (London, Falmer Press, 1989) and *Reforming Open and Distance Education* (London, Kogan Page, 1993).
Email: daryl@mugc.cc.monash.edu.au

Santosh Panda is a Reader at the Staff Training and Research Institute at Indira Gandhi National Open University. He is seconded to the Association of Indian Universities, where he is Director of the Research Division. He is the editor of *Media & Technology for Human Resource Development*, an international journal of educational technology. He has extensive experience in staff development for distance education and educational technology and is the author of many articles in these fields.

Judy Roberts is an independent consultant in distance education, open learning and telemedicine based in Toronto. She has pioneered a number of Canadian distance education projects and has worked with technologies ranging from satellites to print and with applications from telemedicine to corporate reports. Her publications include *Classroom with a Difference* co-authored with Elizabeth J. Burge, and government reports such as *Distance Education and Open Learning* completed for the Council of Ministers of Education, Canada. Most recently she and Erin Keough co-edited the book, *Why the Information Superhighway? Lessons from Open and Distance Learning* (Trifolium Books Inc., Toronto).
Email: 102412.2033@compuserve.com

Andrew Robinson is Assistant Director (Europe) at the Open University in the UK. He has held posts in three British universities, as well as in the private sector (Rolls-Royce Ltd) and in England's largest regional development agency (the Northern Development Company) as Head of Research and Industrial Development. Before joining the OU in 1993, he was Head of the European Community office in the north of England. He is an evaluator for the European Commission's Esprit Programme in Information Technology.
Email: a.h.robinson@open.ac.uk

Robyn Walker teaches in the Department of Management Systems at Massey University in New Zealand. She teaches in the undergraduate and postgraduate extramural programme and has research interests in distance education and also in quality management in service and manufacturing organisations. Robyn has managerial experience in small business. She has particular research interests in productivity and quality, including best practice, which span both the manufacturing and service sectors. Robyn is a member of the editorial board of the *Journal of Distance Learning*.
Email: R.J.Walker@massey.ac.nz

Charles Wong is the Director of the School of Continuing and Professional Education, The City University of Hong Kong. He played an active role in the development of non-credit distance education programmes in Hong Kong during the 1970s and 1980s when he was in charge of distance education at The Chinese University of Hong Kong. Although his present portfolio is no longer restricted to distance education, he retains a strong interest in distance education research.
Email: cello@cityu.edu.hk

Foreword

Distance education has come of age. Traditional educators and government leaders the world over are its latest advocates as they struggle with the challenges of democratising higher education in increasingly difficult fiscal conditions. There is scarcely a modern university that is not significantly involved in distance education and many political leaders envision a virtual university of the future, one which is much more cost efficient and technologically based.

In such a context, one would expect such recent converts to look to experienced practitioners to understand better the lessons they have learned and to seek their advice in implementing new systems and programmes. To a certain extent, this has been the case, but too many of the newcomers are looking at distance learning through rose-coloured glasses as the new panacea for all the ills facing their educational systems today.

As one often asked to speak about distance education and the application of new technologies to learning, I frequently disappoint my audiences – many of whom are technological zealots – by adopting a critical stance and using my experience in distance learning to demonstrate its shortcomings and the importance of student support and effective design. I emphasise that distance learning is simply another means to encourage students to become independent lifelong learners and that one must start with the learning needs of the students, not, as is so often the case, the fancy new technology itself.

One should not be too surprised to encounter such zealotry, however, for distance education itself has not been particularly characterised by a critical perspective. Open universities were so successful from the outset that there was little tendency to worry about completion rates or the quality of interactive learning they represented. The success of the British Open University and its many offshoots around the world was attributed by many to its innovative 'industrial' approach to learning, with its emphasis on team-based course design incorporating the principles of behaviourism and competency-based learning.

This success, however, may have been as much a product of providing access and opportunities to already self-directed learners who were simply waiting for the chance to prove themselves than to any breakthrough in learning theory. Understandably, as in any fledgling field, early work was primarily advocacy for distance learning but, with maturity and experience, more and more theorists focused on the quality of the learning experience and helping students to avoid the one-way tyranny of printed materials and isolated learning situations.

Terry Evans and Daryl Nation are among the best known of a small group of theorists who have greatly raised the profile of the critical perspective in distance education and open learning. Building on the work of theorists such as Anthony Giddens, and on the work in distance education of David Harris, Alistair Morgan and others, their first book, *Critical Reflections on Distance Education*, became a rallying point for distance educators with similar concerns around the world. Their own longstanding collaboration at a distance is an example of the approach they advocate. In this new contribution, they have maintained the unique model of dialogue and constructive criticism among the authors from the many countries, thus achieving a varied international perspective within a common core of concerns, ideas and experiences.

This, the latest in their series of edited texts and part of the Routledge studies in distance education, is an admirable effort to broaden the debating platform by reaching out to those in mainstream institutions less familiar with distance education. The universities that most effectively emphasise learning rather than teaching, that find ways to change radically their prevailing cultures and which make the most effective use of faculty time will be the leading institutions of the future. They would be well served in these endeavours by the lessons from open and distance education represented in this text.

It is an honour for me to write the foreword to this book and I am grateful for the opportunity to recognise the leadership role that Evans and Nation continue to play in ensuring that, in promoting and developing distance education, we never lose our critical perspective.

Ross Paul
President
Laurentian University
Sudbury, Canada
December, 1995

1 Opening education

Global lines, local connections

Terry Evans and Daryl Nation

The emergence of mass education opened new possibilities for the rising generations to become members of their developing industrial societies. All children were taught to read, write and calculate, and to understand something of their history and culture. Practical domestic and industrial skills were taught, and religion retained a place in the curriculum. In these senses, mass education fuelled the emergence of democracies and the technological bases of industrialising economies. Literate citizens and workers could use and contribute to the stored – essentially printed – stock of knowledge of successive generations. They could form political ideas in more codified and collective ways, and give effect to them through the struggle for and within democratic political structures. They could become members of a more adaptable and productive workforce and, increasingly, a well-informed and demanding mass of consumers.

Literacy empowered the masses to pursue their own interests, but it also provided power to those who developed and controlled the emerging mass media. They could publish newspapers and journals for a mass readership and, thereby, inform and shape the attitudes, opinions and values of society at large. Radio and television may not require the same sort of 'reading' as their print predecessors, but no-one doubts their capacity to influence the collective consciousness of communities and nations. These electronic broadcast media do not necessarily require a literate audience, giving rise to their power in non-literate societies. Computer-based communications and information storage and retrieval technologies are now providing yet another generation of mass media with the capacity to transmit knowledge of almost incredible diversity, with immense speed, on a global basis.

As the proponents of the information age remind us, the growth in the stock of knowledge stored by and accessible through the information technologies (IT) is profound. Education plays a vital role in enabling this stock of knowledge to be created and used. Without a mass of sufficiently educated people, computer-based communications via the Internet would only exist in small and very specialist forms. This is not to suggest that the entire world's population has good access to the Internet. As Chapter 4 by Ole Aabenhus and Brian Kenworthy shows, struggling nations such as Mongolia have many transport and communications infrastructure problems which make many forms of telecommunications, for example, quite difficult. Angela Castro and Charles Wong (Chapter 10) make the point that even in Hong Kong, Internet access is still something which is beyond the grasp of many potential students, let alone the population at large. The Internet might embrace the globe, but many of the world's places and people remain untouched.

Contemporary educators and policy-makers, in both the 'developed' and 'developing' worlds, need to recognise their place in the emerging computer communications order and in the diversity of knowledge and experience which it avails to people. It is becoming increasingly difficult for educators in the developed world to close their classrooms and curricula to national and global diversities. Their professional responsibilities mean that today's educators and educational managers need to be more 'open' than ever before, not only to learners' needs and contexts, but also to the policies of governments and to the broader global influences on curriculum, pedagogy and educational technology. Although relatively 'closed' educational structures may well persist, an increasing number and variety of educational endeavours – from the school classroom to the university or college classroom and laboratory – are opening their doors to new technologies and approaches. Margaret Haughey and Judy Roberts's chapter (Chapter 6) is testimony to the complexity of national and provincial policies in this regard, evident in nations like Canada. The influence of international, even global, technologies and practices is clearly evident.

This book provides international insights from the experiences of educators, educational managers and policy-makers, who are opening their practices and policies in response to the changing circumstances surrounding them. As we have previously asserted, there is an increasing diversity of knowledge and media which educators today need to heed. This book also reflects a diversity. We have invited contributors from a variety of nations to report and reflect upon the different educational policies and practices in which they are involved. Some of the national contexts are amongst those facing turbulent social, political and economic change: Mongolia, Hong Kong and some nations of Eastern Europe are dealing with such changes. *Opening Education* is an integral part of the process, as Andrew Robinson (Chapter 3) demonstrates with regard to Eastern Europe; the links with Western European educational endeavours in distance education are important resources in dealing with these changes. Although these are particularly noteworthy national and regional examples, it is obvious that all nations face changes at present and have done so to varying degrees, throughout their histories.

In recent times, the speed of change seems to be particularly rapid, although it is arguable that each generation since industrialisation shares a similar view of the rapidity of change. There is a dynamism to the broader social change surrounding us which enmeshes virtually every aspect of society. Education is a major social institution with a fundamental role in these changes. Education is simultaneously a cause, a consequence and a facilitator of change within society. Education is also a 'conservatising' institution to the extent that it is concerned with fostering established values and knowledge in the rising generation. There are serious contradictions in education's role: on the one hand conserving traditions and, on the other, generating change. In several respects this book provides examples in which the tensions between these two positions are explored. To the extent that each chapter is concerned with *opening education* to the demands and circumstances of the future, then these chapters represent people who are wrestling with educational and social traditions rooted in the past in order to achieve contemporary and future goals.

The increasing sophistication and specialisation of contemporary society, especially with regard to the nature of work and new technologies, is producing changes to the ways in which education is used, developed and presented. Lifelong learning, professional development and workplace training have existed for many decades. However, these formerly minor aspects of education are now expanding so rapidly that they now constitute an equal or greater proportion of the profile of many universities and colleges. This is not only producing changes in the types of students or even the types of courses offered in universities or colleges, but is also engendering radical changes in the way these courses are taught. Put simply, educational institutions are being required to 'open' their structures and practices to the needs of these new students, their employers and governments, in ways that are shaking the traditions of those institutions. Indeed, all these groups are now regarded as sources of clients or customers for schools, colleges, universities and other providers of education such as 'information services'.

This newfound openness is often interpreted relatively narrowly, despite the attachment of names such as 'open learning', 'open campus' or 'flexible learning'. Many interpretations are narrow because they often deal with matters of 'access' and 'delivery' in rather mechanistic or 'industrial' ways which are controlled by the institution. Certainly, there are often important improvements for the students in comparison with traditional education, but many of these 'new approaches' differ little, if at all, from distance education as it has been practised for the last three decades. The terms 'open' or 'flexible' have been deployed more recently to serve marketing and political purposes. There are institutions that have been open in more deliberately educational ways and, for example, take issues such as a student-centred curriculum very seriously. James Hall's contribution (Chapter 2) stems from one such institution in the USA. Indeed, the consequences of using total quality management approaches in open and distance education, as Andrea McIlroy and Robyn Walker illustrate (Chapter 11), are a form of 'openness' to the student-as-client/customer which situates student interests at the heart of the organisation's interests.

It is at this point that the role of distance education comes into focus. In several respects institutions that practise distance education have already encountered many of the changes now being faced by traditional institutions as they seek to engage in forms of open education: flexible learning, distributed training, open learning, resource-based learning, independent learning. Distance educators and their institutions have sought to develop different structures and practices in order to provide and sustain worthwhile educational experiences for students who are usually remote from them. However, distance education has increasingly catered for students for whom distance itself is not their major problem, rather it is the scheduling of classes that is problematic. Distance education provides 'time-flexible' learning for these people and enables them to study without having to disrupt their work or family lives in order to attend classes. Of course, distance education institutions have always applied schedules of a kind, often they have been analogues of the traditional campus-based teaching, so that assignment submission dates, exam times, and teaching periods mirrored those of the traditional university or college. But the regular attendance timetable has disappeared, eliminating a major stumbling-block for a host of students seeking to improve their qualifications.

Members of distance education organisations have almost invariably seen themselves at the margins of educational endeavour. Those within 'dual-mode' organisations have often occupied places at the margins within those institutions; others, in 'single-mode' organisations, teaching exclusively at a distance, have had to cope with marginal valuing from their counterparts in conventional institutions and at times from education bureaucracies and governments. It is not surprising, therefore, that at national and international levels, distance educators and their institutions have often worked communally through their professional associations or through forms of collaboration or networking to sustain and enhance their practices. The contributors to this book have all emerged within these networks and their contributions often reflect the consequential communality. In some respects, the marginality of distance education has contributed to a degree of national and international connectedness between its practitioners which is unusual in other forms of education. It is time that this knowledge was shared more widely.

It is not only the marginality of distance education that provides an important incentive for national and international connections between the participants, but also the nature of the practices and technologies of distance education that predisposes both the individuals and their organisations to interact more effectively than might otherwise be the case. As the practices and technologies have developed in recent times, especially in terms of computer and telecommunications technologies, so the capacity for national and international connections has also developed. In this sense, distance education has been at the cutting edge of the globalisation processes which are a feature of the contemporary world. Distance education has marked as one of its distinguishing features – as the term 'distance education' implies – the means to provide education at times and places determined as much by the students as by the institutions they are enrolled with. Changes to time–space relations are a consequence of a long lineage of developments going back to prehistoric times. Means of transport, for example, have usually affected both the spatial and temporal conceptions of those involved. As mentioned previously, the development of literacy and, later, printing had profound effects on human understanding and culture; however, these are also fundamental elements of the development of the means of storage, transmission and use of knowledge. These means are, in turn, fundamental to the practice of distance education.

Print, audio and video materials, computer communications and telecommunications, or satellite television are all media used in distance education, and often in forms of open education. It needs to be recognised that these media are also essential to globalisation. As these technologies come to the fore, practitioners in open and distance education – from schooling through to lifelong education – are rapidly endeavouring to adopt and adapt them to their purposes. The new computer-mediated communications technologies are the ones which most strongly contribute to globalisation and are the ones to which practitioners in open and distance education are becoming most attracted. These technologies are proving to be so attractive and pervasive in the community more broadly that policy-makers and politicians are becoming enthused. The chapters by Viktor Jakupec (Chapter 7) and Richard Johnson (Chapter 8) chart the ebb and flow of such policies in Australia, Santosh Panda (Chapter 9) does likewise about India, as do the chapters mentioned previously concerning other nations, by Angela Castro and Charles Wong, Ole Aabenhus and Brian Kenworthy, James Hall and Andrew Robinson. Traditional educational institutions and their members are seeking ways to embrace the new technologies and, in so doing, they are reforming their educational approaches. This may be seen as *opening education* within those traditional institutions to the extent that broader choices of curriculum and learning are available. Of course, some uses of new technologies can produce or sustain forms of educational closure: for example, some (potential) students may have access difficulties to equipment or communication services. The point is, however, that the very change of medium and technology may be seen to promote or provoke an opening of educational practice within traditional educational institutions. Shifting from the classroom to print, or to electronic media, for example, requires teachers, administrators, librarians and others involved in the educational endeavour to re-think, and possibly be more open in, their practices.

There is a danger here, in that typifying other than open and distance education institutions as 'traditional', ignores not only the conservatism of all institutions, including those involved in open and distance education, but also the progressivism that can often drive educational practitioners and organisations of all kinds. Distance educators have no exclusive right to provision of education outside the classroom. In Chapter 5, Roland Meighan illustrates this point through a discussion of home education. Not only does this form of education have a long history, but also, in part, it was a response by parents to the 'closure' of traditional schooling. Home-based education is, for some, a progressive, independent alternative which is more open to the needs of the children involved. However, distance education in the school sector, as Margaret Haughey and Judy Roberts explain in relation to Canada, is also an opening of another kind to the needs of children in remote and other circumstances who find traditional school attendance difficult or impossible. Of course, this leads to questioning what 'open' means in relation to education. It is probably fruitless to seek out a concise definition as if the term had been constructed to encapsulate a defined set of policies and practices. Rather, terms such as 'open learning' are slogans that are better avoided when critically analysing educational institutions and practices. Indeed, as Mick Campion illustrates in Chapter 12, 'open learning' can even be interpreted as 'closing minds'. This is not to deny that some people have sought to define terms within open and distance education. It may be useful to do so within particular contexts, but in a general sense the use of these terms as slogans means that a large degree of 'slipperiness' will prevail.

In this sense, it would be unwise for us to suggest that the contributors to this book all conform to a universally held view of what fits within open and distance education. Indeed, we have deliberately chosen some contributions because they push at the boundaries of what many within open and distance education would probably consider to be outside the field. We have selected a diversity of examples from the field, and although the chapters could be grouped in various ways – for example, in terms of their sectoral, intellectual or national contexts – the intention is that each contribution should stand alone. We have organised the chapters in a sequence related to our purposes in Chapter 13, but there is no reason why the chapters could not be read in any order. We trust that the contributions provide readers with experiences of the diversity in the field and stimulate them to consider new possibilities in their own policies and practices.

2 The revolution in electronic technology and the modern university

The convergence of means

James Hall

CONVOCATION

A fundamental change in the conceptual structure of the traditional university is now apparent. Because many of our assumptions about the purpose and structure of distance education are rooted in fixed assumptions about the traditional university, it is useful to focus upon the university as it has existed for several centuries. During that time, the prevailing structural assumptions about the traditional university were developed through experience, adversity and opportunity. Today, those very assumptions are being challenged everywhere, faster in some places than in others, but surely and steadily, throughout the world. Few will disagree that technology, having radically altered the way manufacturing and business are conducted, is at last changing the way the university functions as an institution of higher learning. But, aside from the automation of formerly tedious processes, few observers recognise in the university the same structure-shattering technological changes that have already transformed the way business is done in many other sectors of society. The meaning and extent of technologically induced transformation can best be understood if one thinks about the organising concept of the university itself. A changing organising concept of the traditional university will soon alter this contextual frame of reference so completely that distance educators ignore it at high peril.

For nearly a millennium, the organising concept of the university could best be described by the word *convocation*. Beset in its earliest manifestation by an often barbaric and intrusive world, and fearful that, in a moment's time, the knowledge and wisdom passed down from generation to generation, recorded painstakingly in precious, hand-lettered parchment manuscripts, could be suddenly and irrationally erased from the human record, the university has always organised for defence. Small pockets of scholars, huddled together within moated or cloistered, even fortified, walls blossomed over time into a fortuitous calling together of the finest minds, the most precocious students, the distinguished collections of monographs, texts, serials and artefacts that came to be libraries or bibliothèques, and the study spaces, commons, laboratories and lecture halls that both scholars and students cohabited. This convocation of academic people, scholarly things and convening places constitutes what we have traditionally thought of as the university. For this traditional university, the controlling concept has been to bring together, to convene in a single place, for all time, for the select few who could use them, these resources of scholars, students, books and facilities. Even today we celebrate this concept through a symbolic university ceremony of convocation at the start of each academic year.

For example, the State University of New York (SUNY), in the short space of forty-five years, has constructed a major university system, based on the concept of convocation. Today it is a leading, internationally recognised example of a large, multi-campus, public university system. Over US$5 billion has been expended on building SUNY's campuses; its libraries hold in excess of 35 million items; and over 30,000 faculty members are associated with the academic departments. Today, its annual operating budget exceeds US$2.5 billion. In the past twenty-five years, similar huge investments in the traditional university structure have occurred throughout the world.

As an organising concept, convocation has been powerful and pervasive. We appraise the quality of a university on the basis of how much academic wealth it convenes. What does a university own outright, manage, support and preserve? The more world-class the professors, the higher the intellectual profile of matriculated students, the grander and rarer the library holdings, and the finer the instrumentation in the laboratories, then the more generous the appraisal and, hence, the more prestigious the reputation of a particular university.

But throughout history, these attributes of university excellence have been in short supply. As long as universities have functioned, there has been a shortage of the best minds, a scarcity of the necessary books for these minds to use. The scarcer the item, the more prestigious to have it. Those institutions that could call together more of these scarce commodities than their rivals were appraised as the best. Sometimes universities have even engaged in an intellectual shell game, drawing precious scholars from around the world to the highest university bidders.

In fact, all of the university's traditions and practices assume that *scarcity* is the controlling condition of educational opportunity. As a result, the opportunity for students to pursue a university education must be rationed, parcelled out, limited to those most qualified to benefit from it. To a remarkable extent, this sense of scarcity drives the assumptions and understandings about what university learning is and should be. Consequently, convocation is not only a 'calling together' of academic wealth, but it implies, as well, conditions of scarcity. Convocation and scarcity are structural Gemini.

The scarcity of first-quality scholars and first-rate resources has fostered a sense of exclusivity among those who guard the gate. In the United States, when President Franklin Roosevelt proposed opening universities to returning World War II veterans, Robert Maynard Hutchins of the University of Chicago said that the university would be admitting 'intellectual hoboes'. Too often, the most critical qualitative measure of a university's excellence is how few of its student applicants can become matriculants, and the relative achievement profile of each year's entering class in comparison to that of an institution's closest competitors.

In these ways, convocation describes the university as it has been known in the past: calling together the scarce elements of intellectual excellence, promoting possessiveness and exclusivity. Through convocation, this traditional university guards its gates in ways not fundamentally dissimilar from the ways that nations have guarded their borders. Indeed, today's rivalries on the athletic field give physical reality to the more cerebral, intellectual competition behind the ivy-covered walls of academe.

Gradually, over the past century, the university of convocation has sought ways to lessen the problems of scarcity. It has attempted in many ingenious ways to open its doors to more students. The primary responses to student demand have been to increase the number of campuses and the size of the institution. Within SUNY, thirty two-year community colleges that offer essentially open admissions to close-to-home students, have lessened the pressures for places that might otherwise descend on the baccalaureate-level institutions. These colleges have also helped to keep the costs of an associate degree relatively low and so accessible to more people. But these responses, valuable as they have been in responding to democratic demands for enrolment, have increased the qualities of excellence only at the margin.

In fact, one of the most critical debates, over the years, has been with regard to the importance of size in the university. Many years ago, a college or university of relatively small size was considered highly desirable. But when the numbers of students seeking entrance to a university education increased exponentially following World War II, very large institutions became the norm. Not only could these rapidly expanding, often publicly supported 'Land-Grant' giants bring together vast troves of educational resources, they could also pay the biggest academic salaries, attract the most renowned scholars, and maintain the most extensive collections of bibliographic resources, especially scholarly journals. Most remarkably, they could do all of this and yet remain surprisingly cost-efficient. Sheer size of the student body made it possible to support the widest range of curricula, and post-baccalaureate programmes through the doctorate in every imaginable field of study (not to mention a complex of highly competitive athletic teams!). For several entire academic generations, size of student enrolment was usually considered a positive value. The institutional behemoths of the American Midwest are testimony to this massive effort to respond to democratically inspired student demand.

In the United States, even increasing the size of single institutions could not fulfil the demand. Within the boundaries of the states, many individual institutions were forged together into enormous university systems, creating mega-universities of prodigious size and academic scope. During the 1960s, for example, the State University of New York became a system of seventy-two physically separate campuses, headed by a single, governing board of trustees and administered by a chancellor. Today, its total student enrolment is 400,000 students. Comparable conglomerates were fused in California, with its three very large systems, and in many other American states. More recently, this same phenomenon has been experienced elsewhere across the world as burgeoning demand for post-secondary access has occurred in political democracies. Recently, Patrick Callan, executive director of the California Higher Education Policy Center, referred to these large centralised and hierarchical systems as 'characteristics of a passing industrial age' (1994, p. 17). And just as technology has caused the passing of the industrial age, so technology challenges convocation as an organising concept of the university.

DISTANCE EDUCATION AND THE TRADITIONAL UNIVERSITY

In this climate of high demand and university scarcity, many nations of the world have created new distance learning institutions. Conceptually, distance learning aimed to extend access to those many students, including those bypassed at an earlier stage of life, who could not gain entrance to a university campus. In the United States, distance learning programmes appear to have been a legitimate response to the needs of many part-time and working adult students who could not travel easily or regularly to a campus. Indeed, these are the 'traditional' distance learning students, and the evidence of widespread success with such students is recorded in a number of published research studies.[1]

Distance education, of course, is one of the most significant ways that the traditional university has sought to respond to scarcity. Distance education is, first and foremost, a movement that sought not so much to challenge or change the structure of higher learning, but a movement to extend the traditional university, a movement to overcome its generic problems of scarcity and exclusivity.

In this sense, 'distance education' is a term that can be understood only in reference to the university of convocation. Distance education is distance from the classroom, distance from sitting at the foot of the professor, and distance from the physical campus. The history of distance education is familiar enough for it to need no further rehearsal here. It is sufficient to this argument to stress that distance education developed as a creative political response to the increasing inability of the traditional university structure to grow bigger. Distance education dealt with the downside of size; that is, too many students in a single physical space. As such, institutions that feature distance teaching have filled an important niche unserved and, in the past, largely unwanted by the traditional university. The university would, in effect, reach out, offering not seats, but the opportunity to learn. Distance education developed when convocation, as an organising concept for the university, had reached its natural limits – limits in size, and limits in resources.

But distance education has itself suffered from shortcomings and scarcities that have made it difficult to operate, expensive to develop, and occasionally difficult to validate. All distance learning institutions have had to grapple with three fundamental problems. One problem is the continuing cost and quality of communications. Whether it be the postal strike that greeted the inauguration of the British Open University, or the absence of reliable telephone services, distance learning is bedevilled by unreliable communications infrastructures. In the most advanced nations, the usually reliable voice, data and postal communications are often less than ideal for student-friendly, teacher-to-student interactions. In developing nations, even the simplest of telecommunications systems is frequently inoperable or absent altogether. Distance education has long suffered from the inadequacy of the infrastructure.

A second problem is how to maintain sufficient student contact and ongoing interaction with those who provide intellectual guidance, timely assistance when needed, and adequate performance feedback. Although distance learning courses overcome the scarcity of faculty instructional time experienced by the traditional university, the problem of adequate student–faculty engagement remains. Specialists have expended a lot of time and effort in attempting to devise ingenious solutions to this problem. But beyond an occasional telephone call to a student, an office visit at a study centre, or the written response to assignments, the lack of timely and frequent student-to-faculty interaction is one of the most difficult of problems to overcome.

A third problem is the availability of adequate resources, beyond the required texts, for extended student exploration and research. Distance courses are limited by the high cost and space limitations of set texts. In resource-rich nations, students do have the option of using the local library; in most of the world, library books are inaccessible and scarce. But even where libraries are relatively accessible, shortages of book copies, of available staff, and limited hours of operation that are convenient to distance students pose serious handicaps. The lack of adequate resources in distance education, as in traditional campuses, is an unsolved problem.

Practitioners in distance education have rightly looked to technology as the means to address and solve these and other problems. They have been among the first in seeing the promise of the technological revolution as a means of unlocking the door of access for students, and to help distance teaching institutions become the leaders of the 'new university'. This may indeed happen. But there exists another scenario that may be far more plausible.

CONVERGENCE

It follows from the argument advanced to this point that the issue for distance educators is not simply how to apply the new technologies to distance education. Rather, one must first consider how technology is redefining the university itself. Technology presents new opportunities not only to distance education. Technology is changing *all* of learning. Through applications of technology, the traditional university of *convocation* is about to become the university of *convergence*.

That this is so is seen in another phenomenon that has begun to appear in the university. Increasingly, students who are enrolled at traditional campuses are using distance courses or course modules. These distance courses or academic modules are used by students in the library, as supplements to classroom-based courses, in residence halls and even at home.

Distance is rapidly becoming a transparent factor in defining where learning occurs, where instruction originates, or where resources are housed and accessed. As a result, distance learning is beginning to lose its significance as a defining characteristic. Rather, resources for learning emanate from many places, some from a distance, some from close at hand.

The fact is that *distance* is rapidly becoming less important as the key descriptor for courses or students. Perhaps *networked* or *connected* learning will become a more accurate descriptor. Networked learning describes the growing availability of aids or alternatives that allow a student to review, speed up or substitute for some or all of what normally occurs in a classroom lecture through electronic links. Such networked options are becoming more commonly available, of higher quality, less costly to access, and thereby of much greater importance to every institution.

Because technology changes the meaning and efficacy of distance, the niche occupied by distance education will become less clear, and certainly less undesirable to the traditional university. In short, the university is in the process of deep structural change, and that change will lead to a new structural concept – the concept of convergence. This change opens new opportunities for distance learning, but it will also bring the full weight of the traditional university into direct competition with specialised distance learning institutions.

Indeed, the newest technology allows the traditional university to address some of its most critical and fundamental operating assumptions. Through applications of technology, possession, scarcity and exclusivity, the characteristics of convocation are replaced by wide access, multiplicity and replicability of resources. Exclusivity gives way to outreach and inclusiveness. Convergence replaces convocation as the organising concept of the university. As technology makes possible these new and very different conditions, the very structure of higher education is undergoing fundamental change.

One can visualise the university of convergence as a place of vast, perhaps limitless, exchange and interconnection, where research conducted by the most brilliant faculty is shared almost instantly with the relevant scholarly community and with the larger world. The exchange of ideas around the most cutting-edge research is immediately available throughout the world's intellectual community. The rarest texts are available within a short time, and increasing numbers of serials are available electronically the minute they are published. All of these resources will be available to anyone, anywhere, and, within limits, almost without financial restriction. Students in the university of convergence will learn to engage with information, understand how to use it, and gain the skills and intellectual competencies always associated with a university graduate. The faculties of the university of convergence will also take on aspects of the teaching role that have heretofore been less prominent or essential. The role of intellectual guide or mentor to the student will become more important as students pursue much of the formal instruction, formerly communicated through faculty lectures, in a variety of self-paced, student-directed modes. In fact, student planning and academic planning are likely to move to the very centre of the educational process for students and faculty as both seek to find and use the most useful available resources. The traditional university never gave this critical function more than lip service. Most faculty time was committed to direct instruction and research with little time reserved for direct engagement with individual students. The university of convergence will require a dramatic shift of time commitment towards advice for students.

Possession will not be the limiting fact of the university. Because possession is no longer critical to success, scarcity will also no longer be a controlling condition of the university. No longer will it be necessary for the university to aggregate intellectual wealth behind walls originally designed to defend and protect scholars from the assaults of a barbaric external world.

So, although technology offers solutions to the problems and limitations of distance education institutions, technology will also allow the traditional university to address its limitations as well. With technology, the university of convergence will be able to overcome the historic problems that made distance education necessary in the first place. Simply put, it will multiply the number of seats available to students. It will multiply the heretofore preciously hoarded resources for learning. Most significantly, it will multiply the capacity for students to review and master knowledge through self-paced, interactive study.

None of this will happen instantly or uniformly. Instruction, the most traditionally organised core function of the university, remains largely untouched by the technology revolution. Joseph C. Burke, former Provost of SUNY, calls the classroom lecture the element of university instruction most resistant to change. At least in the United States, scarcity is still defined on the university campus by the limited number of seats in the classroom and by the tightly defined classroom hours of instruction. The tyranny of the classroom hour, as noted by Robert Heterick of EDUCOM, is the remaining but nearly insurmountable obstacle to our overcoming the scarcity of instruction. When instruction – redefined as student learning – is unhinged from the classroom hour, the transforming possibilities of educational uses of technology will be complete. This may be more easily accomplished by non-American universities where the classroom and lecture have always been less important as measures of student accomplishment. In any case, when this change comes to on-campus instruction, as it came long ago to distance learning educators, then the application of technology will have changed the organising concept of the university itself.

How far away is the transformation of the university of convocation to a university of convergence? How many traditional institutions are ready to accommodate such fundamental changes? Are the faculties aware of the implications of these changes? Are they prepared to see their role as lecturer modified?

Until a few years ago, one might have asked similar questions about the permeability of political boundaries, or about the capacity of a dictatorship to control its people. What we have witnessed recently is that technology, in the form of ubiquitous communications, goes where it will. Traditional political controls cannot stop technology. When one organisation, through its dominance or its traditions, resists the use of a breakthrough technology, another organisation creates alternatives that compete with existing forms.

Technology will have a comparable effect on the traditional university. Distance learning, which itself has offered a competing form, will also be deeply affected, even as it pioneers exploring the uses of technology. If the university, in its traditional or distance form, does not adapt to the possibilities of technology, competing structures will surely spring up that can and will perform the tasks of the university.

TESTING THE THEORY IN THE CONTEXT OF THE STATE UNIVERSITY OF NEW YORK

Thus far, this has been a rather theoretical exercise in projecting the impact of technology on both the traditional university and distance education institutions. It may be useful, by way of illustration, to apply these concepts to actual conditions within SUNY. Today, the State University of New York comprises sixty-four distinct institutions, including medical schools, research centres, comprehensive undergraduate colleges of arts and sciences, colleges of technology, community colleges, and one distance learning institution; viz., Empire State College (ESC). SUNY serves a state population of 18 million persons, scattered from New York City and Long Island in the East, to Buffalo in the West, and to the Canadian border in the North.

In the 1960s, SUNY, in trying to reach out to populations that could not be easily served on a campus, and like many of the large, public universities of the Midwest, offered traditional courses at a distance through correspondence education. SUNY even created a 'university of the air', anticipating the use of broadcast television as an instructional medium. In 1971, SUNY established a new statewide institution, Empire State College, to demonstrate new ways of serving the adult, part-time, off-campus student. ESC was empowered to offer degrees through the MA, and to offer instruction throughout the state. Today, Empire State College serves about 10,000 of SUNY's students.

What was unique about SUNY/ESC was its focus on non-classroom and distance pedagogies, rather than on the then prevailing technology. (The PC and digital networks had not then been developed.) Beginning to offer instruction about the same time as the Open University in Great Britain, ESC developed the now familiar processes for which it is best known in the field of distance education: mentoring, contract learning and assessment of prior learning for advanced standing. Perhaps most interesting, however, is that its experiments were designed to move the entire SUNY system towards improved service to the off-campus or distance student. In this regard, Empire State was neither totally separate (as is the case with many freestanding national open universities), nor totally incorporated (as with so-called 'dual-mode' institutions). Its mission established ESC as an experimenting programme for SUNY, but its governance included its own full-time faculties and president. For the past twenty-four years, it has been the unchallenged distance learning institution for SUNY and beyond. But today, as the rest of the university system shifts from convocation to convergence, Empire State cannot assume exclusive service to distance students. Like all distance institutions, ESC needs to develop a new leadership role in meeting student needs.

The State University of New York, as a system, brings special capacities to the task. Its great size and formidable resources are of immense help as it plans for:

- the essential technological infrastructure,
- systems for sharing information, library and other resources,
- instructional course software and
- sharing of distance courses.

The first objective, installing and paying for a statewide information network, seems daunting. But if courses and library resources are to be available to all students, both on the campus (in the library, classroom or residence hall), and beyond the campus (the industrial work site, the community library, or the student's home), and at convenient, asynchronous times, then a wide-band, high-speed electronic network is required to link all sixty-four campuses to each other and to communications trunks that can reach into private homes. Currently, SUNY is testing just such links in three regions of the state. Some of the smaller American states have already installed such networks. The important point is that all universities will have access to this kind of infrastructure within two or three years.

Because no single educational institution can afford such an investment from a single annual operating budget, this technology infrastructure will be financed through long-term bonded debt. Collaboration with all of public and private higher education and with the public schools, as well as with other large agencies of government, will be essential in building and operating the necessary statewide networks.

Once the network is in place, important library, informational and instructional applications can be accomplished. Heretofore, SUNY has concentrated on creating the on-campus library software that allows faculty and students to enter distant databases, reach graphic and information libraries, and explore worldwide bibliographic search sources. Shortly, the libraries will begin to experiment with transmission of full texts of journal articles. In the long run, SUNY anticipates significant savings in the costs of library construction, book cataloguing and book and periodical storage.

A second objective is to reconceptualise the use of technologies. As a system, SUNY spends US$80 million annually for telephones, US$30 million for library book acquisitions and access to databases, and additional millions for computing and video production. It makes sense to begin to think of all these as parts of a whole. Formerly quite separate operationally, telephones and telecommunications, computing and electronic storage, and instructional technology now converge in planning and operations. There is a convergence of technologies.

A third, and certainly much more difficult, objective, is to begin to think of the convergence of instructional modes. Many of SUNY's campuses now express interest in offering courses at a distance, using the satellite, microwave and fibre-optic networks currently under development for system-wide use. Until recently, such interest was unheard of. Now, a number of campuses propose to form regional educational networks, sharing the costs of course development. For example, *EngiNet*, a new programme offered collaboratively by several SUNY schools of engineering, will soon provide live graduate-level courses in engineering across the state, both at participating campuses and at small business locations.

The health sciences institutions are experimenting with various forms of distance communication as well. The delivery of health care is shifting from inpatient to outpatient, and from acute episodic care to longitudinal lifetime care. This shift encourages patient-centred, home- and community-based services, distributed through large, coordinated electronic networks. Even the health professional education process is moving out of the more traditional academic medical centre into distributed, often distant, community settings. In order to deliver high quality, comprehensive care in community settings, providers must be connected by electronic networks which will make patient records, medical data and professional consultation instantly available wherever services are delivered. SUNY is working to provide the learning resources and medical information networks that are the critical components in making this possible. Perhaps the most intriguing demonstration of this distributed principle will be the SUNY rural health network. Such a health-services network will be coordinated by a virtual 'medicampus' that will connect full-time instructors from the faculties of nursing, medicine, allied health and public health. These instructors will practise within the network, and will also provide education for students in health professions located in rural settings.

So, while SUNY currently has in operation only one full distance degree programme,[2] additional already planned programmes will emerge in the near future.[3] Can lectures in the classroom, interactive seminars (both live and on-line), distance courses, and student-paced, multimedia course modules be linked in a wholly interchangeable set of instructional opportunities for students? And will the high-speed information networks be in place to support these academic programmes? Such a convergence of instructional modes and information systems will be the greatest challenge that SUNY has faced.

This challenge is most pronounced in dealing with the problems and issues raised by distance learning. In this area, distance educators are already far ahead. But the traditional university is increasingly active and SUNY is no exception. Three years ago, a SUNY President's Commission on Distance Learning strongly endorsed the development of distance learning across the entire state. The Commission focused on the 'nuts and bolts' of distance learning, including the following:

- Can several campuses share the initial high cost of course development? The investment capital required to develop even very short interactive software is very substantial. Currently, SUNY faculties from several campuses are pooling their expertise and funds to support the creation of new software. Among the most interesting is the development of an environmental sciences course that draws upon the expertise of specialists from the College of Environmental Sciences and Forestry, the Atmospheric Sciences Research Center, the Earthquake Center, the Marine Sciences Center and the River Sciences Center. Such a course will be used as an advanced placement study for talented secondary-school students in their last year of study, or for first-year students studying at a SUNY two-year college. Other examples include the development of a first-year chemistry course, including interactive simulated laboratory studies, and a first course in psychology.
- Which faculties *own* the degree course? Will it be acceptable for a distance course to be sponsored and credited by multiple academic departments located at separate campuses?
- How will otherwise competing institutions receive credit for student enrolment and for collected revenue? Since each campus receives its public budget appropriation based upon the number of students it teaches, can new accounting systems be developed to recognise the enrolment of students who work at a distance?
- How will courses be validated or accredited? Will the imprimatur of a sponsoring academic department be sufficient, as in traditional accreditation, or will alternative measures be needed? Can these costly courses be maintained and updated periodically, so that currency is sustained?
- How will faculty workload assignments and related contractual issues be determined? Since these are traditionally issues that are regulated by the collective bargaining agreement, involvement of the unions from the outset is an important requirement.

- Will it be necessary to synchronise the varied institutional academic calendars of each campus? Or will the new software be adaptable to different calendars? In the past, distance courses have required identical start and stop dates to accommodate the marking of assignments and administration of examinations. But this has been a straitjacket, severely limiting the use of such courses by multiple institutions.
- Can students take courses at multiple universities, compiling a whole degree from the offerings of different faculties? Such a pattern challenges the most fundamental concept of institutional integrity and may be the most difficult question to resolve.

Closely linked to all these questions is the fourth objective of faculty and staff training and development. Development has risen to the top of urgent matters that need renewed attention. If major changes are to occur in instruction itself, the faculty will need extensive opportunity to learn to cope with new systems and strange technologies. The established academic culture relies on the traditional lecture, both as a method of conveying to students the latest research and information, and as a strategy for teaching analysis and problem-solving. The university of convergence will require different forms of student–faculty and faculty–faculty interaction, including considerable asynchronous communication. Shifting away from the old pattern will require an extensive cultural change on the part of faculty and administration. Thus far, most opportunities for training have focused on introductory uses of computers and electronic mail, access to the Internet and access to distant databases for research. But the new, interactive modes of teaching and learning will require faculty expertise in authoring course modules, manipulating video images in the lecture hall and conducting complex experiments at a distance. No graduate schools have ever taught these skills to the current faculties of the university. Moreover, few faculties are trained to help students find and use multiple-learning resources and instructional aids beyond those normally associated with the classroom. Yet it seems clear that the emerging faculty role will begin to replace the older patterns of teaching through lecture and discussion. The faculty role will shift towards one of its most critical, but underdeveloped facets – that of mentor or intellectual guide.[4] In similar fashion, the librarian role will shift towards helping students and faculty navigate through a sea of information riches. Both faculty and librarians will focus much more on steering students, one at a time, through customised, often interactive or self-paced learning and research opportunities.

This shift of pedagogy will require training and development that go far beyond learning how to use the Internet, or discovering ways to manipulate the newest software-authoring system. These capabilities must be supported, of course, but the university must also prepare its faculty for a transformed teaching and learning environment.

CONCLUSION: WHAT IS THE FUTURE OF DISTANCE EDUCATION?

What, then, is the future for established distance education, as it has come to be known, when the so-called traditional university is no longer traditional? What will happen to distance education, firmly rooted within the traditional, when convergence, as an organising principle, replaces convocation? One might deduce, from the analysis thus far, that distance education, as it has been known, has a dim future. Indeed, that might be true, were it not for the distinguished track record of achievement during the past several decades of the now large and prominent existing distance learning institutions, which have a long head start on the traditional university in using multiple pedagogies. That lead will not last, but it will ensure, at the least, that distance institutions are in the game. That timing gives distance learning institutions an opportunity to lead the way, themselves becoming universities of convergence, fully engaged in networked learning.

Collectively, distance educators have great expertise in solving problems associated with education beyond the classroom. This expertise could be applied to help all of higher learning solve the intellectual, developmental, financial and logistical problems associated with convergence.

Moreover, distance educators can participate in this effort in less isolation than in the past, involved more fully with the intellectual mainstream. Significantly, distance educators will also have access to more financial resources by working with partners who, at the end of the day, control most of the resources available for higher learning.

Distance educators can also focus greater attention on comprehensive planning, and give attention to often ignored, but essential, research. A great need exists for information on the effectiveness and related costs of distance or connected learning. While a great deal of research has focused somewhat narrowly on comparisons between distance and traditional learning, or on the logistics associated with older systems of distance instruction, very little study has examined the new relationships between pedagogies that the new technologies make feasible.

In sum, distance educators need to forge new partnerships with the traditional university, collaborate in creating new systems, academic course software and supporting networks for information transmission. Such partnerships will hasten the day when the essential new systems to support a university of convergence will be available, not only to distance students, but to *all* students.

Distance administrators can also be a moral force in promoting the uses of technology to support the values of the university, rather than allowing technology to dictate its values. Workers in distance education know what is needed by students who are working on their own, away from the support structures of the campus. There will be lots of opportunity ahead to use this expertise, especially if the university is to prevent opportunists from commandeering the world of the virtual university.

In the end it will not be its traditional physical trappings, nor its extended distance forms, neither convocation nor convergence, that will guarantee the university's continuing significance to our global society. That significance will be assured by maintaining the central values of the university: viz., helping students to learn and grow intellectually, creating a climate within which scholars can create and test knowledge, and reaching out to enlighten a civilised community. The convergent, networked university, in which all must be full partners, can help achieve that worthy purpose.

NOTES

1 In particular, the studies found in *Open Learning*, *The American Journal of Distance Education* and publications of the International Council for Distance Education (ICDE) are useful references.

2 An upper division degree programme in Business and Management, offered by Empire State College through its Center for Distance Learning, and communicated via SUNY by satellite, a university-wide vehicle jointly sponsored by the Center for Learning and Technology at Empire State College and The New York Network of the Office of Educational Technology.

3 A list of the distance learning or student self-paced projects proposed by SUNY campuses and funded by the Office of Educational Technology is available in a brochure entitled *1993–94 Campus Technology Development Projects*. A large number of SUNY campuses in all sectors are involved.

4 For a thoughtful and comprehensive examination of this new role as it has developed at one institution, see the report of the Mentor Role Committee (1994).

3 Policy implications for distance education in the European information society

Andrew Robinson

AN EMERGING PRIORITY

In this century some defining ideas, with their origins in Europe, have assumed global force, often after periods of intense conflict: communism, fascism, capitalism. All have contested, not all have endured as internationally accepted concepts. Technology, however, has internationalised social habits at least in the developed world: in tourism, motor-car usage, the development of a television culture. Although the move towards literacy and a better educated workforce has a worldwide reach, the national apparatus to cope with the changes of the information age are now showing signs of friction. Perhaps unusually, schools, universities and, crucially, cross-border recognition of qualifications have largely resisted the pressures of internationalisation. In Europe, where the idea of the university began, this is a growing dilemma, particularly as the technology for information and education is redefining the role of teacher, learner and the academy as a whole. The European Union (EU) seeks a clearer role for itself as the wealthiest integrated economic area of the world, though one still retaining national educational systems struggling to cope with global economic forces now often dislocating and debasing Europe's employment patterns. Recent analyses and policy recommendations by the EU underline a growing sense of urgency in seeking to readjust educational frameworks largely set up in the nineteenth century to meet the challenge of rising joblessness and technology-driven opportunities in new ways to learn.

It would be attractive, but deceptive, to regard the recent importance given to distance learning, and to allied tele-activities in European policy-making, as a deliberate attempt by institutional Europe to strike out for politically safer ground after the contested adoption of the Maastricht Treaty. In fact, the Maastricht Treaty pays particular attention (Articles 29b, 129c) to Trans-European Networks in transport, energy and telecommunications, from which the link to distance learning (listed as an area for European Council (EC) action under Article 126 of the same Treaty) has emerged (European Union, 1992). Monetary and economic integration, a central theme of Maastricht, is understandably accompanied by traditional cohesion measures to accompany EU integration, particularly between its peripheral and central regions. What is now proposed adds a new and challenging dimension: spurring across the EU a convergence of education and tele-industries, and a reprofiled appreciation of open and distance learning (ODL) as an agent for educational access, technology transfer, regional development and the creation of jobs.

During and since the Maastricht conference and its ratification process, however, other external pressures have forced a change of emphasis to fill a gap in implementable policies, able to be presented at the next intergovern-mental conference of 1996. High unemployment in Western Europe, the simultaneous collapse of communism, the economic challenge of the USA, Japan and the 'Five Dragons' of South East Asia were all factors in this change of emphasis. Into this semi-vacuum were placed elements from the single market programme, the Single European Act, and some of the less con-tentious areas of the Treaty on European Union itself. A clear theme emerged: if the internal barriers were coming down, cross-border connections of all kinds needed to be made good. In the specific case of education, train-ing and work as the nature of work was changing across Europe, accelerated by the information technology (IT) revolution – the issue would be to see how lifelong learning could be allied to IT so that life and job chances could be broadened, and skills updated around 'portfolio' careers.

CONSENSUS AND CHALLENGE

Here was the genesis of a broad challenge – physical, intellectual, techno-logical, educational – around which an unexpected consensus was to emerge. It has also created a political consensus because it has the capacity to satisfy both the free-marketeers and would-be protectionists. Transnational net-works expand economic activity, reduce barriers to trade, yet at the same time require and enhance economic, educational and social integration. They also accompany and spur deregulation of telecommunications organisations (telecoms), hardware's and software's growing sophistication, and are a valuable sales platform for equipment producers. The latter is a particular opportunity for EU producers, though simultaneously an inducement for non-EU involvement.

At the same time, less spectacular internal changes have underlined the shift of emphasis: the EC structural funds, having been doubled from 1988 to 1992, have subsequently undergone substantial review, particularly for the types of infrastructure spending to be sanctioned, away from too heavy reli-ance upon physical infrastructure towards a balance between infrastructures and infostructures. Synergistic alliances between the structural funds and the research and development programme, the current form of which is called the Fourth Framework Programme (FP 4), have been suggested and with major priorities for funding given to the learning/IT interface in FP 4. Also, the sev-eral education- and training-related EC schemes (e.g. Comett, Erasmus) have been integrated into a new twin-pillar generation of funding programmes (Leonardo and Socrates), with a strong emphasis on distance learning.

The scene was therefore set for the emergence of a new priority of pan-European dimensions: the 'European information society'. From the European Commission's (1993) White Paper on *Growth, Competitiveness and Employment*, presented in December 1993 both as apologia for Maastricht and as blueprint for the twenty-first century, to the Bangemann Report of 1994, there has been a continuity and consistency of approach which appears to match that accorded the Delors/Cockfield plans for the single market, almost a decade before. But whereas the Cockfield implementation plan had in its sights the reduction across the board of internal barriers, the European information society is both generic and strategic, taking education, information, transport and health as the defining 'horizontal' policy areas. It is no co-incidence that Commissioner Bangemann's name is attached both to the EC's *Industry Policy Report* (1992) and to the *Report on the Information Society* (Bangemann, 1994).

THE BANGEMANN REPORT: IMPLICATIONS FOR DISTANCE LEARNING

The report is very ambitious: it claims significant benefits from the information society for Europe's citizens and consumers, for the content creators (such as open universities), for Europe's regions in terms of cultural expression and closer integration, for the more peripheral areas and for governments and administrations operating closer to local needs. As for business, the gains are set out in general terms for small and medium enterprises (SMEs), Europe's telecoms, satellite and cable operators, and for equipment and software suppliers.

To achieve all this the policy framework is to be driven by wider collaboration with the telecoms sector, interconnection and interoperability, harmonisation of tariffs, a public awareness campaign and a worldwide opening of information opportunities. Trans-European-based services would be provided through wider use of 'building block' technology services including Email, file transfer video services, Euro-ISDN, promotion of the Global System for Mobile Communications (GSM) in Europe and internationally, and common objectives by Europe's satellite industry.

Ten applications to launch the information society were called for, with distance learning ranked number two, after teleworking. Other applications include university and research networks, telematic services for SMEs and trans-European public administration networks. As to funding, the report believes the private sector and market forces should resource the programme, though it agrees that some EU funding may be required, with virement under the structural funds and the FP 4.

The European ambitions for distance learning will have to learn from best practice. With a track record of success in particular national contexts, especially where there is strong political support, it is evident that distance learning can only succeed if it is bold, ambitious and properly funded. It is both a content creator and a provider, in alliance with a deliverer (e.g. the Open University and the BBC in the national context of the UK). In a European context, broad strategic partnerships should now occur with EU's leading IT companies. And, as distance learning enjoys a leading priority in the report's action plan of applications, it is in a position to stimulate public demand and acceptance of the whole programme. As for funding, given the traditional acceptance by all states of the need for public funding for education, it is unlikely that the private sector alone would or could provide the necessary resources. The best alliance would be a mixed-economy solution of national and EU public support linked to private-sector European equipment providers.

THE WIDER CONTEXT

The information society challenge, like that of the single market, is also, as shown in 1994, a clear response to external challenges – to the US plans for 'information superhighways' and the more recent, but similar, projects in Japan. The distinction lies essentially in the concepts involved: the EU plan is for a European information society, in which citizens – as end-users – are held to be the beneficiaries – socially and economically – in the information age. In fact, 'knowledge society' would be a better descriptor than 'information society'. For the USA, the prime consideration appears to be the provider of the 'superhighway'; the societal gain may be assumed, but is not the enabling force.

The internal dynamics for the creation of the European information society, and of the role of distance learning within it, assume three broad 'drivers' in the following areas:

Policy

* Skills shortage.
* The unemployment situation.
* Remaining competitive with the rest of the world.
* Equality of opportunity.

Technology

* The European information technology industry is trying to compete with the rest of the world.
* The telecom companies are investing large sums of money into high-speed networks.

Education

- Movement towards more flexible approaches to learning.
- Movement towards lifelong learning.
- Emergence of the learning organisation and knowledge workers.

A salient feature of the European plans is that they revive the promise of broad social improvement by allying information, education, work and technology. This is almost a throwback to the visionary period of the 1960s, before oil price rises in the 1970s introduced a long period of retrenchment from such goals, enabled by the mixed economy.

TECHNOLOGY IN EDUCATION

The challenges facing the EU in making distance learning one of the motors of the information society are considerable. The current situation indicates how relatively little is currently spent on technology-based training in the EU:

- Within the current European Union there are about 85 million people taking part in some form of education and training every year, which accounts for just over one-third of the current population of the EU.
- The total European expenditure on education and training is estimated at 250 billion Ecus.
- Expenditure on open and distance learning adds up to about 1.7 billion Ecus. This is only 0.68 per cent of the total expenditure on education and training.
- Technology-based training amounts to 300 million Ecus, only 0.12 per cent of the total expenditure.

The media, and particularly television, are all-pervasive, of course, but not pervasive enough to widen access to education for all. In fact, broadcasting and other media, supported by ever-changing technology, are increasingly playing the role of an uncontrolled 'pirate teacher' and their strong influence should not be underestimated. In France, for example, statistics indicate that children spend almost as many hours per year watching television as

---

Annual statistics in France

Primary school pupils:
850 hours at school
790 hours watching TV

Secondary school pupils:
960 hours at school
930 hours watching TV

Source: Le Monde de l'Education n° 205, June 1993, p. 41

attending school. The opportunities for television to provide many hours of high-quality educational programmes have generally been missed. Whilst this scenario shows the scale of the challenge, some building blocks for the educational dimension to the European information society have been put in place, often through EU action.

These include currently:

- Research and development into using new learning communication technologies (FP 4).
- Developments towards the idea of a European training network.
- Partnership building between European open universities.
- Developments towards the idea of a European open university network (EOUN).
- Pan-European satellite-based education and training networks.

THE OPTIMIST'S PROMISE

The impact of the information revolution will be felt in essentially all aspects of human endeavour, not least in education. In most parts of the European Union, the current allocation and use of PCs in classrooms is generally small: most teachers and education officers know little about computers, and budgetary constraints are common. This will change as knowledge about equipment standards in competitor nations grows and Europe's educationalists become more attuned to IT. This trend will be reinforced by growing parental knowledge of IT, the continuing demands of the students themselves, the increasing availability of PCs and modems in homes and the universal availability of broadband network services capable of delivering cost-effective and easy access to on-line information services and distance learning techniques. There is widespread acceptance that the old pattern of lifetime employment will no longer be predominant; periodic retraining will be the norm in a globally competitive society. Only broadband communications to the home, school and factory offer the means of providing this.

PLUMMETING PRICES

In the field of electronics manufacturing, technology is delivering massive reductions in the costs of producing things. The microchip is a stunning example of mass production: it is now possible to make about 10 million identical transistors simultaneously by roughly the same set of processes as were required to make one, thirty-five years ago. The result has been progressive price reductions, to the point where today's highly complicated microprocessors at the heart of most computing tasks can be bought for roughly the same price as their simple predecessors of twenty years ago; and individual bits of electronic memory are priced at about a millionth of an Ecu. Moreover, the fibre-optic cables, on which broadband networks are based, are so efficient that the real cost of a telephone call, once determined by the length of copper wire over which it travelled, is now largely independent of distance.

Informed observers of the IT industry are unanimous in predicting that similar price reductions will continue for the foreseeable future. Sheer cheapness, which has already done much to motivate our acceptance of electronics and IT generally, will continue to drive the development of the information society.

EUROPE'S TECHNOLOGICAL BALANCE SHEET

These and other developments can rely upon 'tools' for telematics in distance learning now becoming more widely available, such as studio video-conferencing, desktop video-conferencing, satellite-based delivery and live interactive systems, audiographics tools and audio-conferencing.

The equipment manufacturers of Europe could be major beneficiaries of the Bangemann challenge, though they start from some weakness of market demand, supply and critical mass. Apart from big groups such as Philips, Alcatel, Olivetti, Hachette, British Telecom and STET, and alliances such as France Télécom and Lyonnaise des Eaux, or Deutsche Telekom and Bertelsmann, Europe's companies have a marginal position in the global multimedia market. In terms of the network providers, however, Europe has a comparative advantage in telecommunications, and especially satellite communications, and one it can exploit both internally and in the context of Eastern Europe, particularly as satellite costs fall.

Consumer demand for multimedia products and services is also lower in Europe than in the USA. Thirty-five per cent of US homes have a personal computer compared to only 15 per cent in Europe. Also some 60 per cent of all US workers are 'knowledge workers' today, according to Vice-President Gore's analysis, again a higher percentage than in the EU.

Telecoms manufacturers worldwide now realise that equipment becomes less important – and less profitable – than the services that feed into the equipment. This is found already in PCs and cellular telephones: the profits are most evident in providing the software or telephone networks, rather than making the hardware. It follows that the owners of networks will be the main beneficiaries, followed by those who provide the services. For Europe, a crucial challenge is therefore to develop quickly the ODL products and trans-European networks and to become the global centre of integration between its – and perhaps the world's – own education/training/development needs, its own industrial suppliers, and world-class suppliers attracted to Europe to provide both hardware and software. To bring this about, a programme beyond Bangemann is required, combining the industrial, consumer and network provider groups with the creation of at least one new European research centre to coordinate the necessary elements and programmes.

THE NEED FOR BOLDNESS

Giving an effective kick start to the ambitions of the European information and knowledge society requires boldness and breadth of vision to make any real impact. The challenge is extremely broad, given not only the economic strength of the EU, but also its cultural and linguistic diversity, its capacity for fragmentation, and the political tensions between the EU institutions, member-states, and regions. The Intergovernmental Conference (IGC) in 1996 promises to be contentious, especially on issues of defence and a single currency, and there may be little room to advance specific proposals in the field of training and education. At the same time, there is a strong case for saying that the creation of a European information and knowledge society, capable of creating jobs and confidence and forward-looking in its reach, should be the precondition needed to create the Economic and Monetary Union as outlined in the Maastricht Treaty.

The new policies may be the foundations capable of maintaining the EU consensus, not least because the UK, often a recalcitrant member, has a strong position in some of the key areas: the dominant role of the English language itself, a tradition of lifelong learning, deregulated telecoms, and recognition of the role of the private sector in leading or facilitating change. Much of the Commission's White Paper in 1993 reflected a more 'Anglo-Saxon' approach to economic growth and job-creation, and a reduced role for state intervention. That Jacques Delors was able to present such a paper says much for the change in attitudes brought about by higher and ever higher unemployment in the EU, and particularly in countries such as France and Spain.

The specific ingredients of the building blocks will have to address the real dilemmas facing national or regional educational authorities: operating systems often ill-suited to the emerging realities of the European single market, the globalisation of markets, and the information revolution. But member-states have put a veto on the EU embracing education; it remains a domain for national, sovereign action. Unfortunately, economic reality means that the workforce has increasingly to operate in a trans-European context, and regions and cities are obliged to develop European or international development strategies to attract industry. The North of England, for example, has had to switch from being a national champion in producing coal, steel and ships in the nineteenth century, to being an international and European champion in attracting companies like Nissan, Fujitsu, Samsung and Siemens. Yet still the human resource context and aspirations lag behind: knowledge of foreign (European) languages remains low, the EU has still to develop a popular profile, and there is much to do to ensure that training has the same status as academic education.

FUTURE CHALLENGES

The new Socrates and Leonardo programmes of the EU, which started in 1995, are laudable attempts to inject a European dimension to education and training, building on earlier successful programmes such as Erasmus and Comett. But both new programmes are relatively underfunded, and are still overshadowed by the scale of the EU's structural funds, particularly the European Social Fund and the European Regional Development Fund. Both are starting to develop an awareness of IT and multimedia/open-learning needs, but will need to change their emphases much more to give real impetus to the challenges of the information society. Equally, the legal process will have to catch up with open and distance learning, ensuring that degree courses and students of open universities are awarded the same rights and recognition right across Europe as the degrees from traditional universities.

To underpin the high ambitions of Bangemann, the private sector alone will not suffice: the EU will have to play a seminal role, as imaginative as when the Monnet plan was conceived in the 1950s, dealing with largely Fordist economies, or the single European market in the 1980s. A new set of de-centralised joint research centres will have to be created, as they were for atomic energy and materials in the 1960s; the southern regions of Europe will have to learn about lifelong learning, and access for women, from the new Scandinavian entrants. The rising numbers of elderly Europeans will have to be provided with all the tools of lifelong learning, if they are not to die of boredom, literally as well as metaphorically.

THE CONSEQUENCES OF INACTION

There are several dangers if the EU fails to make a success of the information society project. First, the USA, having developed the means to create, operate and supply its own vast internal network, will, by 1997, then turn to exploit the EU market and, beyond that, the markets of Eastern and Central Europe. US Vice-President, Al Gore, has himself talked of the transition from a national information infrastructure to a global information infrastructure. The US model is built mainly on private-sector funding, creating a national information infrastructure (the 'information superhighway'). Second, the suppliers would be American, giving European companies little more than subcontracting opportunities even in their own continent. Third, the sensitive understanding of the needs of Europeans, as students, consumers, producers and knowledge-workers, would probably take second place to purely commercial considerations. The educational dimension is then likely to be very secondary to that of news or financial information and entertainment. Fourth, without strong EU action, the emphasis may revert to being essentially national, a feature already seen in some member states' plans to create a national educational 'highway'. It would then be very easy for an alliance between a US corporation supplier and one member state to pave the way to European market domination, but without the products having been determined to service the needs of Europeans.

THE EDUCATIONAL PROBLEM

The evidence from research carried out for the European Round Table of Industrialists, in its report, *Education for Europeans* (1995), strongly points to the need to change the strategic direction of the education systems in Europe.

- The world of education is highly complex but deeply entrenched in national systems where priorities are much determined by political expediency and the need to balance national budgets.
- Educational institutions spend a great deal of their time organising how they teach, not learning how to teach differently, and their connection with the realities of working life often seems weak or non-existent.
- In many European countries schools are part of a centralised state system enmeshed in bureaucracy, and this makes them slow to react, or even impenetrable to external demands for change.
- Far too often, schools encourage specialisation, hemming young people into a line of study at too early an age from which they later find it difficult to escape. Teaching equipment, especially for science, in schools and colleges is often poor in quality, or simply inadequate, largely due to underfunding.
- Educational standards vary enormously across Europe and inside each country in Europe. The structural inequality in final educational qualifications obtained by the mass of European pupils is disturbing and raises questions about the different levels of achievement of education systems in each country. This inequality alone could give rise to the possible creation of discriminatory situations between young European citizens.

PROMOTION AND UNDERSTANDING

There will be a need for a major information and promotion campaign about the purpose and benefits of lifelong education and distance education. Already 1996 is designated by the EU as the European Year of Lifelong Learning. It is worth noting that as the EU extends in a general north-easterly direction to take in Scandinavia, it is embracing geographical areas where open educational traditions allied to IT are strongly championed, and seen as corollaries to their society's openness and local democratic traditions. Across Europe there is thus a varied pattern: a 'northern arc' of Scandinavia, the UK, Ireland and Benelux; a group of countries (Germany, France, Italy, Austria) with a relatively cautious approach to ODL; recent EU entrants which have introduced a national distance learning service (Spain, Portugal) or are actively considering it (Greece). Thanks to drastically lower costs for satellite broadcasting, prospects for integrating Eastern Europe into the European distance learning programme appear good. It is certain, however, that unless the broad mass of current EU countries promotes, invests in and manages the framework of a common approach to lifelong learning and distance education in an EU framework and sharing basic goals, it is external beneficiaries who will gain from the ensuing greater fragmentation.

SUMMARY

For distance learning on a European scale, the agenda to the year 2000 will be as broad as it is strategic, and tackling issues such as:

- the major alliances to be created between networks, equipment suppliers and course producers to create real critical mass and credibility;
- allocations within the structural funds to IT and training (along the lines of an IT/education fund) in Objective 1 and Objective 2 areas;
- the impact on course length, production and language used, particularly, for example, if a key market is that of distance learning for SMEs;
- coping with linguistic and cultural diversity;
- adopting the subsidiarity principle to national champions within a European dimension of collaboration and selected integration;
- retaining the essential element of human contact, guidance and counselling in any effective distance learning operation;
- ensuring that the emerging networks (e.g. of existing open universities, EOUN, Euro study centres) lead to course production and delivery on the scale required.

CONCLUSION

Crucial to the realisation of this strategy is the political will of member states and public and private sectors to implement the Bangemann Report, including its commitment to distance learning. Several issues need to be cleared up to pave the way for open and distance learning's rightful place in this whole programme, including clarification on its legal standing across the EU, privacy laws regarding information about individuals, and data protection. Education is a function and reflection of democracy; its alliance to IT does not distort that basic point, and is indeed reinforced as the EU now plans for enlargement to the East. If Europe gets the mix right, a goal of major value could be within reach: making Europe not only one of the several 'information societies' of the world (principally with the USA and Japan), but the global centre for the interpretation, integration and transmission of knowledge, with distance learning one of its key avenues for social progress. In this field, as in its track record since 1945 in the political and economic sphere,

Europe can legitimately aspire to a global reputation in a new and equally demanding form of integration, as a realistic working model and ambition for its own enlarging shape, and – why not? – for the world's own pluralism and diversity.

4 Distance education in Mongolia's political and economic transition

Ole Aabenhus and Brian Kenworthy

INTRODUCTION

This chapter had its genesis in two studies undertaken on behalf of United Nations Educational, Scientific and Cultural Organisaton (UNESCO) in late 1993 and early 1994. The first of these studies was carried out by the two authors and resulted in a needs-assessment document which was presented to UNESCO in November 1993 (Aabenhus and Kenworthy, 1993). This study provides the background for the major part of this chapter. The second study was carried out in March–April 1994 by Ole Aabenhus and Soren Waast, a short-term consultant to the Gobi Women's Project, a UNESCO/DANIDA (Danish International Development Agency) project which is discussed in some detail later in the chapter (Aabenhus and Waast, 1994). This second study, *Capacity Building for Distance Education in Mongolia*, builds on the recommendations contained in the needs-assessment study and presents a project proposal for UNESCO and potential donor agencies. The proposal focuses on the development of distance education as an instrument in the overall development of Mongolia; it is concerned with strengthening the planning, monitoring and coordination capacity of the Ministry of Science and Education; with the development of knowledge and skills in the design and production of distance education teaching materials; with methodology development based on the special conditions of Mongolia; and with the development of a testing and evaluation capacity. Both studies therefore are concerned with capacity building within Mongolia and attempt to provide solutions that are attainable given the local conditions.[1]

The authors have considerable experience of working within developing countries throughout Asia, the Pacific and Africa and are cognisant of 'the problematics of distance education in the developing world' (Guy, 1991). As Guy has pointed out:

> There are no guarantees or proven methods for success in dealing with problems in the developing world. Reflected within this diversity are responses to distance education which are at times arrogant and mis-conceived and result in failure. At other times, responses are sensitive and informed but none the less result in failure. This diversity and problematic

nature should not be viewed as a disadvantage of distance education, but be recognised for what it is and used to refine and reconstruct the methodologies and pedagogies of distance education.

(Guy, 1991, pp. 162–3)

There are no guarantees that the plans and proposals put forward by the authors to the government of Mongolia and UNESCO will be successfully implemented and have some impact on the educational problems discussed within the chapter. However, what cannot be ignored is the increasing globalisation and internationalisation of education, particularly through distance education. Koul (1995) comments upon the momentum being developed by distance education as an educational endeavour in developing countries:

More and more open universities are being established all over the developing world and more and more non-educational agencies, governmental as well as non-governmental, engaged in in-service training/instruction are now turning to DE to meet the overwhelming pressure of numbers, diversity of needs and growing awareness about the importance of professionalism. The overall scene points to what may be called a 'utilisation explosion' of DE courses and DE methodology all over the developing world, involving millions of people in various capacities.

(Koul, 1995, p. 25)

FORMAL EDUCATION SYSTEM

The formal education system in Mongolia, which was based on a Russian model, has provided for a high level of education, particularly when one considers the nomadic nature of many of its 2.3 million people, the high population growth rate and the harsh climatic conditions. At the foundation of the socialist state in 1924 only 1 per cent of the population was literate; following a sequence of nationwide campaigns, this situation improved progressively to 90 per cent literacy by 1990. In 1994 approximately 25 per cent of the population were attending some form of schooling and approximately 19 per cent of the labour force had completed secondary education, with a further 16 per cent having a higher education qualification. An important feature in the Mongolian education system has been, and remains to this day, the boarding school. Located in every *sum* (district) and *aimag* (province) centre, these schools have provided access to education for rural and nomadic children from kindergarten through secondary schooling.

The state education system is administered by the Ministry of Science and Education (MOSE), which is shifting from a role as an implementing agency to that of a regulatory and policy-monitoring authority. Many of the MOSE's earlier financial and administrative roles have been decentralised to the *aimags*, while the higher education institutions have been given increased independence. The formal education structure includes kindergarten for children aged 3 to 8, followed by six years in primary education, two years of middle school and two years of general secondary education. The higher education sector includes eight university level institutions, two colleges authorised to award degrees, and a number of post-secondary colleges, most of which are now being brought under the control of individual universities.

NEEDS-ASSESSMENT STUDY

At the request of the Mongolian government, the United Nations Development Program (UNDP) and UNESCO fielded a mission in October–November 1993 to undertake a study of distance education taking into account the areas addressed by the *World Declaration on Education for All.* The study was required to focus on the potential for using radio and television to assist in the delivery of educational programmes.

Following discussions with the Basic Education Division of UNESCO in Paris, the UNDP resident representative in Ulaanbataar (capital of Mongolia) and the minister of science and education of the government of Mongolia, it was decided to design the study to 'map out the potential area of distance education in Mongolia, i.e. describe the adequacy and the feasibility of using radio and television in support of basic education (formal and non-formal) in Mongolia' (terms of reference for consultants).

The team undertaking the study consisted of the two authors who were employed as consultants to UNESCO. As well as liaising closely with MOSE and the Mongolian Radio and Television agency (MRTV), the consultants met a number of times with an Asian Development Bank team which was responsible for the Mongolian Education and Human Resource Sector Review completed in late 1993.

Mongolia has been in transition since the early 1990s, from being a socialist state of the USSR to an independent parliamentary democracy with a developing market economy. In the process, it has lost Soviet financing, responsible for about 30 per cent of GDP. The consequent economic crisis has meant that food for the centralised boarding schools and heating, essential in the Mongolian climate, cannot be provided from a reducing educational budget. In addition many of the nomadic herders, who make up 40 per cent of the total population, want their children at home to assist with managing livestock. Most of the former collective farms have been handed over to the herders and they need all the labour they can muster to manage their newly acquired herds. There is also some degree of dissatisfaction with the Soviet-inspired school curriculum and many parents – both in rural and urban areas – fail to see the relevance of much of the education currently being provided. This, and other factors, have led to a situation where children – particularly in rural areas – are dropping out of school at both primary and secondary levels. MOSE estimated the drop-out rate as being about 93,000 in 1993, which is very disturbing when one considers that the total population of

Mongolia is only 2.2 million. Indeed, this drop-out rate represents about twenty-two per cent of school-age children.

Mongolia has a proud tradition of education for all and one of the highest literacy rates in Asia. The present crisis in education, particularly the large number of dropouts, has motivated the educational authorities to seek alternative systems of education. One of the alternatives, perceived by senior staff within MOSE, was distance education. However, the consultants found little understanding among the education officials of the nature and extent of the infrastructure required to support successful distance education programmes. Despite a number of perceived similarities, particularly geographical, between Mongolia and countries such as Australia or Canada – vast distances and scattered rural populations – there is no evidence of any previous attempts to provide any level of education by distance or correspondence education. As Bolton has pointed out:

> North America and Australasia pioneered those techniques of correspondence education which were the forerunners of distance education as we know it today. This was not simply an environmental response to the problems posed by long distances; the Russian Empire, with a population scattered over the largest land area of any single political unit in the world, was conspicuously slow about spreading educational advantages among its subjects. To some extent this may reflect technological backwardness. The establishment of distance education in any reliable form presupposed the existence of railways over which mails could be carried. The United States possessed three transcontinental railways and numerous minor lines by the 1880s; Canada was linked from west to east by the 1880s. By the same decade the Australian colonies each boasted significant railway systems radiating from the major seaboard cities, though a transcontinental system would be long delayed because of the breadth of gauge problem. In Russia the Trans Siberian railway was not completed until the first decade of the 20th century, and, although metropolitan Russia was not ill-provided, the social structure of Czarist Russia and the slower speed of literacy held back the possibility of developing a demand for correspondence education. Distance education is essentially a product of democratic societies, and specifically those democratic societies with a strong interest in primary production and influential rural groups. In such circumstances the demand would arise that the old imbalance between city and country should be remedied in terms of the provision of access to educational facilities.
>
> (Bolton, 1986, pp. 5–22)

However, despite the models of distance education practice available, it is interesting to note that the Russian-controlled system in Mongolia remedied the imbalance between city and rural provision of educational access, identified by Bolton above, by relying on a model totally different from the developments that occurred in both North America and Australia. It established a centralised system of boarding schools that attempted to replicate the educational experience for both rural and urban areas, but in the process removed young children from their families for long periods of the year. As well as the developments in correspondence education in both North America and Australia which Bolton has mentioned, an early feature of rural education in both societies was the establishment of small one- or two-teacher schools, a tradition that has continued until relatively recent times. It is interesting that with the removal of Soviet influence, the Mongolian educational authorities are exploring the same concepts and developments that occurred at a much earlier period in both North America and Australia. It can also be argued that the growing interest in distance education is part of the globalisation and internationalisation process currently being experienced within Mongolia as it is undoubtedly influenced by those outside agencies from whom it is seeking advice, expertise and assistance.

We would however take issue with Bolton about distance education being a product of a democratic society. This is a predominant western view which is contradicted by developments like the Chinese Radio and Television University System, which is probably the largest provider of distance education in the world, and developments which occurred in the Soviet Union as early as the late 1920s. As Perraton has observed,

> Since 1929, correspondence education has formed a significant component in the Soviet educational system. Many universities have correspondence sections, and there are some fifteen external polytechnic institutes that teach both part-time and correspondence students.
>
> (Perraton, 1982, p. 8)

It was from the perspective of developments that have occurred not only in North America and Australia, but also in a number of third world countries, that the consultants identified a number of areas where there was some potential for using distance education or distance education techniques to support alternative forms of educational delivery. In addition to the major problem of school drop-outs outlined above, these included: programmes for unemployed youth, some of whom may not have completed secondary schooling; in-service training for teachers; in-service training for other professional workers, e.g. health, local government and agricultural workers; and non-formal education particularly for the rural population.

The establishment of any form of distance education system is problematic because of the lack of appropriate communication systems to rural areas and limitations in access to print-based materials. Mail and telephone systems are not available to many rural communities and those that do exist are deteriorating because of a lack of fuel and appropriate trained technical support. Roads, apart from a few major ones, are very poor and impassable for much of the winter and in any case there are only 1,300 kilometres of paved road in a country nearly half the size of Australia and three times the size of France. This problem is compounded by the difficulties associated with providing any form of printed materials. Paper is in very short supply and the infrastructure required for publishing and printing is in disarray, to such an extent that MOSE had difficulty in producing even a small number of standard school textbooks in 1993. As Castro (1993, p. 3) has also pointed out, 'the development of instructional materials for the non-formal, distance education system cannot proceed until the Mongolian Government has issued more definite and clearer directives for the overhaul of the curriculum of the formal education system'.

Mongolian television broadcasts only to the urban and semi-urban areas for a limited time each day but does have a Department of Children's and Educational Programmes which cooperates closely with MOSE. A small number of educational programmes have already been provided on television and there is the possibility of further offerings particularly in urban areas. However, the situation outside the urban areas limits the potential of television as an option for providing a national educational service.

What does exist, however, is a very comprehensive radio network covering 90 per cent of Mongolia. The consultants visited a number of isolated communities including single *gher* (nomad tent) and *khot ail* (several cooperating herders) settlements and in all cases found that people had access to radios and that radio reception was acceptable (a simple portable radio was carried by the consultants to test reception); in many cases, however, radios were not operational because of the non-availability of batteries. This problem of a lack of batteries will need to be resolved if radio is to be used for educational purposes and the consultants have made a number of suggestions on alternative power supplies that are discussed later. Radio is therefore seen as having the greatest potential, in the short to medium term, for providing some form of educational support, particularly for rural communities.

RADIO'S ROLE IN EDUCATION AND DEVELOPMENT

For a large part of this century, radio has played a significant role in providing some form of educational opportunity for both children and adults throughout the world. As early as the mid 1920s radio was used to support education in schools in Britain. By the late 1930s 10,000 schools were using radio programmes broadcast by the BBC to support classroom teachers. Outside the formal education system in Britain, adult education broadcasts on a variety of topics were popular in the early 1930s leading to the establishment of several thousand listening groups organised to discuss the issues raised in the programmes. Arising from this concept of adult listening groups grew the farm radio forums broadcast in Canada with similar activities following later in India and parts of Africa. The farm forum movement in Canada, which attracted large listening audiences for more than twenty years, adopted the motto, 'Listen, Discuss, Act'. It used radio programmes primarily for agricultural education which were 'designed to stimulate group action towards better agriculture' (Perraton, 1982, p. 10). The All India Radio (AIR) net-

work commenced a similar scheme as early as 1949 with varying success because of the lack of radios in rural areas (predating the advent of transistors).
However, the movement survived and in 1977

> the director of AIR's Farm and Home Broadcasting Department reported
> that there were currently 22,500 registered forums. He had been convinced
> that, rather than be abandoned, forums should be reorganised and made
> part of a more comprehensive program of rural education. They should be
> linked with programs for functional literacy and with the new Farm-
> School-on-the-Air project.
>
> (Dodds *et al.*, 1980, p. 88)

Similar developments have occurred in Africa, the most successful being in
Ghana which had access to a Rural Broadcasting Unit with experience in
developing educational programmes and which, like India, attempted to
provide non-formal education of a general nature in addition to agricultural broadcasts. Somewhat different in approach were the radio learning
campaigns of Tanzania which targeted subject areas as varied as political
education and basic health with short campaigns aimed at attracting a large
proportion of the adult population and promoting issues often leading to
community action.

The Canadian radio farm forums provided the inspiration for the development of the radiophonic schools that were established first in Colombia
in 1947 and later spread to other countries in Latin America. Based on the
beliefs of the founder of the school, Father Salcedo, that basic education
was essential for the progress of the peasants in Colombia, it developed
into an organisation, Accion Cultural Popular (ACPO), which by the
1970s was providing educational support of various kinds to thousands
of rural Colombians. Reporting on its activities in 1980, Dodds *et al.*
suggested:

> not only does ACPO run a radio station, a publishing house, and several
> thousand radiophonic schools in Colombia, but the idea has spread to
> some 25 countries in South and Central America. The radio programs
> are designed to provide information which will help people in their every-
> day life – towards better health, better agriculture and so on – and also
> provide the equivalent of primary education for people who have had little
> or no formal schooling.
>
> (Dodds *et al.*, 1980, p. 97)

Although Dodds *et al.* believe that there is no 'typical' radiophonic school,
they also contend that many of them have been more successful than the correspondence colleges that they investigated

> or the radio forums and campaigns, in creating a curriculum to meet the
> needs of out-of-school students in rural areas. They [the radiophonic
> schools] are not interested in providing a duplicate of formal primary

education, but set out to provide an alternative whose subject matter is agriculture and family life in rural communities.

(Ibid., p. 99)

Radio ECCA commenced broadcasting programmes to support adult literacy and basic adult education in the Canary islands in the early 1960s. Using daily radio broadcasts supported by printed materials and weekly group tutorials the system and materials spread to Spain where the ECCA Centre of Permanent Education for Adults was established in all provinces in 1977. Many Latin American countries have subsequently been influenced by the ECCA system in seeking innovative ways of using radio for basic adult education.

Radio teaching began to show itself little by little as the best method for any educational action in the field of teaching adults as much from the academic as the non-academic point of view – because of its low cost, its efficiency, its accessibility and because of the special characteristics of the Canary Isles' geography which makes it difficult to timetable day or evening classes especially in the rural zone.

(Mederos, 1985, pp. 37–42)

There are of course many more well-documented examples of how radio has been used, particularly in rural communities, for education and development. As shown above, this role can be either formal or non-formal and can span a wide range of subjects and community requirements. However, it must be pointed out that in most of the cases documented above, radio provides a supporting role and the role of the teacher/tutor and the availability of books and other learning resources are both still central to the learning process. The intention of focusing on radio to such an extent is to demonstrate the success of radio technology in supporting the delivery of educational programmes in contexts similar to Mongolia.

TECHNICAL CONSIDERATIONS

Approximately 90 per cent of Mongolia is covered by an AM radio network, the only major 'white spot' being the southwest corner of the country which takes in the sparsely populated Gobi Desert and parts of the Altai Mountains. Television is restricted to urban and semi-urban areas and does not in practical terms reach rural areas. Although reliable up-to-date data are not available, it seems safe to say that almost all Mongolia's 400,000–500,000 households have access to either a cabled or wireless radio. The cable radio system in urban and some semi-urban areas is a radio network based on 'telephone lines', the receiver being a type of small speaker which plugs into a wall socket. The advantage of using this system is that the receiver is very cheap, costing 500 tugrik (about US$1.50) and it does not require batteries. According to the 1989 *Statistical Yearbook* (the most recent available), there were

440,100 radio receivers of which half were cabled and half were transistor radios located for the most part in rural areas.

Compared to many other countries at similar levels of GDP, Mongolia has a technically advanced broadcasting and telecommunications network. Radio signals (AM) are transmitted via microwave links to seven regional transmitters which were installed between 1969 and 1980 and although not as efficient as modern transmitters, they are all fully functional. MRTV-Radio produces seventeen hours of programming a day, broadcast on the national AM network. These programmes are transmitted simultaneously and in full by the seven regional transmitters. The radio division cooperates closely with various government ministries, including MOSE, Health and Environment, and some programmes have been produced on their behalf. It has a total of 141 trained programme producers, seven of whom are located as local correspondents in *aimag* (provincial) towns. There are twelve radio studios, including a drama studio and a concert studio. These are well equipped and functional, but the Hungarian equipment is well used and spare parts are becoming a problem. Field recordings are carried out using sixty portable recorders, of which two-thirds are outdated but serviceable Hungarian models, while the remaining third are semi-professional Sony recorders.

There are two major constraints involved in radio reception. First, batteries for transistor radios are sometimes scarce, particularly in rural areas where their availability is variable. Second, the supply of electrical power, necessary for local relay and re-transmission systems and for powering the cabled radio system, is unreliable and power cuts are becoming more and more frequent. The battery problem may be eventually solved as the transition to a market economy improves barter trade arrangements and as more foreign currency becomes available for importing goods other than food and medicines. However, the consultants carried out some preliminary investigations and believe that there is some potential for small-scale renewable energy projects using both solar and wind power. Very inexpensive solar radios are now available and as most of Mongolia averages more than 300 days of sunshine a year, this may provide a partial solution. Windmills providing electrical power are already being used in some Mongolian rural communities and this source of energy should perhaps be further explored. The use of both of these sources of energy are being investigated in the Gobi Women's Project reported on later in this chapter.

IDENTIFIED AREAS FOR DEVELOPMENT

The major opportunity identified for development by the consultants relates to fostering *gher* (tent) or one-teacher schools with radio providing valuable educational support.

As explained above, the system of one-teacher schools commonly found in many rural communities throughout the world does not exist to any great extent in Mongolia. In developed countries such as Australia, Canada and the USA such schools were a common feature of educational development until transportation systems developed, enabling students to be bussed to more central locations. However, such schools still operate successfully in some more remote regions of Australia and Canada and in many rural areas of other countries. It is also interesting to note that the rural school, albeit in a different form, has come back into favour in Australia with multi-age classes, encompassing all or some of the primary years, being established within regular primary schools. The one-teacher school is currently being discussed by Mongolian educationists as one of a number of ways of providing education to nomadic families and to combat the drop-out problem. An Asian Development Bank sponsored master plan (1994–8) for Mongolian Education and Human Resources pointed out that family schools for nomads could be encouraged; these schools, with or without formal teachers, would move with the families and use parent supervision combined with special home study materials. Bolton also picks up this point when describing developments which occurred in North America and Australia, particularly in regard to the role of women:

> One side-effect of correspondence education which appears to have been less widely publicised than it deserved was its reliance on the labour of wives and mothers as supervisors and teachers. The new democracies have always tended to regard the transmission of culture as an interest for women. It was taken for granted that, as the men of the household would be fully occupied with their farm duties, the children's mothers would accept the responsibility of organising the receipt and dispatch of correspondence materials, overseeing the students to ensure that they got on with their assignments diligently and regularly and, in general, fitting in the role of surrogate monitors with the thousand and one tasks of a busy pioneer wife. Few mothers had previous teaching experience of any kind and many had limited formal education.
>
> (Bolton, 1986, pp. 5–22)

Castro sounds a note of caution with using this approach in Mongolia:

> Distance education for children of rural communities needs the full cooperation of the parents. In other words, parents should make sure that the children are given time to do their self-study and that they themselves are also able to give some academic support. Both seem unlikely when the parents of herder families need the children's labour to help raise their livestock and they themselves are either too fully occupied to help teach the children or may not have the basic academic skills to be able to do so.
>
> (Castro, 1993, p. 4)

As it is difficult to recruit teachers to live in remote rural areas, it is suggested that local people be trained as teachers. Indeed some initiatives have already been undertaken by the Pedagogical University to establish one-year teacher training courses (as against the normal four years of training) for such 'barefoot teachers'. Such schemes are similar to what occurred in Australia and Canada during the early periods of settlement. The authors also believe that there is some potential for travelling local teachers who may provide teaching support to a number of *gher* settlements or *khot ails*, using the ubiquitous horse as transport ('teachers on horseback').

Radio broadcasting to support primary education began in Britain in the 1920s, in Canada and Australia in the 1930s and in parts of Latin America in the 1940s. The consultants believe that a similar approach involving regular radio programmes to support the curriculum and to provide in-service training to the teachers or parent/teachers could be used in Mongolia. This approach could be similar to the schools broadcasts organised by the Australian Broadcasting Corporation together with state educational authorities, which were a regular feature of primary schooling in both rural and urban schools in Australia from the 1940s through to the 1970s. As a young primary-school teacher, one of the authors found such a resource invaluable and many Australians would remember with some affection the enriching experiences that were provided through the medium of radio.

Although the consultants believe that the use of radio has its greatest potential in primary schools, a number of other areas where radio could assist were also identified. These included in-service training for educators, health workers, agricultural extension workers and local-government administrators. Because the Mongolians now have to take over from a system controlled in the past to a large extent by Soviet experts and administrators, there is a great need for in-service training. Such training can be provided by conventional means in Ulaanbataar and other large centres, but distance education could play a pivotal role in delivering appropriate training to *aimag* (provincial) centres and rural areas through the provision of learning packages supported by radio.

In addition, radio could have a major role to play in extension services and community broadcasting for agriculture, health, environmental education, women in development, understanding and coping with a market economy and civic awareness promotion (knowledge of one's civil rights under a democratic system).

However, it is important to reiterate that radio is just one of the educational resources required for development, it should not be seen in isolation from the role to be played by human resources whether they be teachers, community or extension workers. Similarly the role of other learning resources such as books and other print materials cannot be divorced from the potential of radio to support development.

CURRENT AND FUTURE DEVELOPMENTS

As has been pointed out earlier in this chapter the consultants found much interest in distance education, particularly related to non-formal education for adults. A special task force has been created within the Adult Education

Department of MOSE to draw up strategies and examine the infrastructure required for establishing a non-formal education system where new innovative methods of delivering education, particularly the techniques of distance education, can be put into practice.

Arising from this development, a small-scale UNESCO project funded by the government of Denmark through DANIDA, which incorporates some of the elements identified in this chapter, has already commenced. This project, 'Non-formal education to meet basic learning needs of nomadic women in the Gobi Desert', aims at assisting the government in specifically targeting nomadic women, of whom more than 20 per cent are heads of household. Although the average basic education level of these women is from three to four years of primary schooling, many have relapsed into a state of illiteracy or semi-literacy because of a lack of opportunity to practise acquired literacy skills. The immediate objectives of the project are to enable 15,000 nomadic women to acquire basic knowledge in a number of areas, including: improved cattle-rearing techniques; family planning, health, nutrition and hygiene; basic commercial skills arising from the transition to a market economy; and upgrading of literacy skills.

The implementation strategy, which has already commenced, will involve the selection of female school teachers at the *sum* (district) level who will receive intensive short course training related to the delivery of non-formal education. These teachers will have a pivotal role in delivering the programme to nomadic women. For specialised subject areas these teachers will be able to call upon the services of health workers, veterinarians and animal breeding specialists. Self-instructional materials with content appropriate for nomadic women will be developed with the active participation of the teachers. Radio programmes to support the delivery of particular subjects are also planned. These programmes will use interviews with members of nomadic families and regional extension workers in health, education and agriculture. Recording and editing equipment is being made available by DANIDA at regional centres for this purpose. Women living in the *sum* centres who are facing similar problems as nomadic women can participate in training sessions at the *sum* level and benefit from the learning materials and radio programmes. It is anticipated that such resources, although focused on Gobi women, will provide some benefit to the entire Gobi population.

The first distance education seminar and training workshops to support this project were carried out over a two-month period early in 1994 and involved both Danish and Australian expertise. The aims of this activity were to

- train national distance education coordinators at central and aimag levels;
- train broadcast people in distance education techniques in Ulaanbataar and regional broadcast stations in South Gobi and Gobi Altai;
- prepare guidelines for training of selected teachers to be involved in locally produced radio programs;

- produce some distance education radio programs and print materials in close cooperation with Mongolian counterparts, which will serve as models for later productions at central and local levels;
- develop guidelines for further production of distance education radio and print programs for the nomadic women in the Gobi Desert.

(Russell and Waast, 1994)

These workshops proved to be highly successful and, later in 1994, were followed up by further activities of a similar nature in both Ulaanbataar and the Gobi. A further follow-up visit by the Australian educational radio consultant, Nigel Russell, was conducted in August–September 1995. Russell reported that the pilot had been well received by the participants and that the educational use of radio is being perceived as essential to the future success of the project. The local radio team is currently producing over a hundred distance education programmes to be broadcast in 1996.

The Gobi Women's Project is being understood by MOSE as a pilot project leading to the introduction of some form of distance education to support both formal and non-formal education in other parts of Mongolia. It should provide, in the not too distant future, the potential for exploring many of the ideas that have been raised in this chapter and for trialing on a limited basis the potential for using radio to overcome some of the communications problems facing Mongolia during this most difficult transition period.

DANIDA is also providing support to MOSE through the agency of the Royal Danish School of Educational Studies (RDSES). The RDSES collaborates closely with the Institute of Curriculum Development and Methodology (ICDM) of the State Pedagogical University, and a twinning arrangement has been put in place. Up to the middle of 1994 the project has mainly focused on curriculum and methodology in eight schools in three different *aimags* and in Ulaanbataar. However, it is now planned to provide in-service teacher training for the 23,000 teachers in the country. This training, which will address the new curriculum and new methodologies, will make major use of distance education techniques including the use of radio programmes and audio cassettes.

As has been stated earlier in this chapter, a capacity building study, based on the authors' needs-assessment study, was conducted in June 1994. The main feature of this later study is the development of a project proposal for UNESCO which deals with 'capacity building' at both institutional and national levels. The first stage of this proposal is the selection of a pilot region in which a range of activities will be conducted. These will include school broadcasting for family and *khot ail* schools as well as formal schools; out-of-school schooling focusing on dropouts; in-service training for adults; extension activities and broadcasts for community education. The pilot region will be defined as the coverage area of one regional radio transmitter encompassing *gobi* (desert) as well as *khangai* (steppe) lands. The regional transmitter may cover three to four *aimags*; however it is planned that only the two major *aimags* within the region will take part in the trial activities.

The project proposal also provides for the creation of a number of national institutions of focal importance for the development of distance education. These include a national distance education board at government level, dealing with monitoring, promotion and planning. The board would be headed by the minister of science and education while the day-to-day operations would be carried out by a distance education unit within the ministry. Also proposed is a learning resources design and production centre capable of producing distance education packages for national distribution. However, the main objectives of this particular proposal are inexorably linked to the use of regional radio and the support of Mongolian Radio and Television (MRTV) to ensure its success.

CONCLUSION

Mongolia finds itself in a similar position to many other countries in the former Eastern Bloc which are endeavouring to come to grips with political and economic changes as a result of the collapse of the Soviet system. From a relatively stable and economically comfortable position which has been maintained for many years, it now finds itself in the process of a difficult and often frustrating transition to a democratic and free-market society. In such a situation there is a danger that services such as education, which previously enjoyed high status and which endeavoured to provide educational opportunities to both urban and rural populations, could deteriorate quite rapidly. There is no doubt that this transitional period will persist for some time to come. To overcome some of the problems that this will hold for education there is a need for new thinking and new approaches. As Dr Duger from the Institute of Educational Development (MOSE), and coordinator of the project *Continuing Education*, has stated:

> The Government of Mongolia is aiming to establish a new educational system which together with its social and economic development will be able to maintain the national culture and tradition while reflecting the world trends in education. The present educational system is not suitable to the needs of the country because it is based on a Russian educational system which does not take into account students' interests and talents. Due to the political, economic and social changes of the country it is therefore necessary to change and reform the educational system. This educational system should meet the requirements of the population with an efficient combination of non-formal and formal education which is both a flexible and continuous process suitable for scattered nomadic cattle-breeders, seasonal workers, groups of people requiring social care and for those who require continuous improvement of their education.
>
> (Duger, 1993, pp. 1–2, edited version from Mongolian translation)

There are now a number of other initiatives being planned, developed or implemented from both within and outside the government which are attempting to deal with the problems which have been described. These will no doubt be strengthened by the major review completed under the sponsorship of the Asian Development Bank. A number of these initiatives have identified distance education as a key element in educational delivery. If these plans are to come to fruition and have any impact, the authors believe that a capacity-building programme, focusing on infrastructure support and human-resource development, is urgently required and that distance education in some form will need to play a major role. What form this will take will no doubt be influenced to some degree by issues related to globalisation and internationalisation. For many developing countries the concept of distance education 'remains alien and its methodology primitive and static – alien in the sense that DE in developing countries continues to depend on models developed and tested elsewhere without indigenising them, and static in the sense that innovations are hardly ever attempted, and so the potential of DE in difficult and diverse settings remains unexploited' (Koul, 1995, p. 25). The challenge in Mongolia is to utilise this potential through approaches that are innovative in what is indeed a difficult and diverse setting.

NOTE

1 The information presented in this chapter presents the views of the authors and in no way should be attributed to UNESCO.

5 The implications of home-based education effectiveness research for opening schooling

Roland Meighan

> Trying to get more learning out of the current system is like trying to get the Pony Express to compete with the telegraph by breeding faster ponies.
>
> (Fiske, 1992, p. 15)

INTRODUCTION

At the same time as the debates about schooling have been taking place in the UK and elsewhere concerning the 'regressive' ideas (see Meighan, 1993) of a National Curriculum, 'obsessive testing', 'back to basics', etc., some families have just quietly been getting on with a 'do-it-yourself' approach to education. In the USA over a million families are reported to be 'home-schoolers' as they are known across the Atlantic. As regards the UK, the number of families opting for home-based education has grown from about ten families in 1977 to about 10,000 in 1995. In Australia, 20,000 home-based educators are reported, and in Canada, 10,000 are officially known whilst the real total is estimated at 30,000. In New Zealand the figure quoted is 3,000. In all cases, these figures have been rising steadily over the last twenty years. Every time the subject appears in a newspaper article, or is the subject of a radio or TV programme, more people come on board convinced that this option is worth trying in an attempt to deal with their educational dissatisfactions. They are surprised to find that it not only works, it works very well. Increasingly, this has become publicly recognised. Thus, a letter from Boston University's undergraduates admissions director proclaims:

> Boston University welcomes applications from home-schooled students. We believe students educated primarily at home possess the passion for knowledge, the independence, and self-reliance that enable them to excel in our intellectually challenging programs of study.
>
> (Smith, 1993, p. 4)

Partly because of its low profile in the media in general, the actual *significance* of home-based education has hardly begun to be recognised. It questions all the fundamental assumptions underpinning the institution of compulsory schooling as well as pointing to ways of reconstructing education systems.

HOME-BASED EDUCATION IN THE UK, 1977–95

Most people in the UK have come to believe that schooling is compulsory and are often taken aback to find that they are quite wrong. The families concerned get rather tired of quoting the law to correct this myth. Section 36 of the 1944 Education Act (England and Wales) states that: 'It shall be the duty of the parent of every child of compulsory school age to cause him to receive efficient full-time education suitable to his age, aptitude and ability, either by regular attendance at school or otherwise.' The law is clear, education is compulsory; schooling is not!

Education Otherwise

In 1976 a self-help, mutual-support organisation was founded for home-schooling parents in the UK. It took its name from the clause in the Education Act and was therefore entitled 'Education Otherwise'. When I began to research into this development there were about ten families involved. Now there may be ten thousand or more.

Some findings of the research

The research undertaken since 1977 has included:

- collecting information from questionnaires sent to members of Education Otherwise;
- interviewing families;
- telephone interviews;
- attending meetings and conferences of home-based educators and making notes;
- collecting newspaper, magazine, radio and TV reports;
- getting research students to do similar activities for their theses; and
- preparing detailed case studies for use by lawyers defending families.

As a result, a considerable bank of information has been built up and scrutinised and the patterns that appear in the data have been analysed (Meighan, 1992; Holt, 1982).

Social class

As regards social class, no clear pattern appears. People from all social classes are represented although there are a few more from lower middle-class and upper working-class backgrounds than the others.

Attitudes to school

Most of the families are not opposed to school in general but turn to home-based education because their children are very unhappy at school, or learning little, or both. At the outset, they would prefer a school that gave them a better deal, but cannot find one in the locality.

Attitudes to teachers

Families often express sympathy for teachers, particularly those who are forced by circumstances rather than preferences into their actions. They often see teachers as victims of the system and understand how they are corrupted into doing police work because of the nature of the school model currently in use. It is recognised by many families that such teachers would do a better educational job if their situations were more favourable by adopting a less rigid model of schooling.

Occupations and status ambitions

Some parents educating at home have high-status occupations as an ambition for their children and aim at university entrance through examination work. Others favour alternative lifestyles and work to develop the skills of self-sufficiency. Some favour the lifestyle and satisfactions of various forms of work not requiring a university degree.

Educational methods

If examinations are the priority of a family, then correspondence courses may be purchased or ready-made courses obtained from bookshops. Help may be sought from teachers who are friends or found via advertisements and these are often built into the learning programmes in varying combinations. Families with other priorities, such as self-sufficiency, fix a programme of practical projects and activities. One of my students training to be a teacher reported that, despite her first-class Oxford degree, the children of such a family had left her feeling totally uneducated because of the stunning range of their practical skills.

In all cases, there is a strong tendency for the learners to take on considerable responsibility for their own studies sooner or later. Learner-managed or autonomous learning is a frequent outcome. Parents rarely try to be a replacement for a team of subject teachers but become 'fixers' instead: that is, they help fix or arrange a learning programme with their children from a variety of learning resources. As one family put it, the parents become the *learning-site managers*, akin to the manager of a building site, making sure the materials and planning and equipment are all coordinated.

Political party support

As regards political party identity, no clear pattern of voting appears and all types of voter are encountered.

The question of social skills

Families tend to encourage a wide range of social contacts with people and groups of all ages. Where families have one child in school and one out, they have always, to date, reported that it is the social life of the one at school that gives them the most concern, contrary to the predictions of most people. Phrases like 'the tyranny of the peer group' are mentioned in contrast to the learner at home who can 'make up their own mind' and 'get on with a wide range of people of all ages'. One parent wrote:

> We feel that the benefits of practising Education Otherwise are enormous. We have one child in school and one at home. The difference in their attitudes both socially and to work are marked. The one at school has less friends. The one at home enjoys every moment of every day unlike the one at school.

Organisation of timetable and curriculum

As regards methods of working, some families use a fixed timetable, others let the timetable emerge from day to day, others timetable the mornings and leave the afternoons for spontaneous activity. Yet others report that they experiment until they find the best way of working for them.

Life philosophy

Families engaged in home-based education demonstrate little consensus on anything and the keyword is variety. This applies to religious affiliation too. Some families describe schools as involved in religious indoctrination and they do not approve. Others see schools as anti-religious and they disapprove of this. There have even been occasions when both views have been expressed about the very same school. Some are religious families from the various Christian denominations, some are from other religions, whereas others are humanists and freethinkers. About the only thing you can safely say these families have in common is that they are home-based educators.

Success rates

Perhaps there is one other thing they have in common: whatever they define as a good education, and this varies considerably, they are then almost always successful at achieving it. The minority of things that homes find it more difficult to emulate involve the large-group facilities and experiences such as school orchestras, drama productions, television programme making, team games, some aspects of physical education, and other activities that require larger groups than one family can provide, such as discussions and simulations. Ironically these are often seen as the 'frills' of schooling. Thus, what is claimed as the hard core of schooling presents no insurmountable problems for an energetic and resourceful family.

FIRST REACTIONS FROM THE UK EDUCATIONAL ESTABLISHMENT: THE ERA OF DEFENDING THE MYTHS

At first, members of the educational establishment in the UK tended to oppose home-based education and set out to defend a series a myths about schooling and education.

The compulsory schooling myth

The experience of families adopting home-based education in the UK is that the myth that schooling is compulsory persists and persists. One of the key contributions of Education Otherwise has been to give its members the confidence to quote the law to refute the myth.

The one right way of education myth

In the case *Harrison* v. *Stevenson*, the charge against the Harrison family was based on a second myth – that there was one right approach to education, known to the trained professionals and implemented in schools. It was authoritarian in nature, being imposed on learners by adults, and using the medium of formal instruction to transmit the supposed wisdom of our ancestors as codified in compartmentalised subjects. The approach required timetables, textbooks, subjects, instructor-teachers, and long periods of listening, reading and writing. Childhood was conceptualised as a period of reluctance to learn, incapability, avoidance of effort and ignorance. Therefore, children were unworthy of being granted rights in law or general consideration and respect. The Harrisons did not agree (see Meighan, 1984).

Geoff Harrison, in a TV interview, outlined the family's view of childhood. The youngest member of the family was seen as having equality of consideration and a right to be listened to, and have his point of view taken into account. If a contribution from any member of the family was recognised as reasonable then it would be included or accommodated in some way. In the family's view the adults had no monopoly of wisdom and sensible ideas. The Harrisons had gradually established a vision and practice of education that fostered self-direction, self-reliance and self-confidence. The approach was akin to Bertrand Russell's (1916) 'control in the spirit of freedom' because any authoritarian type of intervention was reserved for extreme situations such as personal danger, and seen only as a temporary expedient. The technical name for this alternative non-authoritarian approach is autonomous education, roughly translated as self-directed learning. The Harrisons had to go to court to claim the right to educate in this way because the experts were of the view that the family should adopt the authoritarian approach in order for it to be 'real' education.

The judge's verdict supported the Harrison family's approach:

> We are satisfied that for these children, their manner of education has proved efficient. . . . They have a wide range of practical skills – plumbing, building, mechanics, husbandry – are commercially and financially competent. Any individual gift – such as A.J.'s violin playing – is encouraged and given specialist tuition.
>
> (Meighan, 1992, p. 3)

The professional monopoly myth

Some Local Education Authorities (LEAs) inform families that they cannot educate at home unless they have a qualified teacher to hand. There is no such requirement in law and the officers concerned are committing an offence by trying to perpetuate such a myth. Behind it is the myth of professionalism – that only the qualified can educate. In fact there is a considerable presence of qualified teachers in the ranks of the home-based educating families – about one-third of the membership. But allowing other parents to take on the role of educationalists without formal training seems like an erosion of the claim of teaching as a profession. The legal profession has similar anxieties about do-it-yourself conveyancing in house purchase and the medical profession in the idea of self-help medicine.

The right of veto myth

The Harrison family were criticised by the judge for eventually refusing to cooperate with the authorities and denying access for scrutiny or assessment. He did not go on to say that this was an *offence.* Earlier case law (e.g. *Bevan* v. *Shears*) had established that it was not. Although most families do cooperate, this has come to be interpreted by officials as a right when it is not.

The home educators' consensus myth

A stereotype of people opting to educate at home is often proposed. They are imagined to be radical anti-schoolers and anti-authoritarian activists vaguely labelled as left-wing. The research shows this to be nonsense. One generalisation that can be made about home-based education is that it is diverse. There is a wide variety of motives, methods, aims and experiences. Furthermore, families are not static. They can adopt one position at one stage and revise it in the light of experience, as the following parent reports:

I started with much confidence, trying to stick to a timetable, worried about social life. After a year we were far more relaxed; no timetable, still structuring it a bit, anxious about 'projects'. Second year, all that had gone, completely freewheeling, not a care in the world. Now we seem to have found the balance, i.e. we work at those areas of interest, concentrate more on living life as a whole.

The parental incompetence myth

Another lesson from my research is that parents are undervalued as educators even by those who preach, and practise, parental involvement. The stance taken is all too often the patronising one of how parents can be made useful to teachers in some way as fund-raisers or teaching helpers, rather than how teachers can amplify and extend with parents the work they have begun in the first five years of their children's lives. Thus 'parents as educators' turns out to mean junior partners, not equal ones. Most of the honourable exceptions to this are to be found in early childhood settings such as nursery schools, nursery classes and infant schools.

The 'trust the officials' myth

The research has also revealed the unacceptable face of school management. The correspondence that parents have shown me as part of their exchanges with some head teachers, officials, educational psychologists and others have frequently been shameful for their lies, distortions, ignorance and ugly threats. Time, energy and money is given over to trying to stifle the initiatives of families. There is an impressive irony in an educationalist telling parents that everything will be all right if their children go back to school, when it was the inflexibility and regimentation of the regime there, and its hostile learning environment, that caused much of the damage in the first place. On the positive side, the majority of home-based proposals are at least tolerated by the authorities and occasionally treated with open-minded interest.

Just occasionally, disputes come to court. I have witnessed some dubious justice in law-court hearings when I have been called on to help defend some of the families denied their rights. Although this has usually been redressed in higher-court hearings, it has cost families dearly in terms of both money and personal stress. In one case the family house had to be sold to finance the legal fees and the father died of a heart attack during a succession of court hearings. The irony is that the offence appears to be that of *caring too much* about the education of their children.

THE ERA OF PASSIVE TOLERANCE

Since the research began in 1977, there have been several changes. The first is a change in motivation. Initially, the most common motive of parents opting for home-based education, in the UK, was desperation. Gradually, a group that has been growing in size and influence in Education Otherwise has been that of young parents who plan from the outset to educate their children at home. Some of these parents have themselves been educated at home, whilst others have become converted to the idea.

A second change has been in the behaviour of LEA officials. As they have had more experience of home-based education and its results, their reaction has tended to become more understanding and less hysterical. Thus more than one LEA has devised a home-based education package to help families who elect for the Education Otherwise approach.

Another change is that evidence has been collected that can be used to support parents who have to argue their case. Research students linked with my own research programme have studied individual cases in depth as well as tracking groups of families over seven or more years. The results are impressive. Families rarely fail to achieve the aims they set for themselves. For some this is entrance to university. Others would regard this as the last thing they ever wanted and achieve entry to the other institutions of their choice instead. Those opting for a self-sufficiency lifestyle achieve the range of practical skills they value so highly. Some have children with physical handicaps or with other special needs and achieve the gains in capability and confidence they seek. There are parents who achieve the aim of rebuilding the confidence and stability of a child shattered by school experiences. None of these aims is necessarily achieved easily or without setbacks, but the evidence is now clear: they can be achieved, with only rare exceptions.

A fourth change has been the growth of a small group of parents who offer their children the choice of school or home-based education. Some alternate periods in school with a year or more out. Others, my own son included, choose school but report that the continued option of home-based education redefines the school experience for them: it is no longer compulsory but chosen. The detachment this gives is perhaps illustrated in my son's assessment of whether to continue with school or not when he was 14 years old: 'I am still managing to rescue enough bits from the wreck.'

A final development has been the gradual growth of interest in the concept of flexi-time schooling. Initially this was seen as a flexi-time programme of education agreed between family and school and undertaken partly at home and partly at school. More developed conceptions of flexi-schooling go well beyond this starting point into ideas for regenerating school into more flexibility in all its dimensions, not just the role of parents (see Meighan, 1988).

DOES IT WORK? HOME-BASED EDUCATION EFFECTIVENESS RESEARCH

As a scene-setting device, this letter from a schooled child points to some effective features of a home-based education:

Dear Education Otherwise,

My best friend is Susan and she doesn't go to school; she is taught at home by her parents and is more interesting than someone that does go to school because she knows a lot more.

I sometimes feel a bit jealous of her, because she is more educated than some of my other friends and myself. At school there are quite a few bullies, but Susan doesn't have to worry about things like that. Sometimes I wish I was educated at home as well as Susan and her brother, Paul, as they can spend more time with their parents and pets. At school, you hardly use a computer, but Susan and Paul nearly always use a computer and are shown how to use one properly. They are always learning about new things – at school I always learn about the same things over and over again!

Some teachers are hard to get on with and you don't get any encouragement from them, but your parents always give you encouragement.

(Carol Ann, aged 12, from Bolton, UK)

Home-based education effectiveness: the evidence from case studies

There are several kinds of answer to the question 'how effective is home-based education?' One is to assemble evidence about cases in the past and make reference to the achievements of people educated this way. Some are well-known people (some living, some dead), such as Yehudi Menuhin, Patrick Moore, Agatha Christie, Margaret Mead, Thomas Edison, George Bernard Shaw, Noël Coward, C. S. Lewis, Pearl Buck, Bertrand Russell, John Stuart Mill. There are many more. Reference can be made to current academic successes gained by home-based students in gaining entry to a variety of universities. Reference can also be made to the World-wide Education Service (WES) of the Parents' National Education Union, founded by Charlotte Mason, because they have been educating children at home and abroad for over a hundred years by means of a correspondence course for the parents using similar principles of distance teaching to those of the Open University.

Home-based education effectiveness: the evidence from systematic studies

The issue of social skills

The study by Shyers (1992) showed that home-schooled children had significantly lower problem-behaviour scores than schooled children and that they are socially better adjusted than schooled children. Shyers concluded that the real question was why the social adjustment of schooled children was of such poor quality.

Smedley (1992) used different test instruments but came to the same conclusion: that home-educated children are more mature and better socialised than those attending school. Some possible reasons are proposed in his study:

- The classroom is mostly one-way communication often of a stilted kind and few meaningful interchanges are in evidence. In home-based education the opposite is the case.
- Schools are products of the factory age with batches of uniform products running on the conveyor belt in lockstep motion towards the standardised diploma. It therefore socialises into this kind of mentality. Home-based education, in contrast, works to more personalised educational outcomes.
- An unnatural aspect of school is age segregation. Learning to get along with peers alone does not prepare students for varied interactions with older and younger people in life. Home-based education avoids this trap, for in the home-education learning programmes, people of various ages are encountered in a way that more accurately mirrors the variety of society.
- The emphasis of home-based education on self-discipline and self-directed learning and the personal confidence this produces, creates young people who can adapt to new situations and new people.

Knowles (1993) studied 53 adults who had experienced home-based education to see how they fared in later life. He found that more than three-quarters of the sample had felt that being educated at home had actually helped them interact with people from different levels of society. When asked if they would want to be educated at home if they had their lives over again, 96 per cent; replied 'Yes'. Factors that were commonly highlighted by the adults concerned were the self-directed curriculum, the individualised pace of working, and the flexibility of the home-study programme. None of the sample was unemployed or on welfare assistance, and two-thirds were married – the norm for the age group. Knowles concludes that the idea of there being social disadvantages to home-based education was not supported by the evidence, which rather indicated the reverse.

The issue of intellectual and academic development

The academic excellence of home-educated children has been repeatedly demonstrated by research in the USA and it is supported by case-study evidence in the UK. In summary, the earlier findings were that they consistently score at or above the 50th percentile on standardised achievement tests, with more than half scoring at the 70th and 80th percentile (Alaska Department of Education, 1985, 1986; Hewitt Research Foundation, 1985, 1986). Later studies from the USA put home-educated children at least two years in front of their schooled counterparts in intellectual achievement, and sometimes as much as ten years ahead (Ray, 1991).

Competence in science

Hornick (1993) studied a group of seven families with teenage children in Massachusetts to find out how they coped with learning science. He found that the parents in the sample did not teach science to their teenagers: the teenagers taught themselves. The result was 'inquiry science of the very highest quality'. The students performed as real scientists in exploring phenomena, making hypotheses, designing and carrying out tests and analysing and evaluating results. Memorising texts and doing worksheets was not seen as valuable, but textbooks were used as a source of ideas and reference. The families saw science as a 'hands on' activity.

Science shows on television were used extensively and trips to science museums, farms, nature centres and national parks 'were a staple of the science curricula'. The parents, whose own backgrounds in science were slight, learnt with their children rather than giving any instruction. They saw themselves sometimes as learning coaches and sometimes as fellow inquirers. Parents operated with a sense of the 'teachable moments' when their teenagers' interest and curiosity had been aroused. Every family agreed that locating suitable resources was the key to their science learning and this was the justification for the extensive use of TV and field trips.

Hornick's assessment of the scientific knowledge and understanding gained was that it was of the highest standards, but that the families were largely unaware of this and rather took the quality of their learning for granted: 'When I asked 13-year-old Louis what science he knew, he neglected to mention that he is an expert at identifying medicinal herbs and preparing oils and tinctures; for him this was his small business not science.'

Competence with computers

Marchant (1993) investigated the use of computers by home-educators in a three-part study unusual in its research approach. The first part consisted of a summary of data obtained from a directory of those home-educating families interacting through an education bulletin board. The second was a content analysis of the notes posted on the bulletin board. In the final part, other researchers joined Marchant in posting questions to the home-educators on-line and the responses were analysed.

He found that 185 families from thirty-seven states were exchanging ideas and information on a regular basis without ever physically meeting. The characteristics of this group were analysed without any assumption being made that they were typical of the general population of home-educators. Marchant found that this group was knowledgeable and sophisticated. The parents were a fairly well-educated group who felt that their own formal education had contributed little to their success as home-educating parents. They were well equipped in terms of modern computer technology and know-how, and even though they tended to downplay the importance of this, the impact on the competence of the children was hard to ignore.

A UK study of learning methods

Thomas (1994) interviewed twenty-three families in the Greater London area and went on to carry out observations on ten of them. The research is on-going and also involves a sample of families in Australia. Parents were asked to share in the joint venture of exploring how their children learned. Many observations were undertaken in the kitchen, where so much home-based education in the form of conversations takes place. These were recorded with pen and paper. The qualitative data were subjected to content analysis to identify emergent themes.

Families starting out on home-based education, who at first adopted formal methods of learning, found themselves drawn more and more into less formal learning. Families who started out with informal learning at the outset found themselves drawn into even more informal learning. The methods that both groups grew into had much more in common with early childhood education. The sequencing of learning material, the bedrock of learning in school, was mostly seen as of limited value.

Learning to read was a central concern and some were late in coming to reading: 'Curiously, these children who learned to read relatively late still went on very quickly to read material suitable for their age. Most of the children were voracious readers' (Thomas, 1994, p. 2).

Thomas stresses that his work is in the early stages, but he is already aware that his research challenges one of the fundamental assumptions of schooling:

> This study challenges the almost universally held view that children of school age need to be formally taught if they are to learn. In school this may be the case but at home they can learn just by living.
>
> (Ibid., p. 2)

CONCLUSIONS: LESSONS TO BE LEARNT FROM THE HOME-EDUCATORS

The need to return to the principles of natural learning

Families educating at home often engage in highly sophisticated activity without necessarily being able to articulate what they are doing. Most parents find, as Holt (1991) proposed, that young children are 'natural' learners. They are like explorers or research scientists busily gathering information and making meaning out of the world. Most of this learning is not the result of teaching, but rather a constant and universal learning activity 'as natural as breathing'. Parents, supported by grandparents and others, achieve the remarkable feats of helping their children to walk and talk by responding to this process. This is perhaps the most successful example of educational practice worldwide, and it is achieved by 'amateurs'.

The highly sophisticated activity of parents is described as 'dovetailing' into the child's behaviour. Parents appear to have no predetermined plan of language teaching, they simply respond to the cues provided and give support to the next stage of learning as the child decides to encounter it. This process of natural learning can be hindered or destroyed by insensitive adult interference. Holt identified this as 'unwanted teaching'. The studies by Wells (1986) show that the *least* effective strategies parents can try are general verbal encouragement and demonstration/instruction. Significantly, these turn out to be the most common strategies in use in the formal classroom.

A wide variety of learning styles

Human beings, adults and children alike, differ from each other quite dramatically in learning styles. To date, over thirty such differences have been catalogued. An example would be the difference between those who learn better with some background noise and those who learn better in quiet conditions. Individuals also differ in the kind of light conditions, temperature conditions, bodily positions, food intake and type of companions needed for efficient learning. Bio-chronology is another factor, for some are early-day learners and some late-day or even evening/night learners. Some are impulsive learners and others reflective. It follows that any uniform approach to learning is intellectual death to some, and often most, of the learners, and is therefore suspect.

Therefore, the situation in which one teacher faces thirty children in one room, and is required to deliver the same material within a given period of time to all of them, means that drastic harm to the quality of learning of many of the class, and the resultant loss of a great deal of potential learning, is inevitable. In contrast, in home-based education, the families rather take it for granted that learning styles differ and vary the learning situations accordingly.

The need for the 'catalogue curriculum'

'The idea of a National Curriculum has little educational merit and a poor track record' (Meighan, 1995, p. 38). When I wrote this in *The Freethinkers' Pocket Directory to the Educational Universe*, I detected some squeals of protest. But I actually thought I was being a bit restrained, because I take the view that the National Curriculum is an *anti*-educational concept and part of the regressive educational agenda. This kind of judgement puts the onus on a critic to provide some alternatives. I have done this elsewhere (Meighan, 1988). The lines of analysis are clear enough. An adult-imposed curriculum, whether *national* or not, is part of the *authoritarian* approach to education. The *democratic* and the *autonomous* approaches have some different concepts to offer. Although these can be, and are, given technical-sounding names, we need an analogy that connects with people.

In this endeavour, I have proposed the idea of the 'catalogue curriculum'. Others may have used this description before, but I have not come across it. Glines (1995) has something similar in his 'window-shopping' approach to the curriculum, and the 'shopper's guide' for students. The learners are offered a printed catalogue of learning opportunities including set courses, ideas for making your own courses, instructions as to how to set up a learning cooperative, self-instructional packages and available learning resources and opportunities. Because the catalogue includes pre-planned, negotiated and individual options, it serves the requirements of both the democratic and autonomous approaches whilst also allowing authoritarian offers to be included. It thus serves the flexi-schooling synthesis which is an attempt to incorporate the advantages of all three approaches and types of discipline.

There are several operating examples of the catalogue curriculum approach in existence, although none of them is quite as broad-ranging as I have in mind. Thus, the *City as School*'s initiative in the USA presents its students with a catalogue of hundreds of opportunities for work experience or learning at work placements and any associated college-based course options, from which they devise their personal study programme in consultation with a tutor. A longstanding example is that of the Scout and Guide movements and the catalogue of badges that can be earned. This particular example shows how an authoritarian approach can be dominant – all the badge options are preplanned recipes for learning.

Of course, the catalogue approach is common in further and higher education. Further education colleges all produce a prospectus. The Open University provides a good example of a catalogue approach to devising a personal degree programme using the methodology of distance teaching and learning.

The case for the catalogue curriculum to replace all versions of imposed set curricula is based on the most recent research into learning. Gardner (1991) identifies at least seven types of intelligence. We have known for many years about the thirty or more learning styles in humans. The flexibility a full-blown catalogue curriculum approach implies is now widely recognised as the way forward, in order

- to equip individuals so that they can cope with a rapidly changing world, creatively and imaginatively, rather than with fear, obstructionism and fatalism;
- to match the wide variety of individual learning styles, learning biographies, forms of intelligence and learner aspirations;
- to match the needs of the modern economy for flexible capable and adaptable people;
- to match the needs of a modern, living democracy for people who can operate as participating citizens exercising responsible, informed choice, and acting with all the necessary possible positive tolerance needed to make an open and diverse society work.

Most home-educating families operate a catalogue curriculum. Often the morning programme may be preplanned. The afternoon programme may then be of a more spontaneous kind. The learners sometimes direct their own studies. At other times they work in cooperation with others. The parents occasionally act as instructors, and at other times as facilitators, sometimes as co-learners, and often as sources of encouragement. Only a few schools, mostly the best of the nursery and infant schools, can match the curriculum variety of a home-educating family.

An essential part of the approach of the families working in these flexible ways is the regular monitoring and evaluation of their curriculum. In some cases I have seen this taking place regularly and deliberately at morning coffee breaks supplemented by reviews at meal times. In other cases the planning and review has taken place in a regular Sunday evening meeting to decide the learning programme in outline for the following week.

In these and other ways, home-educators are, without necessarily intending to, blazing the trail for a future flexible education system that provides alternatives for everybody, all the time.

6 Canadian policy and practice in open and distance schooling

Margaret Haughey and Judy Roberts

As is true of many countries, Canada's early involvement in distance education grew out of the need to provide public education to a relatively small
population scattered over a wide geographical area. As the country became
more heavily settled, the need for distance education seemed to decrease.
Since the mid-1980s, however, interest in distance education has been on the
rise. The federal government, provinces, school jurisdictions and individual
schools realise that, if they integrate technology in their programme offerings,
they will increase the potential to provide expanded opportunities within
regular structures and enhance the possibilities for new forms of schooling,
thus developing an education system fitted to the new century. The pace of
change challenged us to select from a rich range of examples for this chapter.
Government initiatives seemed easiest to capture, so we have focused on that
level and have not included references to the many successful school- and
classroom-based initiatives in technology integration.

PROVINCIAL GOVERNMENT INITIATIVES

Across Canada, this renewed interest in distance education manifested itself
in different ways. While some provinces undertook a concerted initiative
for system-wide change, others adopted a more conservative, incremental
approach. These differences partly reflect political party orientations and the
disparities of a federal system where education is a provincial responsibility.

Governmental initiatives in open and distance education have had three
major thrusts: technology infrastructure development, decentralisation of
open and distance education provision, and the development of shared
resources. As we review illustrative highlights from across the country, we
have noted trends such as the revitalisation of small schools, the creation of
consortia, the involvement of the federal government and contributions by
the private sector.

Technology infrastructure development

The changes described in this section benefited from strong starting points. For example, in 1985, Alberta, British Columbia and Ontario had satellite-based provincial educational communications networks whose mandates included schools television broadcasting. Other provinces, such as Newfoundland and Labrador, had terrestrial audiographic networks. Almost all provinces and territories established their own correspondence-course units. Many provinces, such as Québec, had strong track records in pilot project activity. Nonetheless, between 1985 and 1995, all provinces and territories launched major initiatives in technology infrastructure development which were generally preceded by reviews or task forces to identify problems and suggest possible options for innovation.

Ontario's initial focus was Northern Ontario, where 10 per cent of the province's population is scattered over 90 per cent of its land mass. As a result of a commission of inquiry into declining school enrolment in Northern Ontario, a pilot project was initiated in 1982/3 by the government's Independent Learning Centre (ILC), TV Ontario (TVO) and a Northern Ontario school board, the Lakehead Board of Education (Department of Communications, Canada, 1983). The Lake Superior Alternative Delivery Project was designed to address the impact of deteriorating buildings and transient staff on declining enrolments. Students in three schools used ILC correspondence lessons and TVO television broadcasts, as well as accessing 100 pages available electronically through Telidon, a Canadian computer software initiative. They were assisted by an on-site supervising teacher. The most successful part of the project was the involvement of students in self-directed multi-media learning; in 1987, ILC and TVO offered ten multi-media courses to students in small northern schools.

Subsequently, in response to the need for improved access to post-secondary and secondary educational opportunities in Northern Ontario, the government instituted Contact North/Contact Nord (Croft, 1993), and contracted management of the project to four Northern Ontario post-secondary institutions. Established in 1986, this audiographic network now serves approximately 130 communities through 180 access sites. Approximately a hundred secondary schools from urban and remote Northern communities are part of the network. Between 1992/3 and 1994/5, the network distributed fifty-nine secondary school courses (Lamontaigne and Tobin, 1994). From their research, McGreal and Violette (1993) reported that students did as well as or better than their counterparts in classroom courses. Other benefits included working in familiar surroundings with a certain invisibility that lessened the stress of participation and with a feeling of camaraderie due to the small class size (ibid., p. 203). Contact North/Contact Nord also provides an Email service which is being used to support a number of secondary education courses. One of the challenges facing the school sector, however, has been that the Northern Distance Education Fund, established to accelerate the design of courses in a distance education format, was available only to the post-secondary sector.

In its second phase, from 1990 to 1995, Contact North/Contact Nord has been managed, by agreement with the Ministry of Education and Training, by a management committee consisting of post-secondary, secondary and government-sector representatives. Some programme development money was made available to the school sector in various ways in this second phase. A Sunset Review process has been undertaken before the next phase is launched in 1996.

Government policies and practices have been reviewed in other areas as well. For example, the ministry's Independent Learning Centre is working on a re-engineering process for its future plans. Recommendations from the Ontario Royal Commission on Learning (1994) placed considerable emphasis on the importance of technology in the education system of the future. While a full implementation plan for selected recommendations is still being developed, the Ontario government has funded, through the Ministry of Education and Training or other sources, province-wide infrastructures to serve the Franco-Ontarian population (Thomas and McDonell, 1995) and its teachers, trustees and board officials.

While Ontario's initial focus was the establishment of telecommunications infrastructures, Alberta began by identifying problems with the operation of the Correspondence School. In 1987, a task force to develop a vision for the Alberta Correspondence School (ACS) was established and reported (Alberta Education, 1988) that several issues required resolution, many of which could benefit from technology, such as: reducing turnaround time due to postal delivery; exploring the use of technologies for teaching and curricular enhancement; providing student support; enhancing course design; developing local partnerships to support distance learners; and pursuing equity. The report writers concluded that ACS should change its focus from correspondence tuition to the provision of decentralised learning services, and that a renamed centre should focus on the provision of centralised course design and liaison with regional centres. New delivery alternatives such as audio-teleconferencing, electronic mail, telephone tutoring and media resources were to be integrated in this decentralised concept. Notably absent was any reference to ACCESS Alberta, the provincial communications authority. The report was well received by government, which renamed ACS the Alberta Distance Learning Centre and instituted a number of pilot projects to begin implementing the two main thrusts of the report: devolution of responsibility to regional centres and the integration of new delivery alternatives. In 1995, a Legislative Assembly implementation team on Business Involvement and Technology Integration published a discussion paper recommending appropriate ways to integrate technology into education. Alberta Advanced Education and Career Development (1995) has sought reactions to a concept paper for the development of a virtual learning system.

In contrast, Saskatchewan focused first on the development of a provincial network and then explored the problems of correspondence education. School infrastructures were developed as part of larger initiatives. In 1984, the Saskatchewan White Paper on communications policy proposed a satellite and fibre-optic cable network to serve fifty-two communities with 62 per cent of the province's population. Satellite was used for the northern half of the province since fibre-optic cables could not be buried underground given the ground cover and climatic conditions. In January 1989, the Saskatchewan Communications Network (SCN) was established as a Crown Corporation with the mandate to provide equal access to all residents through the use of satellite and fibre-optic cable based on the province's existing telecommunications system.

SCN has developed into two distinct networks, the Training Network which delivers interactive credit and professional development courses, and the Broadcast Network which distributes educational programming via satellite from the University of Saskatchewan to provincial cable companies which transmit to their subscribers. Some Broadcast Network programming is targeted at school or post-secondary students, but the majority is for general audiences. The Training Network, in contrast, delivers programming to specific sites. In 1994/5, there were fifty-four receiving sites operated by the regional colleges and institutes, and twenty other sites. In addition, there were thirty-four high-school classroom sites. Programming is primarily university and technical institute credit courses from the Universities of Saskatchewan and Regina, and the Saskatchewan Institute for Agriculture, Science, and Technology. There were over 2,300 registrants in the academic year 1994/5 (SCN, 1995).

In October 1987, a Distance Education Council was set up to encourage expansion of distance education activities, provide advice on technological developments and make recommendations for government grants. The council was replaced in July 1989 by a Distance Education Program Review Committee whose mandate was to focus on post-secondary education and 'to formalize and ensure effective communication between the newly created Saskatchewan Communications Network and the educational community' (Saskatchewan Education, 1991, p. 1). The report, *Leading the Way: A Blueprint for Saskatchewan* (Consensus Saskatchewan, 1990), included the recommendation that communities must have access to *all* levels of education through distance education. Saskatchewan continued its policy of development for the post-secondary level by issuing a response (Saskatchewan Education, 1992b) to a discussion paper (Saskatchewan Education, 1991).

In September 1990 the minister announced the formation of a Provincial Advisory Committee on Distance Education. Its mandate was to advise on distance education in general and on the Saskatchewan Government Correspondence School in particular. In June 1992, the committee made a number of recommendations concerning these objectives in its report, *No Distance is Too Great* (Saskatchewan Education, 1992a). These recommendations included: developing a strategic plan based on a provincial-needs assessment; working in concert with the curriculum and instruction branches in course development; evaluating presently-used distance education materials especially for media enhancements; pursuing the acquisition of non-print resources; increasing public awareness and access through partnerships with school systems; changing the name of the Correspondence School to better reflect its mandate; and reassessing tuition costs.

Subsequently, the work of the committee and of a distance education and technology planning group were incorporated into a single multimedia strategy. Saskatchewan Education, Training and Employment (1995) issued a multimedia learning strategy which envisaged three key initiatives, two of which are focused on infrastructure development. The latter are a telecommunications enhancement to enable schools and regional colleges to develop a telecommunications infrastructure and a Multimedia Learning Network to build on the province's existing facilities to facilitate access to education and training opportunities.

These three examples, Ontario, Alberta and Saskatchewan, illustrate the opportunities and challenges experienced by the school sector when they are part of multi-sectoral initiatives. Significant consortia-based infrastructures are being put in place elsewhere across Canada.

Newfoundland and Labrador schools became involved in distance education only recently, although a province-wide audiographic conferencing network has been in place since the mid-1970s. Telemedicine/TETRA is now a network of over 200 sites in more than 110 communities. Its backbone is an audiographics conferencing system with interactive video-conferencing at selected sites (Boone and Keough, 1994). The province's schools and teachers benefit from a computer messaging and conferencing system, STEM–Net, which aims to connect all Newfoundland schools to each other and to other networks such as SchoolNet (see p. 74) and the Internet by December 1995. Most recently, a consortium of schools, colleges, universities and others have hired an executive director of the newly created Open Learning and Information Network (OLIN). Operating under a mission to facilitate access to any source of learning, OLIN has two-year funding under a federal–provincial Human Resources Development Agreement. The school sector is also a stakeholder in Operation ONLINE (Opportunities for Newfoundland and Labrador in the New Economy), a task force established by the province's ministry of industry, trade and technology.

This partnership between the public and private sectors in educational activities that are linked to economic policy is also evident in other provinces such as New Brunswick. Benefiting from a decision made by NBTel to install fibre-optic cable well before many other provincial telephone companies saw the need for an 'electronic highway', New Brunswick established TeleEducation New Brunswick (TENB) in 1993. The culmination of several years' work by the New Brunswick Distance Education and Tele-Health Committee, TENB, created under a federal–provincial funding agreement, includes elementary- and secondary-education applications in its mandate. Examples of its work at that level are the provision of two final-year courses to three Francophone schools using TENB's audiographic facilities for exchanges between students in New Brunswick and Newfoundland for French and English conversation practice (McGreal, 1994; CMEC, 1994). TENB's mandate to support the delivery of multimedia courses to community centres, schools, colleges, universities, and private businesses is considered a key component of the province's economic development strategy which includes creating a courseware and advanced technology industry.

The Nova Scotia Department of Education, through its Education Media Section, on behalf of the Nova Scotia Educational Communications Agency, has been involved in initiating Network Nova Scotia, an audiographic conferencing network linking eighteen college and university campuses (Nova Scotia Education, 1992). Working in conjunction with Network Nova Scotia, three rural school boards coordinated their planning for their six small schools. Two other schools have since joined, and all are linked together using desktop video-conferencing (*Vis-à-Vis*) to teach approximately sixteen senior courses (CMEC, 1994, p. 29).

For the past few years, stakeholders in Manitoba's education, training and telecommunications technology sectors have participated in a broad range of pilot projects. For example, in 1991 interactive satellite broadcasting was piloted to combinations of forty-five school sites as an initiative of the province's Teacher Mediated Program (TMP) which supports the provision of distance education courses in partnership with local school jurisdictions. Courses originated in Winnipeg or Brandon with teachers linked electronically to classes of approximately twenty students made up of seven or eight sites. The system has since been formalised as the Manitoba Satellite Network (MSN) which provides a one-way video, two-way audio link to approximately seventy-two sites in sparsely populated areas and to twenty cable outlets. In 1992/3, the Network offered programming for twenty-seven courses to over 600 high-school students in sixty-five schools representing twenty-nine school divisions, three remote school districts, one aboriginal band school, and three private schools. Students use the Manitoba independent study course materials in conjunction with monthly live satellite broadcasts and bi-weekly audio-conferencing sessions. Between sessions, teachers and students can correspond by Email on the provincial system, MINET (Manitoba Education and Training, 1993a).

The satellite network has provided high-quality course options to students in remote areas. One notable feature has been the rise in course completion from an average of 25 per cent to 75 per cent. The use of such a centralised technology, while being cost-effective in its provision of a wider range of courses, raises issues of scheduling, local autonomy and recognition of the need to integrate distance education into the school. Moreover, costs associated with such technology are high, if cost-effective.

In April 1992, the minister of education and training for Manitoba established a task force on distance education and technology to make recommendations for the future development of distance education in that province. The task force envisaged the 'establishment of community-based infrastructures for lifelong learning which provide high quality education and training programs for all Manitobans' (Manitoba Education and Training, 1993b, p. 3). It stressed the importance of partnerships based on existing infrastructures and initiatives such as the Midland School Division's inter-active television system and the Souris Valley audio-conferencing distance education programme, both pilot projects of long duration. The task force recommended that an appropriate administrative structure would be region-ally developed consortia that would be responsible for developing the lists of course offerings, for providing appropriate technological and support systems, and that would bid for funds from government and private sources.

The task force noted that to provide 'effective client-centred service to the lifelong learner' (ibid., p. 10), it was essential not only that programme selec-tion, student support and administrative control of the distance learning system be local, but also that there be a province-wide coordination of efforts in the areas of resource and information sharing. It proposed a provincial council with representation from the consortia which would deal with provin-cial coordination issues and whose primary task would be information shar-ing. It also recommended that the ministry work with other government departments such as 'Northern Affairs, Health, Justice and Family Services, and Rural Development, to provide support and policy direction for distance education' (ibid., p. 13). Although it recognised the use of audio-conferencing and computer conferencing networks, the task force proposed the development of a province-wide network of video-conferencing capabil-ities based on the initial exploration of satellite, fibre-optic, compressed digit-al and amateur radio technologies by various institutions in the province. From a distance education perspective, the most interesting of these is the possible development of a wireless microwave system which would carry full-motion television, telephone and computer data at a fraction of the implementation and operational costs of a telephone-based system (W. Warren, personal communication, 16 March 1995).

Some of these recommendations have been acted upon. MERLIN, the Manitoba Educational Research and Learning Information Network, was es-tablished in April 1995 as an entrepreneurial enterprise within a public-sector mandate. Reporting to the minister of education and training, it operates on a cost-recovery, fee-for-service basis, and brokers network services and rates, copyright negotiations and facilities scheduling, etc. A Council on Distance Education and Technology has been established, with membership drawn from a broad spectrum of education and training stakeholders, including community groups and local businesses. The Manitoba Educational Inter-active Television Network is being established to serve the rural and northern schools not served by MSN.

The above accounts illustrate developments occurring in the selected prov-inces and territories. Québec, the Northwest Territories, Yukon, Prince

Edward Island and British Columbia are also progressing with technological infrastructures for schooling.

Decentralising distance education

Each Canadian province is responsible for its educational services, but there is a trend towards decentralising distance education further. Between 1986 and 1995, British Columbia, Alberta, Québec and Manitoba have sought to place responsibility for distance education closer to the clients by relocating their offices or by giving increased responsibility to individual school boards.

In 1986/7, British Columbia decentralised government services to nine centres. One of the first to be restructured was the provincial Correspondence School. Two centres, Northern British Columbia at Fort St John and Central Interior at Prince George, were opened in 1987; by September 1990, all nine centres were operational. Each of these centres was affiliated with a local school district and was responsible for distance education students in that region (Restall *et al.*, 1987). One result was that the Distance Education Centre staff had more immediate contact with students through visiting schools and through a shopfront office in the regional centre. Course materials preparation remained coordinated from the main ministry office in Victoria, but most of the marking was done on a piece-work basis by teachers employed by the local Distance Education Centre. Centres also began experimenting with audio-conferencing to increase interaction, and facsimile machines for the submission and return of assignments.

In Alberta, the move to implement the findings of the 1987 task force on correspondence education took on new urgency in 1989 as it became increasingly evident that the government would not be able to sustain its level of financial support for educational innovations. Pilot projects were initiated to test the feasibility of infrastructures based on partnerships among schools, and to explore a number of factors: the utility of multi-graded student learning centres in schools; the use of computerised testing and databanks for mathematics students; and the promotion of audio-conferencing and audio-graphics for teaching (Clark and Haughey, 1990). In October 1989, when the project was entering its second year, the minister implemented a provincial policy on distance education with an equity grant of C$8 million for the 135 Alberta schools which had fewer than a hundred high-school students, a small financial tax-base and whose jurisdiction fell within specific funding parameters (Alberta Education, 1989, p. 22). He provided one-time-only funding to allow school jurisdictions to purchase the necessary hardware and also encouraged districts to form consortia to provide distance education services so that tutoring and marking could be provided locally.

This announcement heralded the transformation of the mandate of the Alberta Correspondence School that had been recommended by the 1987 task force mentioned above. The Alberta Distance Learning Centre was relocated from Edmonton to Barrhead and reorganised into two units: Instructional Services and Support Services. Instructional Services (formerly ACS) continues to provide full services to adult students and those school students unable to access a local provider. Support Services provides curriculum development, instructional technology and student support services to regional centres, schools and consortia who provide the courses to students. This unit uses desktop publishing to develop instructional materials, and is responsible for expanding the databanks of questions in secondary-school courses, and exploring alternative technology formats including desktop video and CD-ROMs.

This model is not unlike that recently instituted in Québec. In 1991, the responsibility for distance education college-level courses had been transferred from the ministry office responsible for correspondence schools to a new school attached to an existing college. In January 1995, the responsibility for offering distance education services at the secondary level was transferred to the school boards, with fifty-nine electing to offer such services. While course delivery has devolved to the school jurisdictions, the development remains centralised. However, the governance of this central unit is managed by a non-profit organisation formed by the participating school boards and is no longer part of the ministry of education (CMEC, 1994, p. 28).

Manitoba, in contrast, has chosen a different model. Manitoba's Distance Education Unit contains two programmes: the Independent Study Program provides services directly to students; the Teacher Mediated Program provides services in cooperation with schools. In 1991/2 the Independent Study Program was relocated from Winnipeg to Winkler. As there is a concerted provincial effort to introduce real-time distance programming through video- and audio-conferencing, the services of the Independent Study Program are not likely to be influential in any future multimedia programming mix.

In all four provinces, the strategy to decentralise and relocate operations was a mix of political and economic policy initiatives designed to demonstrate that the governments were trying to diversify economic opportunities to rural areas. However, since government business is largely based in the capital cities, decentralisation has made it more difficult to integrate distance education with telecommunications, since responsibilities for the latter are often in a different unit or government department. People are, however, increasing their use of technology for administrative meetings, and are learning how to compensate.

Sharing resources

This decade's revitalised interest in distance education, which has come at a time of diminishing economic resources and public concerns about the need for common curriculum performance indicators, has led to greater cooperation among provinces in course-materials development. The Maritime provinces have formed a consortium to develop courseware which will fit their curricula, and the four western provinces and two territories have a similar initiative.

Prince Edward Island is a partner with Nova Scotia and New Brunswick in the Maritime Provinces Educational Foundation, which has been formed to develop selected common curricula to obtain improved quality with fewer resources (Prince Edward Island Department of Education and Human Resources, 1993). Newfoundland and Labrador also participate on a project basis. As well as developing common science courses, the Foundation has also been involved in a national initiative called SchoolNet. A programme to assist New Brunswick elementary teachers to become familiar with hardware and software has been supported by Industry, Science and Technology Canada (New Brunswick Department of Education, 1993).

In western Canada, the Manitoba Distance Education unit purchased the grades 1 to 6 curriculum materials developed in Alberta to replace outdated materials that were too costly to revise. In 1992/3, the Manitoba Distance Education and Technology Department formed a partnership with their own Curriculum Services and the similar units from the provinces of Alberta, British Columbia and Saskatchewan to develop computer-assisted learning materials in mathematics for grades 9 to 12 (Manitoba Education and Training, 1993b). This project, completed in 1994/5, was only one of a series of projects where the ministers of education for the four western provinces decided to pool resources to develop common curricula which would meet the requirements of all four provinces.

The Council of Ministers of Education, Canada (CMEC), established in 1967 to enable provincial and territorial ministers to consult on matters of mutual interest, published a report on open and distance education in Canada (CMEC, 1994). The three critical inter-jurisdictional issues identified were: collaboration in development and accreditation of programmes and/or courses, telecommunications across provincial boundaries, and information sharing. CMEC has already begun the development of a manual of best practices on partnerships; a briefing paper on telecommunications, regulatory issues and federal legislation; and a process for sharing information (Roberts, 1995).

FEDERAL GOVERNMENT INITIATIVES

Woven through provincial initiatives are examples of collaboration with the federal government: for example, the Telidon software mentioned in the Lake Superior Alternative Delivery Project and the Newfoundland and New Brunswick federal–provincial Human Resource Development agreements. While education is a provincial responsibility, the federal government has authority for areas such as training, telecommunications and industrial development. Federal–provincial partnerships are, therefore, feasible and necessary. Indeed, the federal government has shown, through projects such as the Hermes satellite experiments of the 1970s (Roberts and Keough, 1995), that its leverage can have a significant impact on educational infrastructures; the federal-government involvement in the ANIK satellite series influenced the development of the provincial telecommunications agencies.

While technologies such as Telidon and Hermes were the focus of federal funding in the 1970s, between 1985 and 1995, the federal government became more focused on policy studies and processes, partnerships with industry and the roles of education, training and technology in supporting job creation and economic competitiveness.

A series of national reports (Economic Council of Canada, 1992; Corporate Higher-Education Forum, 1990; Fournier and MacKinnon, 1994; Prosperity Initiative, 1991,1992; Stahmer *et al.*, 1992) identified the importance of technology for changing the way policy-makers should think about schooling. These reports highlighted, for example, that educational achievements were closely tied to economic prosperity and urged that all social partners collaborate in raising the quality of Canada's education and training systems. Technology was seen as a way to address issues of quality by improving access for learners, bringing more resources into the classroom and providing cost-effective workplace training opportunities.

This linking of technology initiatives and a possible increase in Canada's competitive edge received much press in the late 1980s. Concern was expressed that Canada was lagging behind its competitors with respect to the development of a national 'electronic highway'. While, according to the media, businesses were in the vanguard demanding instant access to global information and, in particular, trading and commodity pricing information from around the world, educators were also interested in the opportunity to access library resources and share scarce expertise no matter where they might be located. Several initiatives have arisen from this focus. Although the federal government has a leading role in them, it has chosen to operate in broadly based consortia. To illustrate this trend, we profile CANARIE, the Information Highway Advisory Council and SchoolNet.

CANARIE (Canadian Network for the Advancement of Research, Industry and Education) Inc. is an industry-led and managed consortium of over 140 private- and public-sector members. It was created in 1993 for the federal government and private sector to collaborate in stimulating the development of the information highway. Now in its second phase (1995–9), with an enlarged membership that includes educational institutions, CANARIE is constructing a National Test Network based on the highly sophisticated network technology ATM (asynchronous transfer mode). To encourage use of the network, and other parts of the information highway, CANARIE is also funding a Technology and Applications Development Programme, the upgrading of CA*Net (Canada's national computer link to the Internet), and an outreach programme to promote the development of infrastructure and the evolution of an information-based economy and society (Industry

Canada, 1994). All these programmes involve partnerships between the public and private sectors; some involve schools.

Another example of government's commitment to technology in education is Industry Canada's leadership in spearheading a cooperative initiative of Canada's governments, educators, universities, colleges and industry called SchoolNet. SchoolNet aims to link all of Canada's estimated 23,000 public schools, libraries, colleges and universities to the Internet by 1998. Industry Canada created SchoolNet's National Advisory Board to guide its development and to enhance educational networking opportunities and achievements available to all schools. As of January 1995, nearly 4,500 schools were on-line and over 500 different types of curriculum-support services were available. The number of connections to the SchoolNet Gopher has been growing at an average increase of 65 per cent per month.

The SchoolNet National Advisory Board, together with the Canadian Educational Network Coalition and the Stentor Alliance, prepared a submission (Reidlinger and Weir, 1995) advocating that education be rated separately from the current residential and commercial categories which govern telecommunications rates. Currently, education pays this commercial rate, a cost that many schools cannot afford. The Canadian Radio-Television and Telecommunications Commission, which regulates telecommunications rates in Canada, received the brief and has since issued a report on convergence (1995) which did not exclude the possibility of a preferential rate for education and health, and also established the conditions for such a proposed rate. Soon afterwards the Commission called for proposals from provincial telephone companies.

In addition to participating in the implementation and regulation of infrastructure, the federal government is actively engaged in policy development. In March 1994, Industry Canada established a national Information Highway Advisory Council to report to the minister of industry on fifteen issues organised under three categories: the infrastructure building, the content transmitted and the benefits. One of the council's five working groups concentrated on learning and training, and included members from industry, education, research and labour. The council's final report (1995) contains over 300 recommendations. One focus that affects educators relates to the need for all teachers to become technologically literate as quickly as possible. The report emphasises the potential of job creation, the export of learning hardware and software, and other economic benefits that will accrue if education, government and the private sector all accelerate their use of information and communications technologies. While access and universality – the traditional priorities of distance education – are also policy concerns, there is a new focus on economic impacts.

Independent of government is a national cable project targeted to serve schools. In an effort to reach students directly, Canada's cable companies in cooperation with specialty channels have launched a non-profit venture called 'Canadian Cable in the Classroom'. Currently, about 3,200 of

Canada's 16,000 schools have cable service. The fifty-one cable operators participating in the project expect to increase the number to 7,000 by the end of 1997 (*Globe & Mail*, 28 September 1995, p. A8). Through the project, cable companies provide each school with one free basic cable-service connection and access to approximately twenty-five specialty channels with commercial-free programming.

These developments indicate the federal government's commitment to the use of technology in education. Its partnerships with the private sector, as well as provincial ministries of education, are designed to stimulate Canada's national economic policy and the development and implementation of provincial infrastructure policies.

CONCLUSION

Distance education is evolving in Canada's schools in a complex environment. The explosion of interest in the Internet among the general public and the rise in the numbers of personal computers in homes, estimated in 1995 to be 33 per cent of homes with children under the age of 18 (Statistics Canada, 1994), is creating pressure on schools to acquire the same facilities. The growth in CD-ROM players and their 'edutainment' applications, and the intense competition between telephone companies and cable television providers for the provision of their services to homes, businesses and schools, intensify the demands. Added to this mix of 'high cost demand in a time of low budget supply' are cultural issues such as the threat of the 'Black Stars' – satellites beaming American programming directly into Canadian homes and schools. There is therefore an enhanced awareness of the issues of technological gateways to business, entertainment and education (Andersen Consulting, 1995).

The private sector is becoming increasingly involved in education. While it has a strong interest in issues such as the quality of the graduates, business is increasingly a force in the introduction of technology to schools. Schools themselves are responding by establishing partnerships that cross traditional sectoral boundaries. The concomitant emphasis on resource-based education is one indication that the notion of school-based distance education and resource-based learning may converge in the wired classrooms of the near future.

However, not all segments of society are gaining access to the same level of technology. The availability of computers in the homes, for example, varies with income from a low of 7.5 per cent in homes with annual incomes under C$10,000 to more than 50 per cent in households with annual incomes above C$90,000 (Statistics Canada, 1994). This trend in Canada is magnified globally when first- and third-world countries are compared. Social goals such as universality and access are still important, but, perhaps because of new national and global economic realities, they are being surpassed by the economic attractions of technology.

The degree of attention paid to technology by the mass media seems to be a significant factor fuelling government initiatives. Coverage of topics such as the trends to a global economy and a technological society, the demands for a better educated workforce, and the need for lifelong learning reinforces the messages contained in federal-government and private-sector documents of the last five years. A recent Gallup poll indicated that 63 per cent of the public is most interested in the educational services on the information highway (Andersen Consulting, 1995).

These pressures on schools will only increase in the next decade. They will be asked to develop new models of distance education which involve techno-logy integration in the classroom and which can be more easily accepted by learners and by taxpayers. They will be encouraged to use approaches such as desktop, or classroom, video-conferencing which emphasise real-time instruction and to employ more technological multimedia support so that students can be engaged more actively than is thought possible with the pencil and paper format.

In the face of these pressures, provincial policy initiatives will change focus from an emphasis on access to courses. They will increasingly move to concerns about working with private-sector partners to provide infrastructure access to computer and video technologies, and to cooperating with other agencies for the provision of educational multimedia materials for resource-based learning. The convergence of federal directions, provincial concerns and business and industry preferences will provide a major boost to open and distance learning. The major challenge for distance educators will be to ride the whirlwind into the next century.

7 Reforming distance education through economic rationalism

A critical analysis of reforms to Australian higher education

Viktor Jakupec

INTRODUCTION

From the second half of the 1980s to the early 1990s distance education in Australian higher education has been changing rapidly. In 1987 distance education came under increasingly severe scrutiny by the government, as part of a general attempt to reform higher education. Following unfavourable economic comparisons with the operation of competitive markets, politicians argued that higher education was not contributing fully to economic development. More precisely the Hawke Labor Government in Australia, acting in harmony with the New Right elsewhere (such as Thatcher's Conservative Government in the UK and Reagan's Republican administration in the USA), argued that there was an 'overload' of demand for taxpayers' money to support free higher education and there was considerable inefficiency within the higher education sector. Despite the transparency of the political economic rationalist agenda, the government attack led to the restructuring of not only the total higher education system, but also the distance education provision within the system. Therefore, it seems to me a worthwhile task to attempt a critical analysis of Australian government policy and its effects on distance education from the second half of the 1980s. In broad terms the critical analysis will focus on higher education policies of the Australian Commonwealth Government, drawing on some policy development parallels in overseas countries.

AUSTRALIAN HIGHER EDUCATION POLICY IN THE 1980s: AN OVERVIEW

It would be impossible to find a period in the development of higher education where everyone was satisfied (Reeves, 1988). It is apparent, however, that during the 1980s we witnessed an increase in the level of criticism directed towards the universities in many western countries (OECD, 1987). In Australia the criticism came from the Commonwealth Government and interest groups with a specifically economic rationalist stance (Marginson, 1993). Their first critical question, borrowed from the OECD with its 'New Right' ideology, was whether Australia could afford free higher education. This was, of course, not only a question of money but one of ideology. In essence the values of equity and participation, as they had existed since the Whitlam Labor Government in the early 1970s, were to be rewritten. Equity and participation in higher education were, contrary to the Labor Party 'Platform' (Australian Labor Party, 1986), no longer to be seen as a basic right but a right upon the condition that individuals made a financial contribution. The second critical question was how Australian higher education should be restructured to better serve the economic 'national interest'. The economic rationalist stance was the major force within the policy-formulating government departments of the time (Pusey, 1991) and, thus, the timing of the first question was critical for any plans in relation to the second; in order to pay for a restructured higher education system the government needed to increase its funding. This situation led to the introduction of the Higher Education Contribution Scheme (HECS), whereby an individual who benefits from higher education is required to contribute on the basis of current or future income (for full discussion and funding arrangements see Wran, 1988). Already embracing an economic rationalist ideology in other policy domains such as health, housing and social services, the Hawke Labor Government and the then Minister for Employment, Education and Training, John Dawkins, were following a pre-determined pattern.

Pursuing deterministic economic and labour market reform, Dawkins succeeded in reducing the meaning of the term 'higher education policy' to that of a rational calculation of means to achieve given economic ends. On the basis of the assumption that the higher education sector could make a significant contribution to economic recovery and future growth, Dawkins constructed a Unified National System (UNS) of higher education which was to meet economic needs through the production of a highly skilled labour force. Even if an economic recovery was not guaranteed through the UNS, the view was that the chances for a competitive labour force would be maximised by the adoption of the correct economic strategy and higher education structure.

The Hawke government's higher education policy was firmly based on a competitive free-market model similar to policies adopted in Thatcher's Britain and Reagan's USA, but with a twist. In embracing Thatcherism and Reaganism, the government tried to fulfil two economic objectives. First, it tried to force the higher education sector to exploit the advantages of a competitive (free) market model and, second, it established a distance education monopoly by limiting the number of distance education providers to eight Distance Education Centres (DECs). In proceeding towards the first objective the government attempted to use the profoundly radical Thatcherist approach of destroying those parts of the structure of higher education that were no longer 'profitable' – that is, the institutions and disciplines that do not contribute directly to the 'economic' goals of the government (Jakupec, 1993). This was to be achieved by shifting government funding from arts, education and humanities disciplines to more economically 'profitable' ones such as engineering, management and technology (Dawkins, 1987a, 1988) and by amalgamations of institutions generally and establishment of a limited number of DECs, so that greater economies of scale could be achieved.

There could be some rationality in this approach as long as one agrees that one can compare higher education institutions with business organisations with fundamentally different purposes. On the other hand, there is much that is misleading in this approach, for economic rationalism promises a precise evaluation of the efficacy of its own policy but it does not seem to be able to 'deliver the goods'. Dawkins consistently stated that there were 'compelling reasons' and 'arguments' for the correctness of his policy – he did not, however, offer evidence of its effectiveness as implemented elsewhere. The policy decisions made, therefore, seem to have been based, in reality, on what were no more than 'judgements' made by individuals and interest groups claiming 'rationality' as their justification. In essence judgements were made by economic rationalists on the basis of *their* understanding of national and international economic circumstances, *their* need to protect their own sphere of interests, *their* specialised and thus limited knowledge, *their* loyalty to a free-market economy, *their* intuition, and so on. Thus economic rationalism is no more or no less rational than any other competing ideology (Schluchter, 1981).

ECONOMIC RATIONALISM AS THE ENGINE OF POLICY

The policies pursued by Dawkins towards distance education during the 1980s have to be understood in the context of the general higher education policy formulations of the Hawke Labor Government. From the beginning it is interesting to observe that many of the policies in Dawkins's White Paper were formulated originally in one form or another by the Commonwealth Tertiary Education Commission (CTEC; see for example CTEC, 1986, 1987b) and based on CTEC's own interpretation of the statistics (CTEC, 1987a). Dawkins, as stated previously, followed almost 'blindly' the policies of the Thatcher Government by proceeding with policy formulations without much consideration of Australia's needs and existing conditions. Let me explain. Keith Joseph's Green Paper (see Joseph, 1985) and Kenneth Baker's White Paper (see Baker, 1987) could be justified on the basis of shortcomings such as the 'crisis of confidence' ascribed to universities in Great Britain by Jarratt (1985; Sizer, 1986; UGC, 1987) but the same problems did not exist in Australian universities. As Hugh Hudson, the chair of CTEC, concluded in the CTEC report on efficiency, 'major changes in the current structure of higher education are not necessary' and necessary changes could be achieved through changes in funding arrangements (CTEC, 1986, p. 197). There are two important points to be noted here: first, in Australia the university sector did not suffer from a 'crisis of confidence' and, second, there was no evidence presented that would justify Dawkins's assertion that the higher education sector was poorly equipped to respond to economic and social demands. In fact, the general public was not dissatisfied with the higher education sector. Indeed the Australian Vice-Chancellors' Committee (AVCC) reported that the universities are respected and have amongst the general public a very favourable image (see AVCC, 1989, and for a contrary view see Mahony, 1990). There was a general apathy within the society about government policies to restructure the higher education system.

Dawkins's (1987a) Green Paper followed the ideals of Joseph's (1985) discussion paper and his own (1988) White Paper was ideologically aligned with Baker's (1987) policy paper. That is, without much consideration of Australia's particular needs and existing conditions, Dawkins claimed that there were 'compelling reasons' to restructure the higher education sector. The basic ideology for the restructuring was very similar, if not the same, as that pursued by Thatcher's Conservative Government in Great Britain. Setting aside some minor differences between the respective policy papers in Australia and Great Britain, there was a consensus between the Hawke Labor Government and the Thatcher Conservative Government that tertiary education (higher and technical) must make a significant contribution to the economic growth of a nation. The New Right ideology of the Organisation for Economic Cooperation and Development (OECD, 1983, 1985, 1986) was embraced.

The adoption of the New Right ideology required an attack on the Keynesian welfare state and moderate conservatism, a phenomenon which emerged during the 1970s and 1980s in many OECD countries (Finegold *et al.*, 1993). Reagan's political programme, like Thatcher's, depended on convincing the electorate that the policies of the moderates were not only ineffective, but would precipitate the very problems they aimed to combat (Green, 1987). Both Thatcher and Reagan spoke of economic decline; both used this rhetoric to frighten the electorate into accepting the monetarism and free-market ideology. In Thatcher's Great Britain the monetarist ideology was heralded by Joseph, Margaret Thatcher's 'mentor' (Worcester, 1989). As far as higher education is concerned, Joseph 'internalised' free-market values using Friedman's and Hayek's monetarist ideas (Friedman, 1962; Friedman and Friedman, 1984; Hayek, 1967, 1978). Dawkins, following Joseph's vision of higher education, adopted monetarist ideology by establishing ministerial control of funding for higher education. He persuaded the universities and Colleges of Advanced Education (CAEs) to accept budgetary constraints while allowing market forces greater power in determining the direction the UNS would take. Dawkins's rhetoric on the need of the higher education sector to follow more closely the entrepreneurial ideals of private enterprise was accompanied by a massive increase in government intervention into the day-to-day running of individual higher education institutions (Botsman, 1988).

Both Reaganism and Thatcherism were based on the idea of the infallibility of market solutions by reducing taxes and government spending (Verstegen, 1990). As far as higher education is concerned the economic strategy was to increase human capital through reforms to education, training and technology (Eaton, 1991). However, under Dawkins's reforms the need for investment conflicted with the desire for reducing government spending. The ideal process of achieving the latter is to unburden the government from the responsibility of spending on social commitments such as education, health and other welfare services (Stoesz and Karger, 1993). Thus, the financial burden was shifted to the individual. In Australia the ideological shift to Thatcherism is evident from the contribution scheme (HECS) developed by Wran (1988). The political rhetoric was to reduce the number of institutions, rationalise the system and increase investment in training, education and educational technology. The Hawke Government believed that by encouraging rationalisation of the higher education sector and decreasing the number of distance education providers the UNS would attract market participation in higher education. Institutions within the UNS were viewed as future participants in the markets and, thus, financially less dependent on the government. This again is a reflection of Thatcher's monetarism and bourgeois values of self-discipline and self-reliance (Gilmore, 1992). The acceptance of monetarism by the Labor Government was important for it is a very powerful tool allowing the government to foster a free-market approach to all sectors of society, including higher education.

What emerged in Australia was a 'cult of efficiency' driven by the government's aim to establish a more efficient and effective higher education system – more efficient and effective in the monetarist sense. The system was to become more responsive to the needs of industry, business and commerce interests in line with the government perception of what was required. These government aims gained support from a number of groups who were vigorously pursuing their own interest in isolation of others. Business groups, especially the Business Council of Australia (BCA), called for a reduction of expenditure on higher education to free resources for other forms of investment (see, for example, BCA, 1986, 1988). At the same time, the CAEs, through the Australian Committee of Directors and Principals in Advanced Education (ACDP), argued that they should have the same levels of funding as the universities (ACDP, 1988). Using the economic rationalist views expressed by various interest groups, Dawkins argued that universities had failed to achieve the alternative structure needed for the nation's new economic requirements and, thus, the government had to take the initiative (Dawkins, 1987a). Many individual academics, higher education institutions and their respective representative bodies responded to the arguments by agreeing that there was a need for public debate. This debate was taken up by strong interest groups such as the ACDP (1988), the AVCC (1988), the unions (see ACTU, 1988) and the business community (BCA, 1986, 1988).

There was a critique of government policies on higher education but it came from only a small number of academics and interest groups. There was little criticism from the general public. Furthermore, it appeared that a significant number of academics, including those working in distance education, were casual in their interest (Jakupec and Nicoll, 1994b). For example, Dawkins's decision to reduce the number of distance education providers caught many institutions that were not classified as DECs off-guard. Clearly this situation demonstrates academia's failure to understand the New Right agenda underpinning the restructuring in Australia and other OECD countries.

One has to ask how and why a Labor government was able to embrace New Right policies? There was no indication that there was a solid base of political support for change – the government had no great demand placed on it to press for change – there was no obvious interest (other than ideological) for the government to pursue the restructure. On the balance of evidence presented there was no identifiable problem. Thus the Hawke Government offered a solution to a non-existent problem. This explanation seems to be too simplistic, however. The most likely reason for the restructuring of the higher education sector was the government's perception of how to react to and counteract an emerging economic crisis which was based on a rising overseas trade deficit and less than favourable balance of payment figures. The government argued that Australia's future and long-term economic prosperity would depend on successful competitiveness in the international arena which is only achievable by augmenting the *savoir faire* of technology.

There is a problem with this argument, because there is 'not a single unequivocal conclusion that emerges' from surveys conducted in Great Britain during the 1970s and 1980s that higher education can be linked to economic growth (Aldcroft, 1992, p. 20). If anything, despite the claims for the contribution of education towards economic growth,

> the main thrust of the debate in recent years suggests a more modified role for education's contribution to the economy. Because of different growth trajectories, differences in the quality of educational inputs, not to mention the tricky problems of measurement, one would not expect to find a very strong cross country relationship between education and economic growth, at least among advanced countries.
>
> (Ibid., p. 20)

Despite evidence that education cannot be necessarily linked to economic growth, the Labor Government 'fast tracked' the restructuring of the higher education system. The interesting point is that Dawkins's higher education policy was implemented in just over a year, achieving direct financial control over the entire higher education sector. In the process it abolished a thirty-year history of the working of statutory commissions (such as the CTEC and its predecessor the Universities Commission) that had kept the tertiary education sector at arm's length from the government. Direct and controlling links were put in place between Dawkins's new 'super-department', the Department of Employment, Education and Training (DEET), and individual institutions. Newly developed funding arrangements and formulas – made with little respect for the constitutional rights of the states – enabled the

Commonwealth Government to dictate to the state governments who retained legal control of most institutions. Control of institutional administrative structure, teaching and research profile and size was now, *de facto*, in Commonwealth hands. From the legal perspective there was no compelling reason for either universities or the CAEs to comply with Dawkins's policies. In short, most higher education institutions followed blindly policies which had little legislative backing. This was achieved legislatively by transferring the role of CTEC to the minister and DEET and making the necessary amendments in the relevant Budget Bills.

How was it possible that most higher education institutions implemented Dawkins's policies and all state governments endorsed the wishes of the Commonwealth Government through complementary legislation? The answer to the first part of the question was the government's threat to penalise financially those institutions that did not join the UNS. The answer to the second part of the question may well be that state governments simply followed the wishes (or apparent wishes) of the individual institutions. If this is the case then the institutions would have had to convince their respective state government of either the advantages of amalgamating or the consequences of refusing to join the UNS. There is some evidence that this was the case:

> The Minister has indicated that the [Commonwealth] Government will only consider proposals which have been agreed by the institutions involved and that it will support those proposals which have the potential to generate educational benefits and to make better use of available resources.
>
> (Ramsey, 1989, p. 3)

The Commonwealth Government succeeded in establishing the UNS and DECs by using two Acts: the Employment, Education and Training Act 1988, No. 80, which abolished the CTEC and established the National Board of Employment, Education and Training (NBEET) as an advisory body to the minister, and the Higher Education Funding Act 1989, No. 2. Using the latter, the government identifies institutions which will be funded, establishes the level of recurrent and capital funding for each institution, and specifies administrative and accounting procedures which enable states to manage the grants. Curiously there was no Commonwealth Act that legislated for the massive structural changes in the system overall and the institutional structures, management, amalgamations and governance achieved by Dawkins.

In summary, the Dawkins reforms to the general system of higher education were as follows: the binary system was abolished and replaced with the UNS; there would be fewer higher education institutions – achieved through institutional amalgamations, whereby the new institutions would be larger and sometimes multi-campus institutions; institutional administration within the UNS would be based on corporate managerial structure and governance; the relation between teaching and research would on the one hand be relaxed and on the other there would be a more competitive process of allocating

research funding – the government would provide for a more targeted allocation of research funds; institutions within the UNS would be required to
forge links with industry and to focus in their teaching and research on the
needs of industry, business and private enterprise. In this context, the institutions within the UNS would pursue more 'market oriented' policies in
teaching and research. An analysis of these policies is outside the scope of
this chapter but a detailed understanding of them is necessary in order better
to understand the implementation of policies directed exclusively to distance
education which occurred in the same context.

RATIONALISING DISTANCE EDUCATION

The reforms proposed for distance education in the White Paper were not
new: they had been put forward by CTEC in the mid-1980s. From the early
1980s there had been concerns about the uncoordinated proliferation of
courses and institutions engaged in distance education (see Chapter 8 of this
volume). For example, in 1987 there were about thirty CAEs and nine
universities offering courses ranging from Associate Diplomas to Master's
Degrees in well over three hundred different subject areas. Throughout
Australia individuals could choose from fifty-two offerings of Graduate
Certificate courses in education alone (University of Queensland, 1988).

With the unchecked proliferation of distance education in mind, the government's policy focused on rationalisation which would provide a high
degree of efficiency and effectiveness and, at the same time, provide for
tighter ministerial control over all aspects of higher education. The political
rhetoric, however, was quite different. It emphasised the need to avoid duplication of courses, the need to foster collaboration between distance education
institutions, the need to increase the quality of teaching materials and expand
the range of disciplines available. Dawkins summarised his agenda as follows:

> External studies (or distance education) has a key role to play in achieving
> the Government's objectives of growth and greater equity in higher educa-
> tion. In this context the Policy Discussion Paper outlined proposals for
> enhancing the provision of external studies by reducing duplication, fos-
> tering co-operation between providing institutions and improving the
> overall quality, availability and efficiency of external studies courses.
>
> (Dawkins, 1987b, p. 49)

In order to achieve these aims, Dawkins appointed a committee with representatives of DEET, the Higher Education Council (HEC) and some
independent members (henceforth DEET–HEC, 1989). The committee was
asked to decide which institutions should be designated as DECs and it published a report in March 1989. The committee recognised the political aims
for distance education, namely 'rationalisation' – whereby only about six
higher education institutions would be designated as DECs. Although all
institutions were invited to apply for designation only seventeen were able to

respond because of the selection criteria. The criteria were based *inter alia* on arbitrary national needs, rationalisations, ability to develop and maintain quality and effectiveness of distance education materials and services, competitive completion rates, provision for postgraduate and full-fee-paying overseas students, and cost-effectiveness (ibid.).

By restricting distance education offerings to a few institutions the government was able to relate two objectives: the rationalisation of distance education and the reformulation of institutional profiles. This, in effect, created a drive towards effectiveness and efficiency (in line with government aims) and a rationalisation of courses throughout the whole system. Furthermore, some of the smaller institutions, which required distance education to attract sufficient student numbers to justify their existence, were forced to amalgamate and some were simply absorbed by other institutions which were eager to become DECs. Effectively Dawkins's policy changed the structural framework of distance education through the imposition of a controlling mechanism. Eight rather than six DECs were established. Five of the DECs involved amalgamated institutions and one was a consortium of three universities in Western Australia. The DECs were given the freedom to develop distance education programmes at state and national levels.

The question of how far the government achieved its goal of making the higher education sector more efficient remains open. Abe and Wheelwright (1989) contend that the Commonwealth Government did not rectify the inefficiencies of the higher education system. They argue that the desired alignment of higher education with economic needs occurred only in a peripheral sense. Sweet (1989), who supported the restructuring, lamented that Dawkins did not achieve the paramount goal by forcing institutions to align their courses with economic priorities. Despite this kind of criticism, distance education was significantly affected. Livingstone (1988) concludes that the Commonwealth Government succeeded within the established economic paradigm to restructure distance education so that it became more effective and efficient. He argues that distance education had become identified as a separate and formal part of higher education in its own right with a distinct type of administrative system through the DECs.

Campion and Kelly (1988) advance the argument that the Commonwealth Government challenged the higher education institutions to provide an increased number of student places. However, they argue that a differentiation between face-to-face and distance education contradicts such an aim. Only integration of the two methods would lead to an increase of places. Such an undertaking, they conclude, would be innovative as well as cost-effective. Despite this argument it would have been impossible for the government to accept the proposition as it would have contradicted the desire for intervention and direct control.

As we can see there is little consensus among commentators about the influence of distance education and DECs on access, equity, economic values and efficiency of delivery. We should be mindful that much distance education, as we knew it prior to Dawkins's restructuring, preserved a similarity to face-to-face university education's traditional values and cultural heritage. Thus the erosion of these values through values of economic rationalism encountered resistance; this is where many of the problems with policy formulation and implementation originated.

The changes brought about by the restructuring of the higher education sector during the second half of the 1980s had impacted on the whole higher education sector, yet in end effect the changes to distance education were different from those encountered in conventional institutions. Common factors were: amalgamation of institutions and with it reduction or, at least, potential reduction in duplications of courses; establishing frameworks that fostered collaboration between DEC and non-DEC institutions; enhancement of teaching quality incorporating, under the premise of efficiency and effectiveness, distance education methods into other forms of higher education. From the government's point of view, there was a need not only for collaboration among DECs, but also for a steering and control mechanism. This was to be achieved through the establishment of the National Distance Education Conference (henceforth NDEC) which I will address later.

There was one very important consequence of Dawkins's reforms: they brought distance education from the margins to the mainstream of higher education (Nunan, 1988). How far this was the intention of the government is difficult to judge. What can be said is that the restructuring of the system, as a whole, brought with it a separate identity for distance education. Yet despite this restructuring there was the problem for DEET, as Nunan (1991a) observes, in that a large number of universities that were not classified as DECs refused to abandon their distance education programmes or, as DEET intended for non-DECs, to hand over these programmes to the DECs. It is outside the framework of this chapter to analyse all the possibilities of intervention of DEET into the DEC and non-DEC institutions as far as distance education programmes are concerned. It should suffice to say that some institutions changed the name of distance education programmes to 'extended-campus studies'. This raises the question of how far the DECs were prepared to accept the *Zeitgeist* of economic rationalism. According to King (1989) there was the possibility that DECs would not follow blindly the New Right ideology and would resist the 'devaluation' of academic values. King argued that, regardless of DEET budget allocations and guidelines for the DECs for the development of distance education materials, it is not valid to understand the production of distance education as a narrow linear and industrialised form. He contends that distance education should only be seen in the context of the normative and historical concepts that underpin it

Nevertheless, so as to facilitate changes to the distance education structure, NDEC's membership included not only representatives from the DECs, but also 'consumer institutions' (i.e. non-DEC members) and DEET. The function of NDEC was to develop the rationalisation policies in line with the aims of the Commonwealth Government. This, of course, strengthened the power of DEET to intervene in the future planning of distance education provision in Australia. NDEC was charged with operating as a national distance education forum for consultation and negotiation and, as such, to advance effectiveness and efficiency among DECs, through cooperation and sharing of resources, and to 'advise' the minister 'on Commonwealth support for the introduction of new technologies in higher education in Australia' (NDEC, 1989b, p. 1). Not only did the government firmly believe that application of technology would provide a more efficient distance education system but that this may also extend to the entire higher education system. That is, the 'Commonwealth also considered that the DEC co-ordination mechanism (NDEC) would be well placed to advise on the related issue of the application of technology to the management and delivery of higher education' (NDEC, 1989a, p. 1).

This point was taken up by Fox (1989), who argues that distance education (and open education) because it is legitimised through functionality is 'valued for its pragmatic effects in enhancing the efficiency of the social machine as managed by the decision makers' (ibid., p. 257). If this is the case, then we can perceive DEET as the decision maker and technology as the vehicle by which the 'efficiency of the social machine' came be achieved.

In effect, NDEC provided a framework that: fostered the development of an effective and efficient network of distance education providers at national level; enabled DECs and other interests groups to initiate the development of network mechanisms for distance education, including collaboration in course development and provision, research and resources; provided advice to the government on matters concerning funding and resource allocation, and development of new technologies with the view of enhancing teaching and learning throughout the higher education sector; enhanced national planning for distance education; allowed for investigation of quality issues and norms for the development of distance education materials including study support for distance learners; and provided, as we will see later, a catalyst for the further development of distance education towards open learning.

THE DEFICIENCIES OF DAWKINS'S POLICIES

Dawkins viewed universities as production agencies for industry and commerce. The fundamental issue was to bring the higher education sector and distance education to contribute to economic changes through skilling and 'up-skilling' of the workforce. However, Dawkins failed to explain how the restructuring of the higher education sector could create a distance education system that went beyond mere delivery of distance education teaching material. Although Dawkins's policy on distance education argued firmly for growth with equity, the deficiency of the policy became evident through its implementation, which focused substantially on delivery mechanisms through technology (Jakupec and Nicoll, 1994a).

The contradiction between the concepts of growth and equity, and development and implementation of communication technology, became quickly evident to the government. Within three years of the establishment of the DECs the government had changed direction. Baldwin (1991), as the new minister for higher education, shifted the focus from a policy of growth with equity, based on economic rationalism akin to Thatcherism and Reaganism, to a policy of quality in diversity, underpinned by 'economic technicism'. The government believed that if it implemented technological advances on a sufficiently large scale within the higher education sector it would enhance not only efficiency but also quality of education (Jakupec and Nicoll, 1994a). First, Baldwin questioned the division of higher education institutions into DECs and non-DECs, claiming that it was arbitrary and that the 'withdrawal' of institutions from distance education 'limits the realisation of the potential offered by technological innovation' within the whole higher education system. Thus all universities should be able to offer courses in a diverse mode. Second, he questioned the monopoly of and centralisation of distance education provision within DECs and argued that Dawkins's policies for distance education had an adverse effect upon the whole higher education system (Baldwin, 1991). But as Jakupec and Nicoll (1994a, p. 27) suggest, 'Baldwin's perception of quality in diversity refers to the quality of the diverse technology for educational delivery, rather than quality of diversity in education.'

Baldwin changed aspects of the Dawkins legacy, especially by abolishing the monopoly of DECs. Yet despite these changes, the fundamental structure of Dawkins's reforms remains intact, especially in ideological terms, and this has caused social and moral damage within the higher education sector in Australia. In suggesting this it would, of course, be churlish not to welcome the improvements in higher education through the utilisation of distance education methodology for openness and access that flowed on from Dawkins's and more substantially from Baldwin's policies. This guarded welcome may not induce us to accept the Hawke Labor Government's policies for distance education in the second half of the 1980s; nor do we need to listen too attentively to the New Right, which still dominates the higher and distance education agenda in Australia. Its proponents assure us, on the basis of anecdotal evidence, that through the opening of higher education to a wider population, using distance education methodology, we have somehow resolved the defects of Thatcherism and Reaganism and those who have followed and copied them such as Dawkins.

Distance and open learning, together with flexible delivery initiatives offered in their current form by Australian universities, militate against the assumptions that we have overcome Thatcherism and Reaganism. Recent improvements in open learning and flexible delivery, while welcome, have done little more in many respects than restore distance education to the position it had in Australian higher education institutions prior to the restructuring under Dawkins. It is as though the Hawke Government and Dawkins threw distance education and the whole higher education over a cliff in 1988 and by

1991, with changes introduced by Baldwin, the same government was congratulating itself as distance education, with an emphasis on open learning and flexible delivery, inched its way back up the cliff-face to the point it had started at – being available to all institutions that wish to use them.

CONCLUSION

Almost a decade ago the emphasis was clearly on centralised planning and a DEC monopoly of distance education; the focus was on how distance education could contribute to foreseeable economic and labour-market requirements. Disillusionment with the DECs led to a dismantling and opening up the whole higher education system in Australia to a distance education delivery mode in a new key – distance education principles are now reflected in open and flexible delivery. The confusion between economic rationalism and economic technicism epitomises the view of the New Right. This confusion in the Hawke Labor Goverment was exhibited so clearly through Dawkins's policies and Baldwin's shift to harness distance education through technology for popular consumption within the whole higher education system. In short, there was no inducement to progress in distance education beyond the mechanism of delivery – the university tradition of critical inquiry through distance education was substituted with the simple descriptiveness of delivery of prepackaged knowledge.

On a positive note, one of the main effects of Dawkins's restructuring was that distance education has moved from the margins to the mainstream. The once marginal external studies moved towards being an integral part of face-to-face higher education, thus bringing flexible and open learning principles to the entire higher education sector. The general restructuring of the higher education sector as envisaged and implemented during the Dawkins era has remained mainly intact. The same cannot, however, be said about distance education. That is, the amalgamations have survived well into the mid-1990s and the pre-Dawkins binary system has disappeared; the DEC system has come and gone and access, quality, diversity and equity issues have been enhanced through the introduction of open learning principles.

We should not expect ever to be able to resolve the deficits of Dawkins's higher education policy and the rise and fall of DECs. The academic community and the issues raised are infinitely variable; all we can expect is to be able to grapple with the deficits and problems of the past, present and future by adopting a body of principles including a rationale for distance education, which goes beyond economic rationalism.

8 To wish and to will

Reflections on policy formation and implementation in Australian distance education

Richard Johnson

INTRODUCTION

Writers on spirituality in the Catholic religious tradition used to make a distinction between 'will' and 'velleity'. It is a useful distinction also in policy formation and implementation. 'Will' is the determined effort to achieve a given result; 'velleity' is the wish to achieve the result without commitment of effort or determination. Some decades ago there was a romantic song, *Wishing Will Make It So*. It was a popular song, but it isn't usually true.

This chapter attempts to describe the efforts to develop and implement a policy of rationalisation in distance education in Australia from the early 1980s. It is a story of relatively easy policy formation, and substantial failure of will in implementation. It is a chapter based on personal experience and involvement and is not a work of scholarship.

Up to 1982 distance education in Australia had been provided by the different educational sectors and authorities as a matter of necessity or advantage. The school systems of the various states had to provide for children in remote areas or other isolated situations (e.g. in hospital) and developed the various state correspondence schools and Schools of the Air. The Technical and Further Education (TAFE) systems of the states similarly sponsored a College of External Studies (or similar title) within each state, to bring that level of education to students who were not able to access it on campus; an exception was Victoria, where production of distance learning materials was located in the TAFE Off-Campus Coordinating Authority, but the tutorial process was decentralised to individual colleges.

In higher education, in universities and colleges of advanced education (CAEs), the picture in the early 1980s was different. Each institution was autonomous; and though the advanced education sector was supposed to be coordinated by state bodies, the degree of discipline and system varied considerably from one state to another. Universities did not even face that control, but were coordinated – to the extent that they were – by the Universities Council of the Commonwealth Tertiary Education Commission (CTEC).

In 1975 there were just over 17,000 external students in Australian higher education (8,891 in universities and 8,366 in CAEs), a little over 6 per cent of the total enrolment of some 270,000. They were eclipsed as a proportion by part-time students at 28.6 per cent in universities, 31.9 per cent in CAEs. By 1982 the numbers and proportions in the two sectors had risen to 15,497 (9.3 per cent) in universities and 24,801 (14.7 per cent) in CAEs – almost a doubling of numbers in universities and a trebling in CAEs in eight years, while total enrolment had risen only to some 334,000, an increase of about 25 per cent. External studies or distance education was the fastest growing mode of study in higher education.

At this point I was invited to undertake a study of this phenomenon. The formal terms of reference are set out in the report of that study (Johnson, 1983) but I well remember the less formal riding instructions I received orally from CTEC's first assistant commissioner, Lance Hennessy: 'We don't know what's going on out there, so we want you to find out and tell us.'

THE NEED FOR RATIONALISATION

In its concluding chapter that report said: 'The nation needs provision co-ordinated on a national scale and seen in a national perspective.' There were at that time forty-three higher education institutions offering some courses in external mode (as the language of the time put it). Most of these were in the fields of teacher education and business studies. There was a great deal of duplication – for instance, seventeen introductory courses in accounting – and a dissipation of the numbers of students; yet such numbers, if concentrated, would contribute to the economy of provision by distance means and reduce the duplication of effort in course development. The idea that some rationalisation was necessary was widely accepted.

The dissipated provision of distance courses had arisen for a variety of interacting reasons. There was no question of a need for distance education at university level; from its foundation, the University of Queensland had been legally obliged to offer some courses in that mode at least for the sake of schoolteachers scattered over that huge state. After World War II, when the University of New England left the tutelage of Sydney University and became autonomous, it too was designated to provide external studies for the people of New South Wales. Deakin University, from its foundation, had the same function for Victoria, so did Murdoch University for Western Australia. When all education had been entirely the responsibility of each separate state, it was not surprising that distance education at university level should develop state by state.

By 1981 nine universities were listed by CTEC as offering distance education. Some of these, such as the Universities of Adelaide and Sydney, were not real distance education providers; they simply made short-term *ad hoc* arrangements for individual students who were temporarily unable to come onto campus; in such universities of many thousands of students the numbers of those enrolled in distance mode seldom reached three digits and sometimes not two. Macquarie University offered, by distance means, Law, and Slavonic languages other than Russian – important niche fields of study but not ones of large enrolment. The significant university providers were the Universities of Queensland, and New England and Deakin and Murdoch Universities.

The real proliferation of distance higher education was in the CAEs. These fell into two broad categories: substantial institutes of technology (three in Victoria, one in each other state), all in mainland capital cities, and smaller, less technologically oriented colleges. The latter group had in most cases begun life as teachers' colleges which later expanded their offerings to include business studies and sometimes some liberal studies or applied sciences.

Teachers' colleges had traditionally been part of the state departments of education and therefore subject to the policies of the State Minister for Education. New ones were established only with the minister's approval, and ministers approved them with a rhetoric of extending access to education but with a hard eye on electoral advantage. Thus the pleasant town of Armidale, once the seat of one minister, gained from him both a university and a teachers' college while the neighbouring much larger centre, Tamworth, has had nothing. Rockhampton, Toowoomba, Lismore, Bathurst, Wagga, Gippsland, Warrnambool, all traditionally solid conservative seats, gained colleges over a long period of conservative state governments in the three eastern states.

There is nothing unusual or particularly reprehensible about such political behaviour; Labor governments also bestow favours on loyal or marginal electorates. The point is that Labor's bounty tends to be given in the major cities, that of the conservative parties in rural areas. But rural regions in Australia do not have large centres of population and large local pools of potential students. Even extensive provision for student residences as at Armidale, Toowoomba and Bathurst could not produce enrolments of more than a few thousand on-campus students at these sites. Thus eastern Australia became dotted with small colleges reliant on a few fields of study, at risk from changes of economic climate.

Those changes came in the mid-1970s. The whole nation was involved in economic downturn and rising unemployment. There were several consequences for the regional colleges. Like the rest of the higher education sector, they experienced sudden financial stringency. In a period of rising unemployment, teachers, who had been a volatile workforce (NSW at one point had a resignation rate of 12 per cent per year), ceased to resign their positions, so that far fewer new teachers were required. In the same climate of unemployment, school pupils in country towns who were offered jobs – usually the brighter pupils – tended to take them rather than proceed to higher education. There was a general slackening of enrolments in higher education in all institutions, but it hit the regional colleges hardest.

For this complex of reasons the colleges offered and promoted distance education; if the students would not come to them, they would go to the students, because an institution's viability depended on maintaining its enrolments. In this move they were assisted by other factors.

It had been accepted for decades that training to become a primary-school teacher required a minimum of two years; in the late 1970s, three years came to be regarded as the minimum, and large numbers of teachers already in service wanted their qualifications extended by the third year. It was not possible (because of their personal circumstances) for teachers all around the country to take up a year of full-time study, nor could the teaching services have given them all leave to do so, so they enrolled in distance courses part-time. For several years this large pool of distance students helped to keep the regional colleges viable.

In addition, the Whitlam Labor Government of 1972–5 had sought to extend access to higher education by abolishing tuition fees. This might not have made a great deal of difference to male students; those who were not on some form of scholarship or bursary might expect to be helped by their families, even under difficult circumstances. Families were in general much less ready to support daughters. The abolition of fees and the introduction of the Tertiary Education Assistance Scheme of income support meant that daughters had the same opportunity as sons to enter higher education. But it meant much more; it meant that women of all ages, women with families, women financially dependent on husbands, could seek higher education confident that it would not cost the family any money. From the mid-1970s these women flocked in, and because of their family commitments or geographic location, very many wanted to enrol in distance courses.

This combination of factors led to the expansion of distance education, not only in numbers of students but in numbers of institutions offering the facility, and hence to the concern of the CTEC.

ATTEMPTS AT RATIONALISATION, 1983–4

My 1983 report canvassed a number of possible ways to bring some rationalisation or coordination into the provision of distance education. Some people supported centralisation, either a single open university on the British model or a concentration of all production resources and expertise in one institution with some decentralisation of weekend schools or occasional seminars in other universities and colleges. This would probably not have been acceptable to the existing providers and in the economic climate it was impossible to imagine the government establishing a new institution. No less important, it would have devastated colleges, and with them employment, in a dozen rural electorates.

The report in its draft form suggested a standing committee of CTEC to advise the commission on the future development of distance education. This was not pursued in the final report; CTEC had already knocked it on the head since it did not operate through standing committees.

The state coordinating authorities for higher education argued for the job to be left with them, with CTEC 'entering into dialogue with the states regarding appropriate means of providing for unmet needs and minimising duplication'. This would have resulted in coordination by state bodies (some, but not all, of which were very effective within their states) but would have still left a sixfold repetition of offerings across the nation. The proposal from a much earlier report (Karmel, 1975) for a national institute of open tertiary education was mentioned with commendation but dismissed as unlikely in the economic climate. A position which was strongly though privately advocated by one of the commissioners was to do nothing and let the market sort itself out. In my view, expressed at the time, that would have led to further dissipation of resources.

The position finally advocated by the report was that the providers themselves set up their own coordinating mechanism with some modest financial support (for travel and secretarial services) from CTEC. In the event, the commission was not willing to contribute, and the providers set up not one but two mechanisms: the 'Toowoomba Accord' for the universities (so named because it was formed at a conference held in that city) and a body under the aegis of the Australian Committee of Directors and Principals in Advanced Education (ACDP).

In the next few years these did little if anything to reduce existing duplication, but they did take some measures to limit its spread. The Accord members developed a system of cross-crediting which enabled students to count courses from Accord partners towards degrees in the university in which the student was enrolled; the most notable example was a major in women's studies, using units from Murdoch, Deakin and the University of Queensland. The ACDP developed a scale of tariffs for the sale of courses between member colleges. It is doubtful if it was extensively used.

ATTEMPTS AT RATIONALISATION, 1985–9

Less than twelve months after publication of the 1983 report I was appointed Secretary of the Commonwealth Department of Education and Youth Affairs; and less than twelve months after that appointment, the minister for education decided to remove me from that position. This was not an easy process; at that time the position of secretary was a permanent appointment, and to remove a secretary one had to find a suitable alternative position for him (the language is not sexist; until 1985 all the secretaries had been male).

By that time there was a new chairman of CTEC, who to assist the minister and the displaced secretary was willing to set up a Standing Committee on External Studies (SCES) advisory to the CTEC, and to accept me as chair of that committee and as a special commissioner attached to the commission. Had the need to find me a position not arisen, it is doubtful whether these steps would have been taken. It is salutary for historians to realise that such developments quite often occur for similarly random and pragmatic reasons, not as the outcome of high policy.

The standing committee was then constituted, with an eye to the political correctness of the time: at least one person from each mainland state, at least one from each of the three sectors of tertiary education, one person of Aboriginal descent, three women. That is not to disparage their merits; they were all able people with records of achievement, and worked well together as a committee; but they were selected to fit the formula. Their names are given in the Appendix to this chapter.

The committee met four times a year, and its members were expected to keep in touch with the institutions in their respective states to ensure a flow of information in each direction. Early in its life it established a newsletter which reported to institutions on its deliberations at each meeting and other matters of interest. Its major concerns were: the use of new technology, and coordination in its use; development of policy advice to the commission; and the promotion of enquiries into aspects of distance education, for which it had a modest budget (A$150,000) within the CTEC's Evaluations and Investigations Program.

One thing the committee did not have was 'clout'. If it had commanded some executive authority or control over funding, it would have been a relatively straightforward matter to rationalise distance higher education. Institutions could have been told: 'we will fund you to offer distance courses in these fields but not in those' or 'we will fund this institution to develop a course in this field, and not any other institution; but we will fund any (or several) institutions to offer the course so developed'. There was a range of such possibilities.

The SCES had no power to allocate funds; even the funding of the enquiries just mentioned was subject to the approval of the chairman of CTEC. It had, of course, no power to direct any institution to do or not do anything; CTEC itself lacked that power. It is often not recognised that the successive commonwealth agencies concerned with the funding of higher education, from the Australian Universities Council of the 1960s through CTEC to the present Department of Employment, Education and Training (DEET), have no power to direct institutions in their teaching or behaviour. Australian universities and, in earlier times, CAEs were established under state legislation, with very few exceptions. The Commonwealth has no legal authority to direct them. Even in the few institutions established under Commonwealth legislation (the Australian National University, the Australian Maritime College, the Canberra College of Advanced Education) the legislation gives the institution full control over its course offerings, as to both content and method of teaching.

The only power the Commonwealth has is to fund or not fund particular developments. It has used this power to restrict the number of medical and engineering schools (highly expensive developments) but it is unlikely to use the power to dictate at the level of department or course unit. Certainly CTEC was unwilling to use its funding power to restrict the development or delivery of units by distance education.

So what was left? Moral suasion. Institutions generally prefer to cooperate with the funding authority, or at least not blatantly to defy it. If CTEC indicated a preference for a particular line of policy, institutions generally tried to indicate that they were acting in accordance with the policy. It was therefore up to the standing committee to propose a workable system to CTEC.

THE PROPOSED SYSTEM

The SCES suggested to CTEC the adoption, with modifications, of a system of rationalisation which had been applied in Victoria by that state's coordinating authority. The 1983 report in its Appendix listed thirteen institutions which were 'considered by the Commission to be major providers' and foreshadowed that number would grow to sixteen. In the SCES model, twelve institutions were designated 'principal providers' and were expected to offer a wide range of subjects in distance mode to at least 3,000 students each, and with a high level of expertise in the production and delivery of course materials. Other institutions were designated 'specialist providers' and should offer distance courses only in fields where they had special expertise, and in cooperation with the principal providers who would make available their professional skills in the preparation of distance materials. Other institutions should be encouraged to leave the field and should be given on-campus student load to keep up their enrolments (see SCES, 1987).

The model for this system was a collaboration between the then Hawkesbury Agricultural College and Darling Downs Institute of Advanced Education (DDIAE). Hawkesbury wanted to offer a few subjects in distance mode but lacked the professional resources to do so. They contracted with DDIAE to provide those resources while Hawkesbury provided the course content, tuition, assessment and accreditation. Both sides seemed to regard the arrangement as successful, and there seemed no reason why it should not be extended into a nation-wide system.

The SCES's advice was published as Appendix 5 to CTEC's *Report for 1988–90 Triennium* (SCES, 1987). It begins: 'the aim of the Standing Committee on External Studies is to see in Australia by 1990 a network of tertiary institutions in all sectors collaborating to ensure provision of high quality distance education in a coordinated and economical way'. The committee had accepted figures provided by DDIAE which indicated that using materials and production values usual in Australia, distance education does not become economical until there are at least 50 enrolments in a unit, preferably 150, and that the appropriate infrastructure is not justified with total distance enrolments of fewer than 3,000 in the institution. Below those figures provision is either over-expensive or below a reasonable standard. These figures were queried by many institutions but none of them provided sound alternative figures. The Commission accepted the SCES's advice:

When the proposals are implemented there will be eventually no more than about half a dozen higher education institutions, designated as principal providers, involved in distance education on any large scale. Some institutions having special expertise and/or a special relationship with a client group, will be designated as specialist providers to work in conjunction with the principal providers. Other institutions will be required to phase out of external studies provision.

(CTEC, 1987b, Vol. 1, Part 1, 6.31)

The one surprise for members of the standing committee in the commission's triennial report was the throwaway line when discussing nurse education that there should be 'opportunity for external study through a single principal provider servicing all States' (ibid., 1.53). I questioned all the commissioners at the time and none of them knew the origin of this decision.

In any event, none of this mattered. It was all swept away by a federal election in July 1987 and the coming of a new minister, John Dawkins.

1987–9: THE COMING OF THE DECs

Dawkins came into office with a head full of ideas on higher education gathered from a clique, soon dubbed 'The Purple Circle'. These ideas were consolidated into a discussion paper on higher education (the Green Paper) issued in December 1987. Most of the ideas had been around for some years but had not been drawn into a single statement; nor had they been implemented, though CTEC's now forgotten *Report for 1988–90 Triennium* was advocating implementation of some of them. It is not necessary for this chapter to expound them all, but to concentrate on those relevant to distance education.

The Green Paper (Dawkins, 1987a) endorsed the general CTEC approach: 'the Government's basic objectives . . . are to reduce unnecessary duplication and to enhance the quality of provision' (ibid., p. 36). It proposed 'to reduce the number of institutions offering external studies to a group of providers of less than ten' (ibid., p. 37), which was more drastic than the SCES proposal. This was followed by the bizarre suggestion that 'beyond the base load [of about 3,000], those institutions designated as external studies providers will be able to tender for blocks of external studies students (of the order of 500) in various fields of study' (ibid., p. 37). I have never been able to discover where the minister got that advice.

The Green Paper was a discussion paper, and was followed in July 1988 by the White Paper, the official policy statement (Dawkins, 1988). This kept to the DDIAE figures on economies of scale, abandoned the concept of bidding for blocks of students, kept the idea of contracting between major providers and specialist providers, and reduced the number of providers:

There will be about six Distance Education Centres (DECs) which will be funded by the Commonwealth to develop, produce and deliver external studies. . . . Selection of the DECs will be undertaken on a competitive basis and offers to be designated a DEC will be made for a minimum period of 5 years, with renewal subject to review.

(Ibid., p. 51)

Other institutions were free to offer courses based on materials developed by the DECs but would be funded at a 'significantly reduced rate' to do so since they had not incurred course development costs.

The White Paper traversed the whole field of higher education with proposals which caused upheaval in the sector. Distance education was a small part of it, and not a priority. A committee to select the DECs was not set up until late 1988 and reported in the following March (DEET–HEC, 1989). Fourteen institutions had bid for the designation, on the basis of criteria laid down in the White Paper. The committee visited all contenders. It decided that the three institutions in Perth should be regarded as a consortium and therefore as one contender. There were seven others whose profiles fit the criteria significantly more closely than did the remainder, and it would have been very hard to decide which two of the eight to omit if the target of six had to be met. The minister's office informed the committee that eight could be regarded as 'about six'. On that basis the committee recommended the eight DECs and the recommendation was accepted.

One of the effects of the White Paper had been to produce a spate of amalgamations of higher education institutions, so that, for example, Gippsland Institute of Advanced Education had become part of Monash University, Warrnambool IAE had joined Deakin, the colleges at Wagga and Bathurst had amalgamated as Charles Sturt University. The designated DECs were (using their post-Dawkins titles): Central Queensland University, University of Southern Queensland, University of New England, Charles Sturt University, Monash University, Deakin University, University of South Australia and the Western Australian Distance Education Consortium. These were in fact all the places that had been nominated as principal providers by the SCES three years before; all the flurry of the Green and White Papers had achieved nothing except the loss of three years' progress towards rationalisation.

THE END OF THE DECs, 1989–93

The DEC system was supposed to ensure a concentration of expertise and of specialised resources in a few places, and to make those available to other institutions that wanted to offer distance courses, so that all university distance education should be offered at an appropriately high level of quality. The DECs were to be paid for providing this service to other institutions.

The system for payment devised by an otherwise very intelligent bureaucrat was to fund the non-DEC at 85 per cent of the normal rate for each external student, and divert the other 15 per cent to the DEC with which it was supposed to be collaborating. This system caused intense irritation to the non-DECs and was easily evaded by collusion between the two institutions. It certainly did not cause any institutions to abandon the provision of distance education, or contribute in any way towards rationalisation.

The main mechanism for rationalisation set up by the Commonwealth was the National Distance Education Conference (NDEC) which comprised one representative of each of the DECs, one from a non-DEC distance provider, one from a TAFE system. At its first meetings it was chaired by a senior Commonwealth officer and the secretariat was also from the Commonwealth. The committee had the potential for really strong action to press for enhancement of quality and for diminution of duplication; the Commonwealth representative in the chair could have interacted very fruitfully with the people directly responsible for provision of distance education.

At this point I retired from the Department of Employment, Education and Training and lost contact with the development of distance education for a few years. Apparently the senior Commonwealth officer, after a couple of meetings of NDEC, ceased to attend and left it to manage its own affairs aided by one or two more junior Commonwealth officers as a secretariat. In effect, the institutions were being asked to rationalise themselves, with no way for sanctions or pressure to be applied. Is it too cruel to suggest that one might as well ask sheep to herd foxes?

The DEC system did have some successes. The DECs were put on their mettle, and anyone who compares the current learning materials with those of earlier years can see a rise in the care with which they have been prepared. Electronic technology has been intelligently applied and is now commonplace, with advantage to students. Issues of quality have been addressed by a subcommittee of the Conference, and it is said that the group as a whole has behaved collaboratively.

In 1992 Drs Roy Lundin and Peter Chippendale and I undertook an investigation for the Higher Education Council into the use and potential of distance education materials and methods for on-campus students. One of the terms of reference was: 'whether the present division between external and internal provision should be maintained beyond 1995 with respect to both provision and level of funding', which was a fancy way of saying: 'should the DEC system continue?' In the course of the enquiry all DECs were visited, and many, if not all, were asked what difference it would make if the system were dropped. The answer was, little or none. The DECs would continue their heavy involvement in distance education; many institutions not in the business would not enter it; and the many non-DECs already in it would continue.

The report (NBEET, 1992) therefore recommended that the special funding arrangements be dropped; that any institution be free to offer its courses in whatever mode it chose; 'but that the government, as the funding authority, should endeavour to ensure that all courses, in any mode, should be at the highest standards of content and presentation, and that the potential for economies of scale be realised' (ibid., p. 29). The government has acted on the first two points, but it is not obvious that it has acted on the third at least in respect of distance education. From Karmel in 1975 to now, the government appears to have taken no notice of such recommendations, although it is in a constant froth about economies and quality in conventional settings.

CONCLUSIONS

For more than a decade I have been arguing for more coordination and rationalisation of distance education in Australia. While many in the institutions have not welcomed the measures proposed at different times, the opposition has usually been along the lines of 'rationalise the rest but leave us alone'. Others have argued that since it is impossible to persuade academics to use materials prepared by others, the pursuit of rationalisation is just futile.

There has been one intellectually strong argument against my policies, which has been advanced by a few all through the decade. That is, that technology is developing so rapidly and institutions are so autonomous that they should not be limited in the modes of study they choose; rather, they should be encouraged to offer courses in flexible ways and assisted to do so effectively. That is the position I now take. It is not, however, a position of laissez-faire; it is a position of positive measures in pursuit of what is now termed open learning. There are signs that the government is now edging towards such a policy; its espousal of credit transfer, its establishment within DEET of the Open Learning Unit and an educational technology task force, its establishment of the Open Learning Agency of Australia and its support for the Open Learning Technology Corporation all suggest that at last the government is adopting positive measures, even ahead of some of the universities.

Yet this was advocated almost twenty years ago in the report *Open Tertiary Education* (Karmel, 1975). It recommended the establishment of a national institute of open tertiary education which would have the task of fostering open learning in all its aspects in all tertiary institutions. That was ignored by government in the aftermath of the political crisis culminating in the dismissal of the Whitlam Labor Government in November 1975. Had it been implemented, all the bother from 1983 to now would have been avoided.

There were two other occasions when strong government action to develop distance education on rational lines was possible. One was the CTEC recommendations for the 1988–90 triennium, which were swept away in the Dawkins whirlwind. The other was the establishment of NDEC with a senior Commonwealth officer as the chair. That opportunity passed because the Commonwealth did not wish to be as intrusive as would have been necessary to achieve the goal of rationalisation. It is interesting for one who has had a foot in both camps to observe that while the institutions constantly fear the heavy hand of DEET, DEET constantly fears being seen as heavy-handed!

The reader is now advised to re-read the first two paragraphs of this chapter.

APPENDIX

Membership of the Standing Committee on External Studies, 1985–7. The posts listed for each are those they held at the time. Professor White has since died.

Mr Dean Ashenden, senior adviser on the personal staff of the Commonwealth Minister for Education. Mr Ashenden had joined the Minister's staff from Adelaide and thus South Australian concerns were claimed to be represented.

Ms Delia Craig, Principal of the College of External Studies, NSW TAFE.

Ms Anne Deveson, Director of the Australian Film, Television and Radio School, Ryde, NSW.

Mr Jack Foks, Head, TAFE Off-Campus Coordinating Authority, Victoria.

Professor Fred Jevons, Vice-Chancellor, Deakin University, Victoria.

Emeritus Professor Richard Johnson, Special Commissioner, CTEC (Chair).

Dr Maureen Smith, Director of Continuing Education, University of Western Australia.

Mr (later Professor) Vernon White, Head of the Distance Education Unit, Darling Downs Institute of Advanced Education (now University of Southern Queensland).

Mr Eric Willmot, Chief Executive Officer, ACT Schools Authority.

9 Translating open university policies into practice in India

Santosh Panda

INTRODUCTION

India, a union of twenty-six states and six union territories, is the second most populous and second largest democracy in the world, with a land area of 3,287,263 square kilometres and a population of about 900 million. This magnitude is reflected by the fact that nearly 15 per cent of the world's people live in India (Reddy, 1989). Males outnumber females, and more than three-quarters of the population live in villages. While the Constitution recognises fifteen major languages, as many as 1,652 dialects and languages are spoken; India is a multicultural and multilingual nation. Though predominantly agricultural, there has been rapid industrialisation in the post-Independence era, including the later developments of economic liberalisation towards a free-market system. This brief contextual information indicates how distance education forms part of the policy response of national and state governments to the need to educate India's expanding population scattered across far-flung areas, especially in terms of the emerging demand for skill-based education. India represents the typical South Asian nation in terms of the development of distance education and open university systems. This chapter considers the correspondence between governmental and institutional policies on education and distance education and the actual practices of its functionaries in this subcontinent. The colonial links of the past provide a backdrop for the development of Indian distance education along lines which reflect other more global influences.

POLICIES AND DEVELOPMENTS IN HIGHER EDUCATION

The Indian higher education system is one of the oldest in the third world, and is based on the models of the western world, contemporary changes notwithstanding (Ashby, 1966). In the pre-nineteenth-century period the higher education system was based on Sanskrit, Arabic and Persian. Under British rule, the language of instruction was replaced by English following the systematic involvement of the government and the establishment, in 1817, of the Hindu College (later named as Presidency College) in Calcutta, the then capital of India. The *Mountstuart Elphinstone's Minute* of 1823 pleaded for the establishment of schools for the teaching of English and European Sciences, and subsequently such schools were established at Bombay and Poona, and in 1834 the Elphinstone College at Bombay (Powar, 1994a). The approval of *Macaulay's Minutes* of 1935 shifted the provision of money given for study of Arabic and Sanskrit literature to the study of European literature and science under the Act of 1813, thus making Indians thorough 'English scholars'. The Government of India Acts of 1919 and 1935, passed in the British Parliament, made education a provincial or state responsibility. In 1835, the British Parliament ordered an enquiry into the state of education in India *vis-à-vis* the role of the government, which resulted in *Charles Wood's Despatch* of 1854 and the official large-scale entry of the state in Indian higher education. Subsequently, three affiliated universities were established at Calcutta, Bombay and Madras based on the model of the University of London.

It took nearly thirty years to establish Allahabad University as India's fourth university in 1887. However, during this period the number of colleges rose from twenty-seven to seventy-five. In the subsequent years, there was a steady growth of private colleges and the treatment of education as a joint sector, as a consequence of the recommendation of the Education Commission of 1882, that the state should withdraw from the direct support and management of higher education institutions. At Independence in 1947, there were eighteen universities with a student population of nearly two hundred thousand. In the post-Independence period, the growth of institutions has been phenomenal: by 1995, there were 220 universities or equivalent institutions, including 34 agricultural universities, 15 technical institutions, 13 medical institutions and 7 open universities (AIU, 1995). While the student growth was 10 per cent in the 1950s, it has come down to 4.2 per cent in the 1980s. By 1993, there were 4.6 million students (88 per cent of whom were undergraduate students), and a little over a quarter of a million teachers (Powar, 1994b). Only 6 per cent of school leavers, within the relevant age group, pursue higher education.

Over the past thirty years or so, government expenditure on higher education has dropped from 7.9 per cent to 3.7 per cent of total outlays; which represents 14 per cent of the expenditure on education (Tilak, 1993), which itself is only 3 per cent of Gross National Product. The bulk of University Grants Commission (UGC) funding (71 per cent) goes to 19 university-level institutions and 54 colleges under the central government; only 26 per cent is shared by 144 universities and 4,246 colleges under the state governments, and 3 per cent is for other institutions (Powar, 1994b).

Three dimensions of Indian higher education characterise its post-Independence development: *legalism* (institutes created by Act of Legislature to grant academic degrees); *federalism* (federal character of higher education as reflected in the establishment of central universities by Acts of Parliament and state universities by Acts of State Legislature); and *diversity* (establishment of institutions, other than universities, of national importance and of high quality through the policies of the Central Government) (Mazumdar, 1994).

Although Indian higher education is expanding through an 'open door' policy – which has been discouraged by almost all the education commissions because it is seen as leading to a deterioration in quality – not all who aspire are able to obtain access. Its present stage has been realistically characterised by Altbach thus:

> Indian higher eduction seems like an enigma enveloped in contradiction. Pockets of excellent teaching and research are surrounded by a sea of sub-standard colleges. The best graduates compete successfully in the world job market, but unemployment at home is reality for many. Scholarship is often superseded by politics and, in many institutions, crisis is the norm. A system which was at one time highly selective has opened its doors to a large number, yet at the same time there is conflict and sometimes violence over access to what remains a scarce commodity.
>
> (Altbach, 1993, p. 4)

The above analysis provides a background to further discussion on the development of the distance education system in India.

DISTANCE EDUCATION

After Independence, the government of India initiated educational reforms, especially to higher education, within the development-planning process embedded in the Five Year Plans. Within the Third Five Year Plan, the Planning Commission remarked that 'in addition to the provision in the Plan for expansion of facilities for higher education, proposals for evening colleges, correspondence courses and award of external degrees are at present under consideration' (GOI, 1960, p. 589). An expert committee was established under the auspices of the Central Advisory Board of Education – the highest policy-making body of the government – to look into the matter. The committee strongly recommended the introduction of correspondence courses in arts and commerce at undergraduate level by universities only, with the subsequent addition of science subjects (GOI, 1962). Consequently, with the establishment of the Directorate of Correspondence Courses (to become the School of Correspondence Courses and Continuing Education) at the University of Delhi, the first undergraduate correspondence courses were initiated in 1962. On the basis of the satisfactory examination results and the initial success of correspondence education, the Kothari Education Commission of 1964–6, whose recommendations formed the basis of the *National Policy on Education 1968*, observed that in view of the deteriorating standards of higher education due to the policy of open door access and the limited accessibility to full-time education, opportunities for part-time education through evening colleges and own-time education through correspondence courses should be made available to the ever-increasing number of aspirants to higher education. The use of correspondence courses in technical education, the provision of radio and television programmes and personal contact with the students in holidays and vacations were also envisaged by the commission to counter the possibility of the deterioration of its standards (NCERT, 1966).

The commission also envisaged further expansion of correspondence courses for technical and professional education and, to counter the possible unacceptability of correspondence students in the labour market, it recommended that these students should be given the status of recognised students and be treated on a par with other university students. During 1967–71, the UGC sent three delegations to the erstwhile USSR to study the system of Soviet correspondence education and its implications for India. The reports submitted by these delegations (e.g. GOI, 1968; UGC, 1972) made wide-ranging recommendations for the revamping and further expansion of the system in India. The three delegations were concerned with teacher education, evening and correspondence courses and vocational education and correspondence schooling respectively. The consequences of these recommendations led to continual scrutiny of the system as well as the consideration of establishing a national institute of correspondence courses as a registered society. By 1970, there were seven institutes or directorates of correspondence courses offering courses from within conventional universities. In December 1970, at a seminar organised by the Ministry of Information and Broadcasting and the Indian National Commission for Cooperation with UNESCO, an 'open university' was recommended for establishment on an experimental basis, using the methodology of distance education. Clearly, the British influence in relation to the establishment of the UK Open University was being propagated in a new form in Indian higher education. The methodology of 'distance education', which was eventually to become a global term, is also an example of how India was actively connected to these emerging global trends.

Subsequently, a working group was constituted in 1971 by the government of India, under the chairmanship of Shri G. Parthasarthy, to investigate the feasibility of establishing an open university in India. Keeping in view the increasing demand for higher education and the limited availability of human and financial resources within the formal university sector, the working group recommended that the government of India should establish an open university. The national progress towards an open university was slow, and was overtaken by the government of the state of Andhra Pradesh which not only showed extra initiative by appointing a committee on this in 1982, but also established the Andhra Pradesh Open University (APOU) in that year. This committee had advocated, for such a university, adoption of innovative ways of providing access to the education and initiating new course structures, teaching methodology, organisation of activities, credit transfer, use of modern educational technology and a network for student support services.

An encouraging response to the APOU (later renamed the Dr Babasaheb Ambedkar Open University), the recommendations of the earlier committees, and a proposal submitted by Educational Consultants India Ltd (EdCIL, 1985) culminated in the establishment of the Indira Gandhi National Open University (IGNOU) by an Act of Parliament on 20 September 1985. The IGNOU Act articulates dual objectives for the University: (i) to introduce and promote distance education and open university systems in the country, and (ii) to coordinate and determine standards in such systems in the country. The University, which started offering courses in 1987, uses multi-media teaching–learning methodology at a distance, and has responsibility to coordinate and determine standards for both the distance education offered at dual-mode mainstream universities and the open distance education offered at the national and state open universities through its official mechanism and statutory authority of the Distance Education Council (DEC), established in April 1992. The DEC has also an additional responsibility of providing financial grants to various distance teaching institutions in the country.

Subsequent to the establishment of an open university at the national level, five more open universities have been established at the state level with the objectives of providing equality of educational opportunities, democratising education and designing academic programmes to suit the manpower requirements at regional and local levels. These are: Kota Open University (KOU) (1987), Nalanda Open University (NOU) (1987), Yashwantrao Chavan Maharasthra Open University (YCMOU) (1989), M. P. Bhoj Open University (MPBOU) (1992) and Dr Babasaheb Ambedkar Open University (BRAOU) (1993). The institutional expansion and growth in enrolment in distance education are presented in Tables 9.1 and 9.2 and are drawn from Yadav and Panda (1995).

The establishment of three Correspondence Course Institutes (CCIs) and three OUs since 1991/2 has not changed the enrolment percentage of distance education, nor its characterisation. In 1995, student intake in the four functional OUs was as follows: 91,398 (IGNOU); 57,499 (BRAOU); 43,485 (YCMOU); and 8,557 (KOU) (DEC, 1995).

Table 9.1 Expansion of distance education institutions

	Number of institutions established	
Year	CCIs	OUs
1961–70	9	—
1971–80	23	—
1981–90	11	5
1991–4	7	3

Table 9.2 Enrolment in distance education

Year	Total higher education enrolment	Enrolment in distance education	
		(number)	*(% of total)*
1975–6	2,490,319	64,210	2.58
1980–1	2,918,865	166,428	5.70
1985–6	3,925,987 (27,629)	355,090	9.04
1990–1	4,988,061 (75,417)	562,814	11.28
1991–2	5,289,170 (122,531)	678,063	12.82

Note: Figures in parentheses indicate enrolment in open universities

Structure of Correspondence Course Institutes (CCIs)

There are fifty directorates of correspondence courses or departments of correspondence/distance education, commonly known as CCIs, functioning within the institutes of higher education (i.e. universities and deemed as universities). These mainstream universities have full control over the CCIs, with little or no freedom delegated to the latter with regard to design of curriculum, development of programmes, teaching approaches and support services, student evaluation and certification. The institutional management and, in most cases, financial allocation and expenditure, and staffing of the CCIs are determined by the host institution. Sometimes staff of the university teaching departments, without experience or expertise in distance teaching, are either deputed or transferred (as a punishment) to the CCI. With no freedom of decision-making on major issues or activities, teachers of these institutes find constraints, become lethargic towards the task of distance teaching and are reluctant to innovate.

Based on the university curriculum, usually the teachers of the CCIs and university teaching departments write the course units (known as lessons) without giving much consideration to the principles and methodologies involved in the development of self-instructional distance-teaching material. While format editing is virtually absent, content and language editing are carried out in-house, with minimal involvement of external consultants. Some of the institutes use student-response sheets or assignments with the objective of providing continuous feedback from the isolated students though, in reality, only a few institutes evaluate such student responses (Singh *et al.*, 1994). Personal contact arrangements vary from one week a year organised in one place to regular contact at various places through a network of accredited institutions or study centres. The students of the CCIs study the same courses, sit for the same examinations and receive the same certificates or degrees as their on-campus university peers. There is a complete absence of the use of video or television, and only a few CCIs supplement their print materials with the use of radio broadcasts.

CCIs' staffing ranges from six to more than a hundred. Although staff salaries and other expenditures are kept to the minimum, a number of CCIs are profitable and extend financial support to their state departments of education or parent universities. For the last decade or so, some of the institutes have adopted the objective of earning large-scale revenue from student fees, higher than those being charged by the open universities.

Open university structures

The establishment of the open university system in 1982 ushered in a new era in the history of higher education in India. The open universities have the responsibility for providing access to higher education, of offering functional, needs-based and continuing education programmes, and of reducing the unit cost of education to the lowest possible. They are intended to practise open learning through the methodology of multimedia distance teaching in which there is the possibility of self-pacing and credit-transfer. In India, the emergence of open university education is a response to an ever-increasing number of students aspiring to higher education, within limited financial and human resources available to the sector. It is a response that is part of a global trend towards open and distance education. Unlike the CCIs, open universities are autonomous educational institutions, with authority over their financial, administrative and academic affairs. As an industrialised system of education, it involves a complex network of sub-systems, some of which have distinct features from the formal university system. The practice necessitates teamwork, a specialised division of labour and both individual and team accountability. The management mechanism involves flexibility in both credit accumulation and credit transfer, and giving exemption for study on the basis of experiential learning gathered at the workplace is currently under consideration. It is a shift into aspects of open education, rather than just distance education, which is part of an international development in terms of both policy and practice. It is noteworthy that the kinds of policies and practices unfolding in the more industrialised and technologically sophisticated nations have also taken their own shape simultaneously in India.

Structurally, the open universities are similar in most respects to traditional universities, with a vice-chancellor (president), pro vice-chancellors and other officers, a board of management, academic council, planning board and finance committee. The academic structures are organised through various schools, each with a few discipline areas. The major service divisions include student admission, computer, evaluation, distance education, communication, general administration, and finance. Additionally, most of the open universities have a network of regional and study centres to administer the academic programmes and provide support services to students.

Functionally, while the various schools undertake the task of designing and developing multimedia packages, with the support provided by course writers drawn from outside and media production provided by a service sub-system, the service divisions like distance education, admission, evaluation, computing, course-material printing and distribution provide support to the academic faculty in course-material development, student admission, student evaluation, student records and database, printing and dispatch of materials respectively. The regional services division looks after the implementation of academic programmes, provision for academic counselling at study centres, assessment of assignment responses, and audio- and video-programme support to the students. The administration and allied divisions provide administrative support to all schools of study and service divisions to enable them to carry out their functions smoothly and effectively.

Distance education practices

IGNOU offers nationally almost 55 academic programmes and over 370 courses (in English, Hindi or modern Indian languages), to over 200,000 students with the help of 16 regional centres, 244 study centres located in conventional university and college campuses, over 600 coordinators and as- sistant coordinators, and a panel of 12,800 academic counsellors (IGNOU, 1995). Besides the multimedia packages (comprising print, audio, video), academic counselling, summer schools and practicals, IGNOU broadcasts programmes daily through *Doordarsan* (Indian Television) and radio pro- grammes from AIR stations of Bombay and Hyderabad. Also, the University has already experimented with tele-conferencing technology with extended C-band; has established a permanent audio-conferencing network, linking headquarters with its sixteen regional centres and other state OUs; is constructing a very sophisticated educational media production centre with Japanese aid; has established the Staff Training and Research Institute of Distance Education (STRIDE) and the Commonwealth Educational Media Centre of Asia (CEMCA) with support from the Commonwealth of Learn- ing. In comparison, BRAOU offers fourteen programmes (178 courses), KOU eleven programmes (120 courses), YCMOU twenty programmes (171 courses), NOU one programme and the remaining three open universities are yet to offer courses.

The early correspondence courses through the CCIs were considered, by most of the commissions and committees on education, to need improvement towards becoming good quality distance education courses. Recent studies (Rathore, 1993; Singh *et al.*, 1994) have outlined the impediments in these respects and have made suggestions to overcome them. Concerns have been expressed especially with regard to quality of education and guidelines have been issued for CCIs to achieve the appropriate standards (UGC, 1993; Deshpande, 1994). The main impediment in the way of designing relevant correspondence courses seems to have been the academic and organisational subservience of the CCIs to their host institutions. Recently, the Distance Education Council of IGNOU has encouraged the CCIs to shed their status as revenue-generating entities and to develop into distance education departments. Furthermore, there have been moves to subsume the CCIs under the umbrella of the DEC and link their performances in terms of distance education enhancement to their grants.

The recommendations of the *National Policy on Education 1986*, its revised *Programme of Action 1992*, and the Central Advisory Board of Education's recommendation to establish an open university in each of the twenty-six states in India would lead to a massive expansion of the Indian open university system. Further, as envisaged in the Eighth Five Year Plan, an additional 500,000 students or, in other words, 50 per cent of the additional enrolments (17–21 year olds) in higher education are to be accommodated through this sector (Panda, 1992). Against this background of expansion, and invariably similar policy objectives of all OUs, it is worth examining the extent to which the open universities perform on the major criteria of access, relevance and quality.

Access

Access for students with regard to certain selected variables for three open universities is shown in Table 9.3. The data are expressed as percentages.

The location of IGNOU study centres indicates a skewed access in favour of those who already have access to other town and city resources. In 1990 the

Table 9.3 Student profiles of selected Indian open universities

Variables	IGNOU (1991–2) (All programmes) (N = 62,375)	BRAOU (1992–3) (UG Foundation course) (N = 35,278)	YCMOU (1990–3) (Preparatory course, BA/B Com) (N = 19,356)
Male	75.09	74	75.28
Female	24.91	26	24.72
General	91.82	48	71.32
SC/ST/BC	8.18	52	28.68
Employed	52.67	20	—
Unemployed	47.33	80	—
Rural	38.39	—	23.39
Urban	61.61	—	42.49*
Under 25	9.02 (<21)	79	64.72
26–30 yrs	58.21 (21–30)	11	19.13
31–50 yrs	31.31	9	15.05
Above 50	1.46	1	1.10

Notes: ST = Scheduled Tribe; SC = Scheduled Caste; BC = Backward Caste
     * = information for 6,602 students not available
Source: Panda (1996, in press)

distribution of the 132 IGNOU study centres was as follows: metropolitan cities (17.4 per cent), state capitals (18.9 per cent), large towns (8.3 per cent), small towns (53.8 per cent), rural areas (nil) and tribal areas (1.5 per cent) (Menon and Joshi, 1990).

Relevance

The courses offered by the CCIs range from liberal arts to professionally oriented courses in management, computer science, engineering and tech-

Table 9.4 Professional programmes offered by OUs

Open University	Programmes
BRAOU	Certificate in Food and Nutrition Bachelor of Library and Information Science Bachelor of Public Relations Master of Business Administration
IGNOU	Certificate in Guidance Diploma in Nutrition and Health Education Diploma in Computer in Office Management Diploma in Rural Development Diploma in Tourism Studies Advanced Diploma in Water Resources Management Advanced Diploma in Construction Management Bachelor and Master of Library and Information Sciences BSc Nursing Postgraduate Diploma in Computer Applications Postgraduate Diploma in Higher Education Postgraduate Diploma in Distance Education Master of Business Administration
KOU	Certificate in Computer Science Diploma in Library and Information Sciences Diploma in Journalism Diploma in Labour Law Diploma in Tourism and Hotel Management Master of Business Administration
NOU	Certificate in Food and Nutrition
YMCOU	Certificate in Word Processing Certificate Course in Agriculture Certificate in Grape Growing Certificate Course for In-service Teachers Diploma in Applied Electronics Diploma in School Management Diploma in Office Services Diploma in Computer Operations Diploma in Horticulture Master of Business Administration

nology. The OUs have been slow and cautious about offering professional programmes. Table 9.4 shows the professional course profile of five OUs.

In the case of BRAOU, 98 per cent of its enrolments in 1992/3 were in non-professional undergraduate programmes. In the year 1989/90, at BRAOU, BA students alone constituted 84 per cent of the total enrolment. At IGNOU, although nationwide access for students has been unsatisfactory, professional programmes are more common and the proportion of under-graduate students is smaller. For example, in 1992/3, only 22 per cent were enrolled in Bachelor's degree programmes and 12 per cent were enrolled in Bachelor's preparatory programmes respectively.

Quality and effectiveness

As has been noted previously, the quality of course materials and support provided by the CCIs lags behind the OUs, a matter which the DEC has been seeking to address (Deshpande, 1994). The OUs differ little from conventional universities in terms of institutional culture and work ethics. However, the quality of service offered to students with regard to material distribution, evaluation of assignment-responses and turnaround time, and academic counselling is gradually deteriorating. There is an absence of strong management information systems (MIS), although quality assurance and quality audit mechanisms have been initiated which may lead to improvements. Powar and Panda (1995) have suggested that Total Quality Management should be trialled; the contribution by McIlroy and Walker in this book (Chapter 11) confirms this view.

With regard to cohesive teamwork and team accountability, IGNOU has three groups of people, drawn from three different sectors of society (i.e. a professional team from established agencies, teachers from conventional universities and administrators from government bureaucracy) who form three quite separate entities. Menon observes :

> All these three agencies have had independent existence and identity and through their many years of operation have acquired certain unique and sometimes idiosyncratic characteristics, and more important a certain amount of mutual mistrust and suspicion. An open university is a nascent phenomenon and as such it is quite amorphous in its character. Therefore, different categories of people who constitute it entertain diverse and some-times mutually contradictory perceptions about its goals and functions and their respective roles in it. This makes it extremely difficult for them to readily gel into a cohesive team.
>
> (Menon, 1989–90, p. 51)

Another factor related to quality is student workload. In a recent study (Garg *et al.*, 1992), it was revealed that student workload plays an important role in student learning in the physics elective courses of the BSc programme of IGNOU. The authors observed that 'while on the one hand the IGNOU course materials have been appreciated as better than what is available in the market, they are too exhaustive and dense for the average student' (ibid., p. 93). This finding is applicable to other undergraduate programmes where even students with non-matriculation certificates obtain admission; a finding which might account for the low course completion rates in these programmes.

A few other important aspects, related to the effectiveness of open university education, are briefly noted as follows:

- The per capita cost of correspondence education is lower than for open university education. The annual recurrent cost per student at BRAOU, IGNOU, YCMOU and conventional universities (CUs) for 1991/2 were Indian rupees 777, 2,046, 2,214 and 5,746 respectively. For the same year, the cost per student for three-year undergraduate programmes at IGNOU and CUs were Indian rupees 6,000 and 16,428 respectively (Naidu, 1993).
- The cost of media production (audio and video programmes) is high (Pillai and Naidu, 1991), and such programmes are not optimally utilised at study centres.
- The process of credit transfer between open universities, and between conventional and open universities, is very slow to become established.
- Similar courses are separately developed by different OUs and each one has its own network of study centres without much sharing. A common network of study centres would reduce costs and help develop an integrated, national distance education delivery system.
- Research and development is completely absent, and institutional research is yet to emerge; and controversy persists with regard to systemic vs. discipline-based research (Koul, 1994; Panda, 1995).
- Open university–industry interaction is barely in its infancy, although many conventional universities have well-established links and collaboration with industries.

A CASE FOR CONVERGENCE

The demand for higher education is increasing, while the supply within the conventional universities is short of the demand. In this context, distance education institutions, more specifically the open universities, have to play an important role. Structurally, as well as functionally, both have their inherent strengths and limitations. Discussion of this aspect is beyond the scope of this chapter, although a brief consideration of convergence between these two systems follows. This suggested move towards convergence reflects a broader global debate and shift in this direction. Some suggestions are offered here as a conclusion.

The recent developments in Indian higher education, which would affect both conventional and open universities, include the following:

- The privatisation of higher education, and provision for capitation fees and education charges (Tilak, 1991).
- The reservation of up to 50 per cent of places in higher education courses for the socio-economically disadvantaged groups.
- The strain on resources and the mobilisation of resources from non-governmental sources, especially through greater university–industry interaction.
- The shift of performance evaluation and accreditation to designated external accrediting bodies, with links to performance-related funding (UGC, 1994).
- The move for the establishment of a media-network centre to share television resources amongst institutions, and the proposal for an educational television channel through the government-owned *Doordarshan*.
- The concern for quality and standards in higher education, and for quality assurance mechanisms to be developed.
- The curriculum restructuring by the UGC and the establishment of curriculum-development cells in universities.

Interaction between the two systems occurs at two levels: one, the development of the multimedia packages by OUs with academic support from CU academics, and the use of the materials of the former by the latter; and two, the establishment of OU study centres in CUs and colleges and offer of tutoring/counselling services by the academics of the latter. Both the systems have partly converged through these interactions and are learning from each other, though at attitudinal level each is competing with the other. More specifically, both the systems have converged at two levels:

- The traditional clients of the formal system, i.e. those meritorious students, adversely affected by the recent policy of the reservation of seats in conventional institutions for disadvantaged groups, are moving towards studying at the open universities, thereby shedding the image of OUs as institutions of substandard intake. Further, the continuing education needs of professionals, including the industries and the CUs themselves, would be best catered for through the OUs.
- The OUs have provided a rich ground for educational technologists to design, develop, implement and evaluate multimedia packages and other educational technologies. Within this framework, while the CUs would need more effective self-instructional packages for use in classrooms, the OUs would need effective strategies for training/counselling and group learning at study centres and/or self-help groups.

Another level of convergence noted by Kelly and Smith (1987), moving towards open learning systems, is yet to take place.

Certain measures are suggested below for convergence:

- Pooling of educational media programmes at various levels and subject areas, rather than the present practice of UGC and IGNOU producing and telecasting programmes separately. This pooling would also involve large-scale future use of tele-conferencing.

- Sharing of curriculum development and the preparation of course materials and textbooks for standardisation of a core and needs-based national curriculum, with a small portion left for institutions to develop locally.
- Joint ventures with industries for the design and offering of programmes to their clients. In fact, the industries would, in future, compel both the systems either to compete or to converge for mutual benefit.
- Joint efforts and mechanisms for credit accumulation and transfer between the two systems.
- Collaboration in research and development – both systemic and discipline-based research – for the development of new educational methodologies and the development of new knowledge.

For a successful convergence, all the coordinating agencies – University Grants Commission, Association of Indian Universities, Distance Education Council and National Accreditation and Assessment Council – would own responsibility and have to collaborate.

As has been shown in this chapter, future policies and practices in Indian open and distance education show some moves towards convergence between the conventional and open systems of higher education. However, many countervailing tendencies remain and much work and debate lie ahead in India before any enduring substantial convergence occurs.

10 Policy and practices in open and distance education in Hong Kong

Angela Castro and Charles Wong

The term 'open learning' is normally used to denote access and equity of learning opportunities and flexibility of learning modes, and 'distance education' a physical separation between the teacher and student. When used together or interchangeably to describe the philosophy, pedagogy, approaches and categories of a major sector of non-mainstream education, they could present some methodological problems as well as conceptual confusion. For example, one can have open learning courses that are not taught at a distance, and distance education courses that are not open in most respects. In Hong Kong, the picture is even more confusing as there are distance education courses requiring substantial and regular classroom attendance, and open learning courses with prerequisites for admission. 'Distance' and 'openness' take on new meanings in Hong Kong, i.e. the market is open to many institutions from around the world and their courses are much more 'open' in that admission policies are less restrictive than they would have been when those same courses were offered in their home countries. This range of activities is often referred to in Hong Kong as 'continuing education', covering extension, second-chance or lifelong, part-time courses offered through the continuing education (CE) units attached to post-secondary colleges and tertiary institutions, commercial and non-profit agencies such as the British Council, the Australian Education Centre, the Goethe Institute, trade organisations and government vocational training institutes.

Whatever name we would like to use to describe such activities, non-mainstream, part-time education in Hong Kong has been an important alternative for the working adults of Hong Kong to acquire additional skills and qualifications and, more recently, for enhancing their chances of emigrating overseas before Hong Kong reverts back to Chinese rule on 1 July 1997 under the Special Administrative Region (SAR) government. This chapter is an account of the Hong Kong government and institutional policy and the practice of 'open' continuing education by local and non-local providers in Hong Kong. We will be mentioning the role of telecommunications media in general, and the Internet in particular, for local student support of overseas courses.

CONTINUING EDUCATION PROVIDERS IN HONG HONG

One of the major providers of continuing education courses at both degree and sub-degree levels is the Open Learning Institute (HKOLI), set up in June 1989 by the Hong Kong government after less than a year of planning. The HKOLI was modelled on the British Columbia Open Learning Institute (now British Columbia Open University) in Canada, and has also drawn on the UK Open University (UKOU) for some of its approaches. Currently it has about 330 full-time staff, 800 part-time staff (mostly instructors on short contracts), and over 20,000 students registered on its twenty-four validated degree programmes. The HKOLI received initial financial support from the government, but the funding ceased after the 1992/3 academic year, and it has been operating at an annual budget deficit of about HK\$17 million in the last two years. It could raise its fees to cover the operating costs but has not done so for fear of disadvantaging the students and of pricing itself out of the very competitive market in Hong Kong. Its courses are being validated by the Hong Kong Council of Academic Accreditation (HKCAA), and self-accredited university status is expected to be confirmed in 1996. It should be pointed out that the HKOLI is under the jurisdiction of the Education and Manpower Branch (EMB) and not the University Grants Committee (UGC) which looks after the mainstream universities.

When the HKOLI commenced in September 1989, it had 60,195 applicants for its 4,273 first-year undergraduate places, indicating the tremendous demand of working adults for such a form of education. The HKOLI relies heavily on purchased distance education courses from the UKOU but modifies them slightly to make them more suitable for local students (Timmers *et al.*, 1992). Since 1992, it has added, to its four schools, a Centre for Continuing and Community Education to expand into sub-degree and non-credit courses. In a recent press interview, Professor S. W. Tam, the new HKOLI director, stated that he would place an increasing emphasis on new, home-grown courses taught in Chinese and would seek the help of Chinese teachers from the People's Republic of China.

The main rivals of the HKOLI for the large adult learners' market are the CE units attached to five of the seven UGC-funded tertiary institutions: The University of Hong Kong, The Chinese University of Hong Kong, The Hong Kong Polytechnic University, The City University of Hong Kong and The Hong Kong Baptist University. Many of these units have substantial enrolments each semester (around 15,000) on their short courses which typically involve class attendance of one to two evenings per week with part-time instructors on short contracts. These short courses used to form the main part of CE activities; however, since the late 1980s, these CE units have been offering degree courses from overseas by acting as the local brokers of predominantly British, Australian and American institutions which are keen to market their courses in Hong Kong. The target groups of these courses have been the large pool of people in their late twenties and thirties who were qualified for tertiary education but were denied a place due to an acute shortage of under-graduate places in the 1970s and 1980s, graduates of polytechnics, technical institutes and colleges of education with only a high diploma or a certificate, and, of course, people who have substantial work experience but low aca-demic qualifications. Since there is often little academic input (with a few exceptions to be discussed later) from the local CE unit, there is not an equitable relationship between the partners and the motivation for collabora-tion is mostly profit-driven; so one would hesitate to use the term 'consor-tium' to describe such collaboration (Lee and Lam, 1993). The revenue from these partnership deals is quite lucrative and, in 1993, two directors of CE units were suspended for alleged irregular financial practices in the collabora-tive arrangements.

These institutional partnerships evolved initially from a recommendation in the government's Education Commission Report No. 2 (1989) to encour-age local tertiary institutions to work with overseas institutions so that such activities could be monitored and, at the same time, to restrict the offering of courses by overseas institutions directly. The most logical unit within a Hong Kong institution to take on this collaborative task has been the CE unit. Most of the CE units do not enjoy a great deal of support by the central adminis-tration or the teaching departments in their home institutions, and as a con-sequence, what they could bring to the partnership has been limited. How-ever, the representatives of the overseas award-granting institutions would often mislead their superiors that they have secured the full range of re-sources from a local tertiary partner institution with a large campus. Some of the CE units in Hong Kong are also slow to recognise that there are signifi-cant differences between running short courses, which they have been doing for many years, and these award-bearing courses and have not therefore geared up the necessary human and other resources to adapt to the change. The non-involvement of senior management and faculty at local host institu-tions has been a major reason why many good overseas courses have not fared well academically in Hong Kong.

Some overseas institutions, including very reputable ones, have taken advantage of the lack of government legislation and opted for direct service by setting up their own local offices or working through local commercial agencies to handle marketing and registration. There are also problems with this arrangement as the regular rental of lecture and tutorial accommodation is very high. Hotel rooms are therefore frequently used as interview or tutor-ial rooms for the overseas staff on their flying visits. A small number of distance education providers, to save on local operational costs, have simply asked students to register with them directly, and course materials are sent to the students' homes from overseas.

There are many reasons for the popularity of overseas degree programmes. As the number of degree places has expanded greatly in the last few years, those who only have sub-degree qualifications are eager to upgrade to stay ahead in the workforce. Many who had planned to take one or two years' leave from work to earn an overseas degree can now earn such a degree without leaving their work or Hong Kong. In general, there is an inflation of credentials in the territory. Many believe, or are led to believe, that such overseas degrees are better than local degrees in terms of international recognition after 1997 and that they will also enhance their chances of being accepted as residents in a foreign country. Lee and Lam (1993) found 2,205 advertisements by 211 institutions from thirteen countries/regions selling their courses in Hong Kong during the period of August 1991 to July 1992.

REGULATING NON-LOCAL HIGHER AND PROFESSIONAL EDUCATION IN HONG KONG

The Hong Kong government enacted legislation at the end of 1995 to regulate the operations of non-local institutions of higher education and professional bodies (NIHEPBs). The objective is to ensure that the standards of the courses offered by the NIHEPBs are recognised by the organisations themselves as well as their own national accredition authorities. The legislation also aims to ensure that the standards of courses delivered in Hong Kong will be maintained at levels comparable to those achieved on-campus in the institutions overseas. The HKCAA has been named as the body which will advise the Registrar of NIHEPBs on the academic validity of the courses submitted by the NIHEPBs.

Exemption from registration under the Education Ordinance for NIHEPBs with local tertiary partners will be allowed to continue after the Bill is enacted, but they must formally apply for the exemption.

Operators of regulated courses wishing to apply for registration must ensure that their courses meet two criteria:

(i) [in the case of a course leading to the award of a non-local higher academic qualification] that the institution is a recognized non-local institution of higher education, and effective measures are in place to ensure that the standard of the course conducted in Hong Kong is maintained at a level comparable with one conducted in the country of origin leading to the same qualification and is recognized as such by the institution, the academic community and the relevant accreditation authority of the country; and

(ii) [in the case of a course leading to the award of a non-local professional qualification] that the course is recognized by the professional body for the purpose of awarding the qualification, and the professional body is generally recognized in the country of origin as an authoritative and representational body of the relevant profession.

(Education and Manpower Branch, 1995, section 12)

One important proposal in the Bill is that purely distance education courses have been excluded from requiring registration. Such courses are defined as those that are conducted solely through the sale of materials in book shops, delivery of mail, or transmission of information by means of telecommunication, without the physical presence of the NIHEPBs or their operators in Hong Kong.

(Ibid., Section 5)

The reason for the exclusion is that the Attorney-General has advised that to include such courses would restrict the 'freedom to seek, receive and impart information and ideas of all kinds' (ibid., Section 5). Should these providers wish to be registered voluntarily, they will be subjected to the same requirements and provisions for the regulated courses as laid down by the Registrar. We predict that distance education providers will wish to register for the sake of gaining credibility, important for their marketing drive and recruitment of students, but the criteria used by the EMB and the HKCAA to assess the acceptability of the more innovative courses using telecommunications and media will probably need to be conveyed very clearly at the onset to the providers who will then be able to inform their students properly before they enrol on a course.

STUDENT SUPPORT FOR COURSES OFFERED IN HONG KONG

In the *Academic Programmes Guide, 1994–1995*, the HKCAA (1994b) has listed 135 courses by sixty-nine British, Australian, American and Chinese organisations, which probably constitute about 60 per cent of the current courses offered by over 300 NIHEPBs. The picture that has emerged from the *Guide* is as follows.

Costs

The fees for an overseas first degree part-time course (with some advanced credit exemption and with between 100 and 400 hours of local tutorials and seminars) marketed directly or through a CE unit within a local institution range from HK$34,000 to HK$90,000 (about US$4,500 to US$11,800). As a comparison, the HKOLI first degree requires fewer on-site tutorials and 120 credits at about HK$750 per credit, but this cost of about HK$90,000 can be further reduced because students can seek up to sixty credits of advanced standing. This still compares well with the cost of a full-time degree in a local institution for three years which has now risen to HK$93,000.

Most popular courses

Business courses constitute half of the total number of courses on offer. The fees for Master of Business Administration courses range from HK$46,000 to HK$120,000.

Registration

Application can be made only at specified periods during an academic year or semester, and there are specified maximum and minimum durations set for the completion of courses.

Entry qualifications

Open entry is generally allowed for non-professional, sub-degree courses. For undergraduate programmes, a school-leaving certificate, proficiency in English and relevant work experience or a trade qualification are required; and for a postgraduate programme, a first degree is expected.

Mode of teaching

Print-based 'distance education' course materials are supplied for self-study and are supplemented with regular tutorials by local part-time tutors and occasional seminars by visiting overseas tutors.

SUPPORT AND FACILITIES

Students usually have access to libraries of the local partnering institutions, the British Council Library and government public libraries. However, such access is not automatic on every course and a special arrangement has to be made in advance; inter-library loan facilities are not automatically included in the arrangement.

The point to note is that while local commercial agencies and offices representing overseas institutions will find it understandably hard to set up facilities for Hong Kong students, those who enrol through CE units in local institutions have only a limited access to their staff resources and facilities. Hong Kong institutions are generally well equipped because they have been enjoying a period of financial bonanza since the government announced in October 1989 that it planned to expand tertiary education by 1994. Salaries to faculty and administration are among the highest in the world in order to retain local appointments and to attract international staff. At five of the seven UGC-funded universities, there are world-class libraries, satellite television, sophisticated science and language laboratories and abundant capacities on the campus computing networks. Digitised video-conferencing has been available at The University of Hong Kong for over a year, although not ostensibly for teaching overseas courses but more for job interviews of overseas applicants; other institutions are soon to install the same facility so as not to be left behind.

HARNet – the Hong Kong tertiary computer network set up in 1986 – has been upgraded to a T1 (1.544 Mbps) leased circuit to the USA. Staff and students in the UGC-funded universities are active users of the World Wide Web, electronic mail and file transfer facilities on the Internet. However, because HARNet is publicly funded, continuing education students enrolled in overseas programmes are not allowed to use the Internet freely. The CE units of The University of Hong Kong, The Chinese University, The Hong Kong Polytechnic University, The City University and The Baptist University have negotiated for a small number of continuing education students on computing and nursing courses to have Internet access for a fee to allow them to receive and send Email, and, in the case of The City University, to use the Web at their own expense.

Generally, the British institutions have been quicker to capitalise on this new way of enhancing communication between tutors, administrators and students, and between students. For example, Henley Management College, University of Gloucester and Cheltenham, and Paisley University all offer electronic mail for communication and assignment submission, and their administrative staff have taken a more systematic approach in providing training and support for local staff and students.

Fax is used by a small number of overseas institutions through the so-called 'fax-a-professor' arrangement, such as the University of Southern Queensland, the University of South Australia and Henley Management College for their MBA courses. The Australian Catholic University in conjunction with Caritas, a Catholic mission in Hong Kong, is the only overseas institution to use video-conferencing for students to communicate with their tutors. The University of Hong Kong has a purpose-built room equipped for telephone seminars on a University of Otago pharmacy course. The HKOLI has telephone tutorials and academic counselling sessions. It has also started to introduce an electronic bulletin-board system for students to send in course enquiries and to check the library collection; however, it has insufficient dial-in telephone lines for its 20,000 students. Such services should be greatly expanded when it moves to its new campus in Homantin in 1996, where an electronic library will be installed.

MENTORING AND CARING FOR CONTINUING EDUCATION STUDENTS

Many educators in Hong Kong may argue that a student support network is not necessary because the geographical distances in Hong Kong are so short, its transportation system so developed, and there is so much face-to-face tuition. However, the authors affirm Sewart's insistence that: 'Students will not easily achieve success if course materials are of poor quality. Nor will they usually achieve success if they are not dealt with individually through the student support system' (Sewart, 1993, p. 10).

Furthermore, the notion of 'temporal' distance is important in Hong Kong. Due to the long working hours of most people it is difficult for them to attend face-to-face meetings in the evenings even though the geographical distances involved are very small. Students can only find time to study late at night and at weekends. In fact, meetings on Saturday afternoons and evenings and on Sundays are becoming increasingly prevalent and this is proving to be very stressful for numbers of students.

Many Hong Kong adult students are also unfamiliar with distance learning courses, having been accustomed to a more didactic teaching in schools and even universities. In the change to distance learning, such students need a lot of help from the outset, as Maree Bentley of the HKOLI has discovered:

> Students really were extremely unfamiliar with the concept of distance education courses. They expected tutorials to be lectures and tutors to be lecturers. They expected to be able to complete the course by reading the textbook and attending tutorials, or by working through study units without referring to the textbook. The concept of getting it all together was very foreign indeed.
>
> (Cited in Timmers *et al.*, 1992, p. 486)

Computer and telephone conferencing and counselling could have helped to sustain interaction and communication, which leads to the central issue of government and institutional commitment to CE in Hong Kong.

CURRENT GOVERNMENT POLICY AND FUNDING

The UGC advises the Hong Kong Government on tertiary funding and coordinates the medium and long-term planning of seven government-funded institutions; but the HKOLI , the newly formed Academy of Performing Arts and the Institute of Education are not part of this remit. In its 1993 interim report, *Higher Education 1991–2001*, the UGC devoted only three short paragraphs to CE. Under the heading of 'Higher education after 1995', it acknowledged the necessity of provision for continuing professional education, but has passed this responsibility on to the CE units of tertiary institutions, the Open Learning Institute (HKOLI) and the industry that wants its staff trained. As a justification for not funding the CE units or the HKOLI, it reiterated the 'user-pays' principle but said that it would be willing to provide some future development assistance:

> Much of the cost of CE or 'leisure' courses should be met by the employer or the student, but there may still be a need for a Government input, particularly in providing for development into new areas. We are undertaking a study for continuing education in Hong Kong and we shall be returning to this matter in our final report.
>
> (UPGC, 1993, p. 7)

It is anticipated that these new provisions will also mean that HKOLI staff would be able to bid for UGC research grants.

The final report has now been postponed to early 1996. There is one major institutional anomaly which the UGC did not address in this interim 1993 report. In The Hong Kong Polytechnic University and The City University, government block grants have been used to support the part-time evening versions of many of the regular degree and sub-degree programmes, taught usually by the full-time staff; yet the government has so far refused to support the same target student group if they enrol for other or similar part-time courses within the same institution offered by the CE unit. However, the UGC has not objected to institutions using public funds to subsidise the core staff salary of the CE units or to make their offices and classrooms available for CE use.

One of the government's hesitations about supporting CE courses may have to do with the recognition of overseas degrees taught at a distance in Hong Kong. It is perhaps not convinced that the majority of courses can be taught satisfactorily in distance education mode, and it is also suspicious of fast-track arrangements offered by overseas institutions. For example, teachers with a Teacher's Certificate (a sub-degree) qualification have been admitted by some British institutions and been able to gain a bachelor degree within ten months (one academic year). Registered nurses in Hong Kong are also able to obtain a nursing degree in Australia by a short period of study in Hong Kong and then only eight months of on-campus tuition in Australia. The government has yet to introduce new rulings to deal with such special arrangements. The Civil Service has therefore established a ruling that it will not accept a distance education degree if it allows more than one-third of advanced standing. The majority of teachers enrolled in Deakin University's Bachelor of Education programme which allows more than one-third advanced standing (for previous qualifications and relevant professional experience) have found their degree unrecognised when they applied for promotion in the Civil Service.

Government laxity in setting long-term policies and the wider promulgation of clear guidelines to all has confirmed what many local CE researchers and operators have been saying for a long time: there is basically no government initiative or commitment to direct the development and implementation of non-mainstream education.Thereby, market forces and economic considerations have been allowed to influence practices, which in turn have given rise to the formulation of contingency regulations. Certainly, with just over a year before Britain hands Hong Kong back to China, the government in Hong Kong has other more pressing issues on its hands. The preoccupation of the University and Polytechnic Grants Commission (UPGC which became the UGC in 1995 after the Polytechnics were designated as Universities) has been the expansion of tertiary places to undergraduates in local institutions from 9 per cent to 18 per cent of the age cohort, or 15,000 first-degree places by 1994, which Morris *et al.* (1994) have criticised as a 'pacifier' in times of political stress.

INSTITUTIONAL POLICY AND PRACTICE

The CE units attached to tertiary institutions have adhered to the UPGC ruling that prohibits institutions from diverting block grants for CE programmes (UPGC, 1993, p. 7) with the consequence that they work as business enterprises rather than public services. Consequently, they have concentrated on profitable business and computing courses; and then education and nursing courses because of the demand for professional-development courses due to the depletion of qualified and experienced staff through the mass exodus of women teachers and nurses emigrating overseas with their husbands.

The relationship between these CE units and their parent institutions is a complex one. Many CE units have found it difficult to solicit the participation of busy and well-paid faculty colleagues in the running of 'franchised' courses. The few staff who teach at the request of the CE units are subjected to quite rigid restrictions and/or the sharing of income with the department. The priority is low for the use of campus facilities. Support divisions such as the library, the computing centre, student counselling office and the mailing office are reluctant to cooperate for fear of being criticised for diverting UGC-funded facilities to 'commercial' undertakings. There are also the difficulties of working out a charging formula for the use of laboratories, related materials and technician support costs, and deciding whether the revenue should go to the support divisions or the institutional central budget. Since CE student enrolment numbers are usually high, there is a fear that allowing these students even a limited access to campus facilities may strain the existing infrastructure, hardware and software resources. For example, the number of telephone lines and ports for off-campus computer dial-in access would need to be increased, not to mention increases in technical and other staff to support the software and hardware.

The exception to the free-standing model of CE units in the five universities with CE units is The City University of Hong Kong (CUHK) where the CE unit is an integral part of the institution. Several teaching departments are involved in the academic coordination and teaching of courses leading to overseas awards as well as (CUHK) awards. Support divisions are more cooperative and the uses of facilities are strictly documented and paid for, based on a formula that is acceptable to the parent institution and accountable to the government.

A NEW INSTITUTIONAL MODEL IN THE MAKING?

The existing arrangement of a separate management structure for CE within most of the UGC-funded institutions has long been a concern. The HKCAA has suggested that institutions should review their organisational structures to cope with the increasing community need for CE:

Another factor which affects the nature of modern post-secondary institutions concerns the increased demands for adult, continuing and professional education placed upon them by the community. (Evidence of such demand in Hong Kong is demonstrated by the significant expansion of extra-mural departments and the emergence of 'self-financed programmes'.) The increased demands for these aspects of post-secondary education and the community links thus developed will require appropriate changes of management and organization within faculties and within the institution as a whole.

(HKCAA, 1994a, p. 4)

The need might come sooner as teaching departments are now attracted to the notion of collaborating directly with overseas institutions without routing the courses through the CE unit in the same institution. Institutions may need to decide whether a distributed model or a centralised model should be used for collaboration with other institutions, including those from China.

Another important development is that at The University of Hong Kong a review of the School of Professional and Continuing Education has resulted in the recommendation that it should offer courses with degrees granted by the University, rather than being brokers for overseas degrees. Should such a path be followed by this or other universities two broad options could be considered which are discussed below.

One option is to offer mixed-mode, 'flexible learning' courses. That is, making the same course and tuition choices (including course materials) available to full-time and part-time students, as has been done in some instances in Australia. Potentially, opening up more options and choices for all students with common degree programmes. For this to occur, staff will have to be persuaded to embrace 'open education' and will need to understand how to transform such courses from a classroom setting to a home or workplace setting. This suggests the establishment of course-development and production units.

The second option will be for universities to let their own existing CE divisions retain their separate administrative structures and continue to control their own budgets, but allow them to develop a few endorsed courses with the faculty members agreeing to contribute to the writing and teaching of those courses. The universities would then accredit these courses and count them towards a degree. However, such courses would need to be validated along with other on-campus university courses.

Both routes would require substantial resources and extensive consultation with the UGC, and probably with the EMB and the HKCAA. The indications are that, despite the occasional noises being made around Hong Kong campuses these days, few changes are likely to take place in the next couple of years because of the 1997 factor.

1997 AND BEYOND

Institutions in China have increased their presence in Hong Kong recently in two ways: through the export of their students and their courses. The first has been helped by the UPGC's recent allocation of funds for Hong Kong institutions to accept and sponsor outstanding graduates from China to pursue master's and doctoral courses. A Hong Kong academic course, and especially one at the postgraduate level with a stipend, is attractive to many Chinese graduates as it could provide a springboard to further studies and probably eventual employment in western countries. On the other hand, some smaller Hong Kong institutions have started to allow their students to study for a second degree awarded by a Chinese university; an example is the Shue-Yan College's collaboration with Beijing University in two law degree courses.

Some universities and provincial governments in China have also discovered a potentially lucrative market in Hong Kong for some of their specialised courses. For example, Xiamen University has been approved by China's State Education Commission to offer in Hong Kong two degree programmes in Chinese and Chinese medicine. The Guangdong provincial government's Department of Justice has decided to offer a degree programme in Chinese law. Chinese academic awards through distance education and self-study opportunities are going to be increasingly attractive as the majority of Hong Kong people who are prepared to stay behind after 1997 believe that a Chinese qualification, or an additional Chinese qualification, especially in Chinese trade or law, will enhance their careers in business and management.

It is conceivable that such courses can be taught via satellite television, which has started to become popular in Hong Kong. Chinese institutions are much more experienced than Hong Kong institutions with televised CE courses because they have been broadcasting them on the satellite-delivered national China Central Television (CCTV) and the China Education Television (CETV). The latter broadcasts mainly the courses of its central and forty-four provincial and municipal Chinese Radio and Television Universities (Wei and Tong, 1994) to about 540,000 students. The Radio and Television Universities have had a setback since the Chinese Government cut their admission quota by 350,000 to 300,000 in 1992. Hence, they may emulate the mainstream universities and recruit Hong Kong students for their economic survival by making the CETV available, alongside the CCTV, which is already received in Hong Kong. When this happens, Hong Kong students will have more programme variety and choices, and at the same time it could present an interesting challenge to the HKOLI which has been able to screen only about a few hours of programming on one of the Hong Kong commercial television channels during the weekends. Wharf Cable, the first cable company in Hong Kong, started a 24-hour Learning Channel on 9 May 1994, broadcasting educational programmes from TV-Ontario and the Hong Kong Vocational Training Council. This channel has now been renamed 'Horizon' and is offering free airtime and production assistance to a number of CE units to offer short courses to its, at this stage, small number of subscribers.

One very rapid development which has the potential to globalise Asian continuing education in the next few years, albeit perhaps for a privileged minority, is the growing popularity of the Internet. For example, the People's Republic of China has been fairly liberal in allowing student and staff use of the China Education Research Network (CERNet) but the scarcity of terminals, telephone lines or leased data lines for such a vast country remains a serious limitation for either mainstream or continuing education use. Some American educators are exploring this mode of communication with their students in Chinese universities with which they have exchange or twinning arrangements.

It is becoming commonplace for administrators and policy-makers in open and distance education, or even in higher education more broadly, to argue that students are becoming increasingly aware of global electronic access to higher education. As this increases, then universities and other providers of education will shift their practices to draw upon this global studentship. The implications of social and cultural kinds are likely to be quite profound. However, the inequities of access to electronic communications will mean that these developments are also unlikely to be uniform, and may well reconstruct new disparities.

Such developments may be a little further off for Asian universities, be they courseware originators or administrative and delivery partners with overseas universities. The electronic support networks that are being established in some British, North American and Australian universities are non-existent at this point in time for Asian CE students.

Quicker uptake of the Internet, CD-ROM and other multimedia technologies for professional and continuing education may come from the private and commercial sectors. There are many new commercial Internet service providers in Hong Kong, China, Taiwan, Japan, Thailand and Singapore, which charge quite reasonable subscription fees for access and data storage, and CompuServe and AT&T are also making inroads into Asia. Currently, communications between Asian countries are routed through the USA, thus incurring unnecessary costs and congestion in trans-Pacific communications. Three major commercial providers in Hong Kong, Japan and Singapore announced in October 1995 the formation of a consortium called Asia Internet Holdings to build an Internet backbone network in Asia with Tokyo as it hub, and Hong Kong and Singapore as regional hubs. Business and professional enterprises will be able to take advantage of these commercial services to deliver international on-line courses for wealthier students who have the appropriate home equipment. Asia could change from being a recipient market of overseas courses to a provider of Asian courses to adult learners in America, Australia and Europe.

The extent of how cable and satellite television and the Internet will be used for CE and how they will be controlled by the Special Administrative

Region (SAR) government after 1997 is very much a matter for speculation at this stage. Evans and Nation believe that in a post-industrial era:

> Communications media and technologies are a fundamental element to structuring a period of change and to transmitting its nature and consequences. Such media and technologies enable people influencing distance education to control, empower, liberate or alienate the learners.
>
> (Evans and Nation, 1992, p. 10)

It is possible that China may not even need to regulate media use because a self-censured mentality has already set in for the people of Hong Kong and foreign businesses operating in Asia. Media magnate Rupert Murdoch's taking the BBC off the Star satellite channel to appease the Chinese government and the recent Hong Kong Government statement about the operators' need for sensitivity and discretion in satellite broadcasting in order not to upset governments in Asia are sobering examples.

It is also difficult to know how the SAR government will treat the overseas CE operators in Hong Kong after 1997. Lee and Lam (1993) predict a three-way collaboration of Hong Kong, Chinese and overseas institutions for CE. However, since many Chinese institutions have separately established direct links with education institutions overseas, there may be no need to involve Hong Kong institutions. For example, the State University of San Francisco already offers three business courses through the Central Radio and Television University in China. Indeed, because the operating costs of CE in China are generally much lower than they are in Hong Kong in terms of classroom accommodation and staff costs, and because China has potentially a massive CE market (in volume rather than revenue), overseas institutions and Hong Kong CE units are likely to establish administrative offices in China to coordinate enrolments and marketing and to use Chinese staff to teach their courses.

The Australian government is taking a very market-oriented approach to exporting its education worldwide through the use of information technology. It is establishing a number of national cooperative multimedia centres and also an electronic network, Education Network Australia (EdNA), to develop products and services for the school and community sectors. These moves, together with the wide availability of Australian television programmes via satellites in Asia and the country's successful establishment of the Australian Academic and Research Network (AARNet), may help to make Australia the leading overseas provider of CE in China and Hong Kong after 1997.

The development of 'open' and 'distance' education in Hong Kong under the British government has reached a plateau. The current situation comprises inconsistent practices and piecemeal, contingent policies. In Hong Kong CE could have been managed better, and the lessons to be learned are salutary to administrators and teachers in the various collaborating local and overseas institutions, not to mention the students involved in CE. Hong Kong has not reached the stage of development where one can speak of 'empowerment' and 'liberation' of the adult learner, and how soon this stage will come probably depends on three factors: the SAR government's willingness to endorse and resource CE with a clear and visionary policy (when so many other new responsibilities will be competing for its attention in 1997 and beyond); the commitment of the UGC-funded universities in embracing, expanding and supporting the mission objectives of their CE programmes; and the extent of the development and quality of full-fees professional education programmes operated by commercial and professional bodies using telecommunications, multimedia and the Internet.

11 Total Quality Management
Policy implications for distance education

Andrea McIlroy and Robyn Walker

BACKGROUND

This chapter stems from previous work by the authors into the correspondence between the broadening of the quality perspective within higher education and the increased regard for quality as a key to business success (McIlroy and Walker, 1993). The impetus for the involvement of higher education, including forms of open and distance education, comes from external economic factors which demand innovative responses from institutions. As business struggled with the new, deregulated environment of the 1980s, higher education too became subject to dramatic challenges for which their existing management systems were inadequate.

With deregulation came drastic reductions in public-sector expenditure. The changed environment brought new players into the tertiary education market, testing the supremacy of the state-funded universities and polytechnics. Students, required to contribute an increasing proportion of their fees, had a greater investment in the education system and became more demanding of their consumer rights.

Globally, tertiary education institutions have reacted in a number of ways to the economic and political reforms. Under the influence of a highly competitive free market, innovative education institutions have examined their core activities and sought ways by which to improve their competitive position. To supplement their incomes, institutions are now exploring new markets and options, including attracting full-fee paying students, often from abroad. As a consequence they may have to offer a greater range of choices and supplementary services to meet the needs of new groups. Distance education has proved another desirable option for some tertiary providers, either building on or extending existing competencies.

Among tertiary distance education providers, the adoption of a business management framework has been a common response to change. Along with this, Total Quality Management (TQM) has entered the domain of educational rhetoric and practice. It appears to have attracted an enthusiastic following including the administrators of a number of universities and colleges in Europe and North America (see, for example, Spanbauer, 1992; Coate, 1990).

Whether tertiary institutions are questioning their traditional internal management practices in the light of a better understanding and appreciation of the effectiveness of business strategies, or whether they are merely clutching at anything that might help to ensure their survival through changing times, is debatable. However, they are adopting different ways of carrying out their role nationally and internationally.

But the application of business solutions to educational problems is contentious. Many educators assert that business has 'no business' in education. Others claim benefits from the application of business models whilst possibly ignoring important educational imperatives. Undoubtedly educators (for example, Irving, 1987) have been concerned about the shift away from traditional values and practices, some voicing strong reservations about it. Baldwin (1994, p. 131) claims that it is 'a process of "colonisation" which may bring with it all of the destructiveness of any colonising movement – a wholesale usurpation of customs, structures, values and perceptions'.

The continuing controversy over how to unite successfully the management and educational objectives of an organisation is fuelled by developments that have resulted from changed government policies. Contestable funding, for example, has made many tertiary institutions seek closer relationships with the business community as they cannot rely solely on government grants or assume that cost overruns will be met. Industry's interest is no longer merely as a potential employer of graduates. It has a role as partial funder. Representatives from the various sectors are increasingly active on advisory boards and in joint ventures with tertiary providers. Its profile as an important stakeholder in the education system has been heightened and business and industry groups are exerting greater influence upon educational policy direction.

It may be that the difficulty in reconciling business approaches with educational objectives derives as much from an inadequate understanding of those approaches and from resistance to change as from a genuine concern for the students and the good of the institution.

What then is Total Quality Management; how is it understood in business, and can it be usefully translated into an educational context?

TOTAL QUALITY MANAGEMENT EXPLAINED

In order to understand total quality management it is helpful to have some sense of its historical development. Quality systems in business and industry have progressed through four fairly discrete phases, each with a different emphasis.

The first phase was inspection or conformance to requirements where corrective actions took place after errors were detected. Quality control, the second phase, focused on monitoring processes and eliminating the causes of unsatisfactory performance at relevant points. The third phase, quality assurance, included the setting of more comprehensive quality standards and both internal and external auditing of quality systems (for example, the ISO 9000 series). Thus it emphasised prevention of non-conformance rather than merely its detection. The most recent progression is into Total Quality Management (Dale *et al.*, 1990).

Total Quality Management developed as a strategic option for manufacturing industries. It incorporates all the features of its antecedents and includes as its primary focus achieving total customer satisfaction.

> Total quality is a set of philosophies by which management systems can direct the efficient achievement of the objectives of the organisation to ensure customer satisfaction and maximise stakeholder value ... it becomes a way of life for doing business for the entire organisation.
>
> (Lewis and Smith, 1994, p. 29)

As Lewis and Smith stress, it is a philosophy rather than a tactic. It is an approach to quality that does not just focus on minimum requirements but on excellence and innovation at every level. '[It] is total in three senses: it covers every process, every job, and every person' (ibid., p. 28). It provides a framework within which to optimise the achievement of the organisation's objectives be they social, educational or economic.

Notwithstanding the evolutionary nature of TQM, its perspective on quality is relatively new. Total Quality Management became popular in North America, Europe and Australasia in the 1980s as a way of improving competitive position and, in particular, as a response to the enormous success of Japan. This success was due in large part to the implementation of quality management strategies and techniques developed in Japan by American quality gurus, W. Edwards Deming (1986) and Joseph Juran (1989).

In their work with Japanese manufacturers Deming and a Japanese colleague, Ishikawa, emphasised continuous improvement. Challenging traditional beliefs and practices, they recognised that the people best placed to identify the need for improvement and make the necessary changes were those closest to the tasks. Quality management and improvement became the responsibility of all the firm's employees, and not just senior managers or those in the Quality Control Department. This, according to Deming and Ishikawa, gave more autonomy and responsibility to employees, put less emphasis on hierarchies and allowed for a greater degree of decentralised authority and decision-making.

Juran also embraced these ideas and emphasised the importance of satisfying customer needs. Quality was 'fitness for use' (1989, p. 15) and quality management included identifying customers' needs, planning to meet those needs and verifying that the needs had been met.

Under TQM quality is defined by the expectations and perceptions of the end users. In addition it goes beyond concerns with outputs and focuses on the *process* of providing the service or producing a good. Therefore the *means* are just as important as the *ends*. While it is difficult to sum up all the features of Total Quality Management, Scurr's definition does capture the essence: '[TQM is] continuously meeting agreed customer requirements at the lowest cost by releasing the potential of all employees' (Scurr, 1990, p. 17).

TQM has several themes:

- *The customer (both internal and external)*. Juran (1989) defines anyone who receives or is affected by the product, process or service as a customer. External customers are not members of the organisation or company that produces the good or service whereas internal customers are.
- *Continuous improvement*. Innovation and excellence are valued at all stages. Improvement is a way of life which may ultimately result in a product or service with 'zero defects'.
- *Staff training and development*. The success of TQM is dependent upon continual employee involvement and education. An obligation is thus placed on the organisation to invest in its staff. The intention is to reinforce employee commitment and have a positive effect on morale. This will lead to productivity gains.
- *Teamwork*. Group involvement and co-operation is believed to be the best approach to deal with improvement activities throughout the organisation and with external interest groups.
- *Measurement*. The success of any total quality initiative is dependent upon the ability to monitor progress and review objectives.

As the name implies, 'Total quality management requires that the principles of quality management should be applied in every branch at every level of the organisation. The process would extend beyond the organisation itself to include partnerships with suppliers and customers' (Dale *et al.*, 1990, p. 5).

Contributing to a revolution in the way organisations are structured and managed, TQM has irreversibly changed our perception of what quality means. It is widely applied in service industries including the public sector and there is now an accumulating literature about the application of TQM to tertiary and distance education.

QUALITY IN HIGHER AND DISTANCE EDUCATION

The concept of quality is not new to educators. Traditionally they have been intensely interested in the subject. However, pedagogical issues have tended to take precedence over the broader institutional and economic systems within which education occurs. From a business perspective, this could be seen to have resulted in a narrow focus – one which assumes that pedagogy is somehow separate from the systems within which learning takes place.

Even as late as 1991, Nunan (1991b) identified this as a fundamental problem in the literature about quality in distance education. He claimed that writers seldom took a comprehensive view of the whole enterprise, tending instead to focus on a particular aspect of distance education. Much of the emphasis was still on outputs, such as the number of graduates produced, or more particularly, on production and delivery processes.

Over the years, many writers focused on better course design of instructional materials, the use of improved communication technologies and more sophisticated use of print materials. Guri, for example, describes the complex system of quality control that Everyman's University in Israel applies to its distance education courses. The emphasis is on developing the best possible course materials according to predetermined standards and goals. Thus a quality-control approach was taken by adjusting operations to predetermined criteria (Guri,1987, p. 16).

Guri also discusses the difficulty of applying quality control mechanisms in distance teaching universities because of the concepts of academic freedom and professional autonomy. This point is also made by Nunan (1991b) who argues that these concepts in effect mean self-regulation, as judgements about the value and worth of distance education courses are made by those who also design and teach them.

The link between evaluation and quality is explored by Lewis (1989) who argues that evaluation is a process of making judgements about the effectiveness of programmes. In other words, evaluation must involve making statements about quality. Like quality-management proponent Juran (1989), he defines quality in terms of fitness for purpose.

Another prominent theme emerging from the literature of the late 1980s and early 1990s is that of quality deriving from the learning process (for example, Bradbery, 1991; Paul, 1990a, b; Mills and Paul, 1993). Paul (1990a) defines institutional success in terms of producing independent learners. He claims that the process of interaction between students, the materials and tutor 'produces' the course as much as the course writers do. Thus knowledge is viewed as a process rather than a commodity.

Viljoen, Holt and Petzall focus their conception of quality on the process of interaction between the learner, the materials and the facilitator, highlighting some distinctive aspects of education as a service:

> quality is as much determined by the input of the customers as it is by the providers of the experience. Educators can never guarantee that their product will work to a pre-specified level of performance because consumers of the product must play a significant and active role in maximising their learning from the product.
>
> (Viljoen *et al.*, 1990, p. 503)

The importance of learner interdependence and the collaboration of educators had earlier been stressed by Burge (1988) along with the importance of encouraging self-responsibility in learners.

However, it is in arguing for critical reflection as a means of achieving 'quality of emancipation', that Jakupec moves towards a broader view of quality in distance education. Individuals should be able to 'reflect critically on society in order to change, however mildly, the world for the better' (Jakupec, 1991, p. 6).

Nunan and Calvert (1991) also subscribe to the opinion that a broader view is required. The literature of distance education has generally focused on 'quality in terms of what [outputs]'. They argue that distance education must now focus on quality 'for whom' and 'in whose interests' (ibid., p. 9). These socio-political questions are inextricably interwoven into any education system and determine institutional responses to the issues of the day. Measures of effectiveness for these more value-laden quality issues are considerably more difficult to define than are tangible outputs. It is clear that quality considerations for distance education systems will encompass a complex array of factors and processes as they are in the interesting position of offering their clients both a product (good) and a service.

This leads to the question: what are the assumptions upon which higher education, particularly university education, are based? Some of these are that students will be trained in higher-level thinking, that they may make a contribution to knowledge or develop new ideas, that they may excel and that they may apply creative solutions to problem solving. These assumptions help determine how quality is defined. In addition, most students in tertiary distance education are mature adults and will determine quality according to their own needs.

What distance education system is capable of meeting individual, institutional, societal and even global needs? Evidence suggests that each of the two broad models of quality in higher education that have historically influenced the development of quality assurance in Australasian tertiary education can be found to be lacking on at least one of the above dimensions.

The French model of quality advocates standards imposed by an external body (van Vught, 1993, p. 3). This has benefits in terms of accountability, but it is limited in that it may discourage self-control on the part of individuals and their institutions. The introduction in New Zealand of external bodies for standards setting and auditing (e.g. the New Zealand Qualifications Authority) reflects this approach. By defining aspects of the curriculum and endeavouring to set quality standards, these bodies constrain educational institutions. Paradoxically, in New Zealand, this has happened in the wake of deregulation.

It should be unsurprising that such developments have met with resistance from Australasian academics. Opposition comes largely from the fact that they tend to derive their approach to quality from the alternative English tradition – that model embracing the notion of a 'self-governing community of fellows' (van Vught, 1993). The English model to some extent addresses the issue of self-control identified by Nunan, but risks alienation from the interests of external groups and the exclusion of the interests of stakeholder groups.

Each of the models has its supporters, yet detractors might identify the following weaknesses: in the worst case, the former (French) model provides an environment in which the real issues can be avoided; the latter (English) model provides protection from scrutiny and a culture of elitism (van Vught, 1993). Recognition of the fundamental inadequacies of each model has led to the initial appeal and growing acceptance of new interpretations of quality and innovative approaches to managing quality in tertiary education.

It is the recognition of the service features of distance education that has provided the impetus for some interesting departures on the subject of quality in distance education. Reaching beyond mere process and rejecting undue emphasis on the outcomes of learning, Murgatroyd (1993) looks to enhance the learning experience. He innovatively applies a manufacturing technique, 'quality function deployment' (more commonly known as the House of Quality or QFD), to the instructional design process. Customer-defined quality attributes are designed into all aspects of the product and service. Using this technique addresses his central question of: 'How can we design learning experiences in such a way that learning objectives are achieved?' (Murgatroyd, 1993, p. 34).

The further exploration of innovative adaptations of techniques from business into the distance education arena seems to hold great promise for future refinement of educators' approaches to quality. Where prevailing models may have fallen short in some respects, business has already provided a model which is in principle an integrative one. What are the implications of applying TQM to open and distance education?

APPLYING TQM TO DISTANCE EDUCATION

In order to explore the potential of TQM implementation within distance education, we will pick up on the fundamental themes introduced earlier.

The customer

TQM takes a very broad view of the customer. Consequently, governments, the institutions, learners and societies at large are not the only groups with an interest in achieving quality in open and distance education. The pursuit of quality is made more challenging by the existence of a range of other stakeholders who might have a legitimate claim to concerning themselves with how quality should be defined and measured. Employers and professional groups are constituencies whose needs have a significant influence upon the formulation of policy at the national level, and whose expectations contribute to the formulation of programmes within institutions. Taxpayers also have a vested interest in seeing their tax dollar spent responsibly and fairly. Professional bodies, alumni, accrediting agencies and other universities are among the other stakeholders. However, recognition of the varying needs and expectations of these groups presents challenges for the educational policy-makers and may involve decisions as to which stakeholders should be accorded preference if and when their interests conflict (Piper, 1993).

As the primary external customer, the varied needs of the distance learner must be central to any application of TQM. Students may have any number of reasons for studying at a distance. They may be seeking a qualification, enhanced employment opportunities, personal development or have other motives. In addition students are now paying a greater proportion of their fees. This has made them more conscious of their rights as customers (McIlroy and Walker, 1992) and more demanding of 'quality' courses that meet their needs. The challenge for providers is to meet these diverse needs.

There is no doubt that the idea of an external customer is a familiar concept. However, it is the idea of an internal customer that distinguishes TQM from traditional management approaches. Within the distance education organisation, internal customers can be identified at every level for every employee. For example, teaching staff writing study materials would become the customers or clients of instructional designers, graphic artists, wordprocessor operators, editors and printing staff. Similarly, centralised services such as the accounts and stores sections have customers throughout the organisation.

But the important thing is that every employee in the organisation considers the individual to whom they will be passing work as a customer or client who deserves the highest quality work from them; that is, work that is best suited to the purpose for which the customer (colleague) intends it. The corollary is that everyone in the organisation is also someone's customer. Under conventional management systems, large sections of the organisation tend to focus on the needs of the obvious external customer (the student) to the exclusion of meeting the needs of the important internal customers such as other administrative and teaching staff. Treating colleagues as customers may, TQM proponents would argue, help raise standards and improve service.

In focusing attention upon customer needs, TQM addresses the powerful concept of 'quality of perception' (Townsend and Gebhardt, 1986). In distance education, as with any other service, it is the customer's perception that attributes a *value* to the service or product received. But, as noted by Nunan (1991b), in distance education judgements about value have tended to be made by teaching staff and course designers which leads to a concept of quality defined by the institution. This is 'quality in fact' which relates mainly to meeting the organisation's specifications (Nicholson, 1989). Under TQM the emphasis would change and customer perceptions of quality would become a central focus.

While it may be true that the student is the ultimate customer the reality is that the other stakeholders, including the institution, will also have an impact on how quality is defined and judged in distance education. Measures of quality that reflect the needs and values of all interested parties would therefore be developed and applied.

Under TQM everyone in the distance learning organisation has customers or clients and they deserve the highest quality of goods and services. As Brower (1994, p. 487) emphasises, 'TQM calls for us to be customer focused, customer led, driven.'

Continuous improvement

Continuous improvement in TQM in manufacturing industries is often associated with the concept of 'zero defects' (Crosby, 1979). In service industries such as education this could be an unattainable goal as the customer perception of quality is so dependent on human interaction. However, the TQM philosophy of continuous improvement should be consistent with the underlying philosophy of any progressive organisation in the education industry. This is perhaps most obvious when considering the learning process itself and it is consistent with a learner-centred approach which takes account of individual differences and the learner's stage of development in psychosocial and intellectual terms. Some individuals will be very dependent, some independent and others interdependent as they relate to the course materials and the tutor (Burge, 1988). The interaction between learner and tutor is therefore crucial to a quality learning experience. TQM would encourage innovative and flexible approaches that could be tailored to meet individual students' needs in terms of their intellectual capacity, interest, experience and motivation. This clearly has implications for the design of course materials, support systems and for how 'success' is defined and measured in distance education.

However, any consideration of implementing TQM in distance education must take account of an extra layer of complexity. The student–educator relationship is complex in that the student (the ultimate customer) is also an integral part of the learning institution and a 'provider' in terms of the evaluative process. The educator, then, has a dual role: as both a provider of a service, and as a client in that they can demand a 'service' of the student through, for example, assignments and tests submitted for assessment. Therefore, it could be argued that if the Total Quality Management approach is to be truly implemented within any learning institution it might be expected that the educator would demand total quality of the student. Somehow the educator must be able to communicate the total quality philosophy to students and to instil in them the belief and expectation that they are capable of continually improving and increasing their levels of attainment.

The learning process is just a part, albeit the most important one, of the total experience the student has when enrolled in a distance education programme. All parts of the organisation contribute to the student's perception of quality. A total quality approach would imply that the quality effort of any distance education institution would go even further than the learning processes and outcomes, to achieving quality in every step of every process. Quality must be obtained by the student before and at enrolment, during the course and at the end of the learning phase (Barache, 1988). To achieve this, all service aspects and administrative procedures would be subject to scrutiny in order to ascertain their contribution to quality.

Proponents of TQM would claim that continuous improvement and adjustment aimed at 'zero defects' or total quality carry with them the implication of streamlining all processes so that all customers' needs are served. This implies self-responsibility and cooperation throughout the enterprise. It also necessitates monitoring systems being put in place and maintained. Clearly a major institutional implication relates to the necessity to view the organisation holistically and for change and innovation to become a way of life. Resistance to change is characteristic of most large organisations and this cultural barrier must be overcome for any successful implementation of TQM.

Large organisations tend to be disparate and fragmented which is one of the reasons that TQM emphasises cooperation and teamwork. To achieve total quality it is not enough to improve efficiency within departments or sections if the superordinate goals of the organisation are not being met. There must be unity of purpose and direction. As Deming (1986, pp. 24–5) says: 'it is easy to stay bound up in the tangled knots of the problems of today, becoming ever more and more efficient in them.'

Staff training and development

TQM philosophy asserts that the pursuit of continuous improvement is dependent upon people. Since organisations under TQM must analyse their operations and modify them to optimise the use of resources, it is necessary to provide for the development and enhancement of the human resource.

It is probably erroneous to assume that all staff within educational institutions are predisposed towards personal development and lifelong learning. However, it is plausible to speculate that highly educated academics would value an environment where staff training and development is a way life. For this reason TQM may be more easily accepted than alternative management philosophies.

The employee role within a total quality environment is one of involvement and responsibility for quality in any operation undertaken. It is therefore logical that education institutions would extend opportunities for self-development to all staff.

Rosander (1989) argues that at the heart of quality in service industries is the service provider's behaviour and attitudes. Any successful implementation of TQM will be reliant on the ability of the staff to respond quickly and appropriately, and to solve problems creatively. As errors are inherent in any service enterprise, it is that responsiveness that affects the customer perception of quality. Only a flexible, trained workforce can provide the continual improvement in service provision required to achieve quality outcomes. Senior management must be prepared to make a formal commitment to empower their people through training programmes and other educational initiatives and to make the necessary long-term financial investment.

Teamwork

According to its proponents, under TQM personal empowerment is enhanced and quality objectives achieved through teamwork. Autonomy and
self-responsibility are balanced by a need to share information, skills and
knowledge across organisational divisions. The resultant access to information leads to a much better service for the student who can contact a number
of people who are knowledgeable about an issue and who have decision-
making authority. Similarly, other stakeholders would benefit from open
communication channels which would encourage consultation and a feeling
of involvement with the institution.

If a distance learning institution is to enhance its responsiveness, a hierarchical organisational structure may be inappropriate. Flatter structures are
likely to encourage cooperation and teamwork, open communication channels, increase worker morale and achieve a more effective distance education
operation. However, the role of top management is also crucial. For successful implementation, all managers must demonstrate an active and absolute
commitment to quality that will in turn permeate the organisation.

Apart from the administrative and operations implications, a team
approach could be used to facilitate the educative process for distance
students. Team teaching would potentially bring a richness to programmes
and extend the knowledge base contributing to course materials (Walker and
Cull, 1994). The inclusion in the team of guidance and other intermediary
staff (Sewart, 1983) may also contribute positively by enabling the learner to
have easier access to local support systems and people with knowledge about
the course.

Under TQM, partnerships between teachers and learners would be
encouraged and cooperative planning to set objectives and assessment procedures would be an integral part of the learning process. Such an approach
would be facilitated by the communication technologies that are transforming distance education systems worldwide. Since students and their tutors
would be working within a collaborative learning framework involving
negotiation of objectives and outcomes, relevance to the individual's needs
would be ensured.

The team approach and staff training combined with the necessary focus
on the customer may have implications for the way staff are deployed. Since
there is a greater pool of interested and knowledgeable people on which to
draw, it would be feasible to make greater use of more flexible working hours
and a range of technologies. Students would benefit by having informed staff
available for consultation at convenient times. Burge (1988, p. 19) argues that
'We need not so much to protect traditional roles and skills of educators as to
develop more facilitative ones and expand on notions of professional
responsibility.'

Measurement

Measurement and evaluation must be an integral part of any organisation which implements TQM, for the process of continuous improvement depends on it. This means evaluation of every part of the organisation – staff, students, processes, programmes and systems.

Distance education quality systems tend to have focused on the tangible aspects of their operation, that is, the products. These more objective dimensions of distance education are relatively easy to measure. Standards can be developed and applied to elements of course design, content, durability of materials and to many administrative processes.

But conformance to specifications is more difficult to achieve with the intangible dimensions of the service as they are determined by a subjective assessment on the part of the customer. This assessment is dependent on the interaction of at least two individuals – the customer (student) and the service provider. It is often a lengthy process to which the customer may make a considerable contribution, an 'input' often impossible to predetermine or define. Gummesson (1991) calls this key concept 'interactive production' in which quality contributions come from the concerted efforts of both the customer and the service provider. Aspects such as the image and distinctive features of the product, the degree of customisation, and/or the perceived 'value' for money mediate this important relationship. Therefore, customer satisfaction must be assessed on all these dimensions.

TQM practitioners believe that empowerment and knowledge-sharing enable the organisation to meet the needs of its customers and other stakeholders. In order to monitor process effectiveness under TQM, appropriate measures of effectiveness would be worked out by the teams concerned with the various aspects of the operation.

Benchmarking is one form of monitoring and measurement used in TQM. It is an ongoing 'structured process to measure and improve products, services and work practices by comparing them against the best that can be identified globally so that competitive advantage can be achieved' (Grinyer and Goldsmith, 1995, p. 18). While many open and distance education institutions often compare parts of their operation to those of their competitors, it is seldom done in the rigorous and systematic way demanded by benchmarking. This technique would provide vital information in the quest for continuous improvement and excellence. Benchmarking is a concept now being applied increasingly to the learning process, particularly in relation to standards-based assessment (Wiggins, 1992; Shavelson *et al.*, 1992).

For the learner under TQM the emphasis would be on standards-based assessment, particularly forms of criterion-referenced assessment. This would include competency-based assessment where individuals aim at achieving excellence in terms of pre-specified learning outcomes. By comparison with norm-referenced assessment, these other forms encourage intrinsic motivation rather than extrinsic rewards. Assessment then becomes relevant to the individual student's needs and would be negotiated as part of the collaborative learning framework.

These are some of the operational and educational implications for TQM implementation in distance education. But to become a total-quality organisation requires substantial cultural and structural changes, some of which may take many years to achieve. So what benefits are there for open and distance education providers in implementing TQM?

ADVANTAGES OF TQM TO DISTANCE EDUCATION

When considering the adoption of TQM in open and distance education institutions, the obvious benefits are to students. The effect of implementation would be a learner-focused organisation that retains the capacity to address the needs of its other stakeholders. Under this system learners would be able to negotiate a learning package that was responsive and relevant to their needs. Since staff would be better trained to facilitate the learning process, students would be better served.

For the organisation, the results could include greater customer satisfaction, better retention rates, fewer customer defections and increased staff morale. It could also attract new customers to the institution as it gained a reputation for quality and service, enhancing competitive position. Superior staff would be attracted to the organisation, increasing the status of the institution in the academic community.

Thus, the application of a business-management model can potentially enhance the achievement of educational objectives. In addition, concerns expressed about the erosion of the 'traditional values of university culture' under TQM (Baldwin, 1994, p. 131) may be misplaced. Certainly a move to TQM may imply a redefinition of 'academic freedom' in terms of 'academic responsibility'. This is anathema to some sections of the academic community but is considered long overdue by many stakeholders.

Probably, however, the most persuasive reason for managers to implement TQM in any institution relates to potential savings. Adopting TQM is a major strategic decision. It involves a large capital investment to initiate and implement the TQM programme itself. Each organisation will have differing requirements which will influence the 'up front' costs. Short-term financial gains may be immediately evident, but it may be only in the long term that significant benefits become apparent.

For managers and policy-makers in open and distance education, a major underlying incentive to implement TQM is that, in both the short and long term, costs are reduced by eliminating surplus materials and the need for reworking courses. What some call simply a 'push for profit' (Baldwin, 1994) may be what good managers would call a responsible use of resources, in the interests of all stakeholders.

In the TQM approach, there are three cost-related areas under scrutiny:

- prevention costs
- appraisal costs
- failure costs, both internal and external.

Prevention costs are incurred at early developmental stages, in order to avoid costs in appraisal and in failure. In preparing distance education courses prevention costs would include resources expended on educational design and development, staff development, specification reviews and quality audits. Preventative maintenance activities, such as regular course reviews, keeping abreast of technological changes and close attention to customer expectations and needs, would result in a reduction in failure costs.

In considering the learning process, prevention costs are incurred in the form of time spent preparing, encouraging and directing students before and during the production of their work. Cost savings could therefore be made for the institution as a whole, the student and the educator by way of less time spent on corrections (review), rewrites (rework) and associated administrative processes. Clearly the costs would be highest to all parties if the student were forced to repeat the course.

Appraisal costs in distance education might come from the use of educational developers, editors and the audit and review processes. While this task would be a team responsibility, it could also involve the use of internal and external consultants, specialists, user groups and professional bodies.

External failure costs are problems detected by the customer and these can lead to customer dissatisfaction and subsequent defections. They relate to both the tangible and intangible aspects of service delivery. Technology failure is an obvious example of an external failure. If, for example, video- or teleconferencing equipment breaks down, students might miss an entire session or have to attend at a rescheduled time. This results in personal expense and time costs to the student. Since distance education packages are largely reliant upon printed materials, other problems may show up as misprints or omissions in study guides or course readings.

Internal failure costs, on the other hand, are identified before the product or service reaches the customer and are incurred through wastage, rework, redesign or redevelopment of materials and processes. Examples are printing excess course materials that subsequently have to be scrapped, redesigning standard forms each year for central processes such as enrolment, and frontline staff lacking the relevant information to deal effectively with customer enquiries. Apart from the obvious monetary costs to the institution, failures such as these can lead to customer frustration and dissatisfaction and ultimately to loss of student enrolments.

Arguably, an assumption of organisational failure underlying student drop out is contestable under TQM. It has been suggested that when distance learning organisations are considered holistically,

> If the course choice has been the wrong one, in spite of all the efforts developed to improve the quality of guidance, [and] it is realistic to drop

out and take another course better suited to the individual, ... we can sometimes speak of happy dropouts.

(Barache, 1988, p. 15)

Crosby (1979) states that 'quality is free'. It is non-conformance that costs. Simply doing away with waste and reworking will result in major savings to institutions. Making optimal use of all the resources of the institution, human, financial and material, will result in large gains in effectiveness and productivity, and improve competitiveness. As Feigenbaum (1983) notes, quality improvement has been identified as the best investment for competitiveness and, without it, service organisations make themselves very vulnerable.

CONCLUSION

A reality of open and distance education is that institutions are required to do more with less in an increasingly competitive global environment. Irrespective of educational philosophy or ideology, it is no longer possible to ignore the significance of resource management. However, management should not have to be divorced from educational imperatives. What is required is a system which balances the dual objectives of management and education. Some would see this as resulting in an untenable compromise, others as a desirable marriage.

The fundamental orientation of TQM is to take an holistic, systems view of the organisation. Consequently, it is capable of addressing the needs of everyone with a stake in an educational institution. Implementation could simultaneously address the needs of learners, the future development of the disciplines, the optimal use of resources and also ensure competitiveness in national and global marketplaces. The framework can accommodate the requirements for external accountability without sacrificing to some inflexible external standards such things as academic autonomy and the development of intellectual enquiry and knowledge within disciplines.

12　Open learning, closing minds

Mick Campion

In the USA in 1987 Allan Bloom published *The Closing of the American Mind: How Higher Education has Failed Democracy and Impoverished the Souls of Today's Students.* In this chapter, following some scene-setting, I want to show how the debate about open learning can provide us with a route into the broader, more profound, and more important debate raised by Bloom's work, and then to display how an understanding of aspects of that debate is essential for an understanding of university-level open learning.

Campion and Guiton (1991) have advocated analyses of educational processes which explicitly incorporate the social and political contexts of learning. This chapter moves in a complementary direction by arguing for a focus upon the learner and the curriculum that also attends to the social and political context. Whilst the chapter may lack the orderliness that has come to be associated with academic writing I believe it reflects our shared predicament and in this way encourages a relationship between writer and reader that displays how to keep minds from closing.

Reading Bloom's chapter in *Giants and Dwarfs*, 'The political philosopher in democratic society: the Socratic view' (1990, pp. 108–23), I was reminded that a number of Socratic dialogues begin with a question, such as 'What is profiteering?' which, through the neglect of more fundamental questions, such as 'What is profit?' result in whole discussions being, in a sense, unsatisfactory. It seems to me that much of the debate about open learning up to now may be unsatisfactory for similar reasons. It also has led us to neglect more fundamental questions by encouraging us to attend to matters such as deciding upon criteria of openness, rather than considering the special nature of learning at the university.

Bloom writes on US universities and my work is largely grounded in Australian distance education and open learning policy and practice. However, I believe that in this chapter the analysis is couched at a level that allows commonalities to be displayed. I would also stress that, like Bloom, I am writing about study at the university level. I am not writing about open learning in other contexts. Though it has to be said that one of the key, and in this context problematic, features of the current era in higher education is the blurring of the boundaries between previously clearly defined sub-sectors.

In such an era it is not surprising to find that Bloom's concerns have their parallels in open and distance education. For example, in an influential article, Rumble states, ' institutions which claim to be open-learning-systems in the sense of being open (adjective) learning-systems ... may develop structures and artefacts that result in a closing of doors and minds' (Rumble, 1989, p. 34). Likewise, Harris's analysis of the UK Open University's practice displays how specific types of openness seem to have an opposite side, a tendency to closure (Harris, 1987, p. 3).

SETTING THE SCENE: THE CHANGING CONTEXTS OF LEARNING

Currently, we are being swirled around within unpredictable, rapid and powerful transformations of information technologies; transformations which have implications of incomprehensible proportions for all sectors of society, including education; transformations ensuing from the social relationships within which such technologies are developed.

In addition, there are many interrelated processes which are specific to higher education and consequently affect open learning. For example,

- the shift from an elite to a mass system of higher education provision;
- the blurring of boundaries between institutional sectors as exemplified by the disappearance of the binary divide in Australia, and subsequently in Britain, combined with the general expansion of roles consistent with the notion of a multi-versity;
- the transformation in the nature and size of the institutions within which academics work and the changing working relationships this entails given a changing industrial context;
- the reduced emphasis upon the work of individual academics in favour of work produced by teams;
- and, most importantly, the rapidly changing technological, economic, political and social contexts within which our educational institutions operate, for example, processes related to globalisation.

An awareness of such interrelated processes can be debilitating, but it is increasingly important nevertheless. Careful analysis is required at a time when the rhetoric of open learning is taking such a strong hold that it is closing other possibilities. Although, as Carr (1990, p. 47) suggests, a chasm exists between the rhetoric and the reality.

Johnson (1990, p. 25) points to the conservatism of academia as an obstacle to open learning which may account for the chasm between rhetoric and reality. In previous periods in the history of university education such forces would very likely have combined to snuff out efforts to introduce such changes. Nowadays, however, universities and academics are confronted by interrelated pressures which have the potential, through consequential widespread dislocations and disruptions, to overcome any such conservatism. .Furthermore, in this process longstanding contradictions and confusions in universities' missions are likely to be revealed. The debate about open learning, which might appear to be of relatively minor importance, provides an opening through which we can begin to approach some of these more fundamental issues.

Dominance of business and training

Baldwin describes some critical contours of the paradigm shift in how university education is currently conceptualised. 'University culture is being colonized by the interrelated cultures of business, industry, and advertising.' She claims that this 'is a process of "colonization" which may bring with it all of the destructiveness of any colonizing movement – a wholesale usurpation of customs, structures, values, and perceptions' (Baldwin, 1994, p. 125).

This is the context within which we must comprehend the shift to, and the possible impact of, open learning. The language and structures of business, industry and advertising are now frequently interwoven in the activities of open learning. The debate on open learning between Lewis (1988) and Rumble (1989) occurred when the distinction between university education and vocational training was meaningful; more recently the disappearance of the binary divide between universities and colleges of advanced education and polytechnics, and the repositioning of education within an employment and training framework, indicates an instrumentalist orientation. This makes a defence of the liberal university even more necessary, but even more difficult. Jakupec and Nicoll encapsulate this position thus: 'open learning, defined through the voice of political rhetoric, represents many formal features of the new society and expresses the deeper logic of the underpinning perceptions of the need for a free-market economy' (Jakupec and Nicoll, 1994c, p. 229).

Recent versions of open learning

But what is open learning? Field states that:

> Open learning is used to denote both an educational philosophy and a set of techniques for delivering knowledge and skills. As philosophy, open learning implies greater accessibility, flexibility and student centredness: it implies placing learner rather than provider at the core of educational practice. As a set of techniques, it is characterised by the use of resource based teaching and training, often associated with the use of new communications media.
>
> (Field, 1994, p. 7)

According to Johnson, open learning systems are designed to enhance access to educational services in a cost-effective manner (Johnson, 1990, p. 27). In a democratic age, such an objective would seem highly commendable: it reflects the political outcome of pressure or struggle from below to broaden access to what is increasingly recognised as a crucial resource. However, the rhetoric of open learning appears to suggest that students can study what they want, whenever, wherever and however they want. It is, perhaps, surprising that such a utopian fantasy gains credence in a world full of misery, misfortune and the potential for massive disaster; a world in which informed, disciplined and committed efforts are likely to be necessary, if not sufficient, conditions for even the smallest improvements. Furthermore, and ironically, many of the educationalists commending open learning with all of its apparent freedoms display precisely the commitments that they claim are outmoded for their students.

Johnson speaks of 'the risks of open learning' which may be summarised as follows:

- The conservatism of institutions encourages staff to resist surrendering to students a degree of control over what and how the student learns. The more expert the scholar, the harder this is.
- Institutional autonomy and academic freedom inhibit collaboration.
- An emphasis upon modularisation may inhibit the maturation and integration of ideas.
- A focus upon well-developed course packages possibly reduces support services.
- A failure to maintain standards, given a more heterogeneous student population, could result if institutions do not 'remind themselves all the time that it is their responsibility to help students reach the standard'.

(Based on Johnson, 1990, pp. 25–6)

In relation to the first risk, Johnson counters this with a comparison of the postgraduate supervisor as facilitator, adviser and learning manager. This 'enabling' notion of the teacher will be pursued later. In terms of the second risk, there are issues of balance, but there are strong arguments that can be mounted in defence of the institution, and of the individual academic, and perhaps genuine collaboration would be more likely to flow if both of these were more rather than less secure. However, these first two so-called risks seem to be possible obstacles to the implementation of an open learning strategy rather than risks of such a strategy. The next three risks are relatively trivial when compared with the concerns of Bloom and his opponents, except perhaps that Johnson's notion of 'reaching the standard' hints that something more may be at stake.

Campion and Kelly argued in 1988 that three broad phases were discernible in the history of off-campus education in Australia:

- The External Studies phase (approx. 1911 to the early 1970s) involved teaching off-campus students through the provision of materials originally developed for on-campus students.
- The Distance Education phase (approx. early 1970s to mid-1980s) involved the creation of professionally produced materials for off-campus students

which were ostensibly grounded upon a clear distinction between on- and off-campus study.

• The Open Learning phase (mid-1980s onwards) implied a convergence between on- and off-campus study through the use of distance education materials for on-campus students to enhance the quality and flexibility of teaching and learning and improve the cost-effectiveness of both modes.

(Based on Campion and Kelly, 1988, pp. 173–5)

The subsequent development of the Open Learning Agency of Australia (OLA), together with numerous government reports and pronouncements, superficially suggests that the third phase is now well ensconced in Australia. However, OLA has no necessary connection with the use of distance education materials by on-campus students, and this example clearly demonstrates that notions such as 'open' are being invoked to label a multitude of very different educational enterprises.

This apparent shift in favour of 'open learning' is an international phenomenon. Indeed, Bates (1994) goes so far as to suggest that the days of exclusively distance education institutions are numbered as the distinction between distance education and campus-based education disappears as a consequence of technological developments.

Specific aspects of open learning

The focus upon learner-centred orientations is central to the rhetoric of open learning and implies a power shift from the academics to a range of 'stakeholders', a matter of concern to Jakupec and Nicoll (1994c). The stakeholders may include students, but business and government would seem to predominate, as the following statement from a recent Australian Minister for Higher Education and Employment Services shows:

Those who contribute to the costs of higher education have an interest in ensuring that the system offers value for money. The Government, as the largest provider of funds for higher education, has a particular interest in accountability for the use of public resources. So too do local students making HECS payments, overseas students paying fees and industry whose involvement in higher education is growing. These *consumers* of higher education legitimately expect to be informed and assured about the quality of provision. It is primarily a matter for institutions to satisfy the various stakeholders.

(Baldwin, 1991, p. 29; my italics)

This may seem a reasonable shift in the balance of power away from academics; away from the privileged and cloistered ivory tower, but, as Apple shows, invoking a notion of consumption in relation to education generates different problems:

Instead of people who participate in the struggle to build and rebuild our

educational, political, and economic relations, we are defined as consumers. This is truly an extraordinary concept, for it sees people by and
large as either stomachs or furnaces. . . .We use and use up. We don't
create. Someone else does that. This is disturbing enough in general, but in
education it is truly disabling.

(Apple, 1990, p. xiii)

Previously I have used the work of Illich to display how the gap Carr (1990)
referred to between rhetoric and reality could be used to reveal diametrically
opposed possible outcomes (Campion, 1991). On the one side a continuing
expansion of schooling with education being transformed into training and
on the other an expansion of learning through a process of deschooling. In
the next section of this chapter I turn to the work of a theorist very different
from Illich to demonstrate further dangers of an uncritical acceptance of
current discourse promoting open learning.

BLOOM'S CRITIQUE OF OPENNESS

Bloom (1987) provides a rich, though perhaps flawed, vein of material from
which we can mine lines of inquiry in the analysis of open learning. For example, he suggests that in early childhood education there is currently a lack
of attention to religion, philosophy and politics and that, as a result of this
absence/openness, students are ill-prepared for profound questions, and as a
result, are indifferent to such matters. One consequence is that they approach
later study instrumentally – as a means to an end – and they do not expect
their education to change their views in any profound way (Bloom, 1990,
p. 351). Furthermore, he argues that whilst Americans acknowledge the cultural diversity that exists in the world, they see no need to understand different cultures because, given a commitment to the idea of relativity and all
cultures being of equal value, the lifestyles they create at home are considered
good enough. In this sense he argues that openness leads to closure reflected in
a lack of interest in understanding others (Bloom,1987, p. 34). He sees openness as meaning the acceptance of everything and as effectively generating a
denial of reason's power (ibid., p. 38).

Clearly, Bloom is no advocate of the openness embraced in open learning
rhetoric. The debate about open learning frequently focuses upon questions
of the who, what, why and when in education. This conceptual environment
is one in which profoundly important questions are rarely, if ever, posed. The
marketing of open learning mirrors this 'ideal' conceptual environment with
slogans claiming that people can learn what they want, when they want,
where they want, how they want, as fast or as slow as they want, if they want!

Although the focus here is on the notion of openness it is also the case that
the notion of learning could and should receive closer attention (see Campion, 1996). For example, Duke (1992) reveals that there is a growing trend in
the UK to focus upon notions of the 'learning society' and the 'learning

organisation'. However, the simple juxtaposition of 'the learning society' with 'the learned society' reveals a significant difference. A 'learned society' suggests a degree of scholarship and a non-instrumental orientation to learning that is far from the contemporary notion of the 'learning society' or, using recent Australian political rhetoric, of the 'clever country'. Such notions are overtly grounded in utilitarian agendas which have more to do with profit than scholarship.

Bloom (1987, p. 42) suggests that, 'True openness means closedness to all the charms that make us comfortable with the present.' The openness of 'open learning' would appear to pander to those charms whilst simultaneously holding out the prospect of accredited omniscience to people who may well not understand the degree of difficulty and the impossibility of reaching such a goal.

It is necessary to protect a space within higher education for scholarly critical discourse: not that this is all that higher education should be about. Scholarly critical discourse is an essential element of a higher education system serving the needs of a society that seeks to be thoughtful and just. Such discourse is under threat, and open learning, as it is currently conceived, is part of that threat.

Bellow, in his Foreword to Bloom's work, states that, 'The heart of Professor Bloom's argument is that the university, in a society ruled by public opinion, was to have been an island of intellectual freedom where all views were investigated without restriction' (Bellow, 1987, p. 18). Bloom's opponents might well argue that his proposals themselves undermine that ideal. However, a commitment to the openness of open learning rhetoric is one more factor that further decreases the special role of the university, thereby diminishing intellectual freedom. It does this by, amongst other things, minimising the differences between universities and other educational and training institutions. Jakupec and Nicoll (1994c, p. 219) have perceptively pointed out how proponents of open learning have paid insufficient attention to different types of pedagogical practice and the necessary limitations of such practices. They reveal the potentially oxymoronic nature of such versions of open learning. The proponents of open learning frequently speak in generalities which obscure the crucial differences between institutional sectors.

Learner autonomy

Andresen and Nightingale address a more specific issue – that of student centredness – in the following remark:

> Open learning represents an expression of trust in students' ability to exercise responsibly the autonomy we offer them. We hope and expect this to lead them to similarly value autonomy as a goal for their students.
>
> (Andresen and Nightingale, 1993, p. 34)

Who today would openly question the wisdom of Andresen and Nightingale's expression of trust in students' abilities? But wouldn't we be wise to maintain doubt, at least until we know something about the students? To trust all without any prior knowledge is to begin by refusing, for example, to acknowledge that it may be important to distinguish between attitudes that enhance the prospect of learning occurring and attitudes that may reduce the likelihood of such outcomes.

The deep/surface learning distinction

A familiar tool for contemporary educationalists is provided by the seemingly ubiquitous distinction between 'deep' and 'surface' learning (see Morgan, 1993, pp. 75–80). This distinction may be valuable for the educational developer, but I am concerned that the uncritical usage of this particular dichotomy or continuum in the debates about education restricts the discourse and blinds us to the possibility of a more important set of distinctions: that between the facile and the profound. The deep/surface distinction leaves students and teachers stranded in a discourse that leads nowhere for it has nothing important to say. Furthermore, all too often the whole issue of student autonomy may, in any case, be little more than a charade, as is intimated by Lisewski when he suggests that 'Students need to be carefully prepared for learning independence' (Lisewski, 1994, p. 12).

The distinction between deep and surface learning does not provide students or teachers with a route into the types of profound questions that must underpin fruitful enquiry or learning. One may not share Bloom's view of what these questions should be, but he does at least remind us of the need for them:

> the crisis of liberal education is a reflection of a crisis at the peaks of learning, an incoherence and incompatibility among the first principles with which we interpret the world, an intellectual crisis of the greatest magnitude, which constitutes the crisis of our civilisation. But perhaps it would be true to say that the crisis consists not so much in this incoherence but in our incapacity to discuss or even recognise it.
>
> (Bloom, 1987, p. 346)

The abnegation of responsibility for the curriculum

A powerful illustration of the problem of abnegating responsibility for the decisions about the curriculum is provided by Bloom when he compares 1960s American universities with the German universities of the 1930s. He argues that they both turned over the decision about values to the folk, the *Zeitgeist*, the relevant (Bloom, 1987, pp. 313–14). Bloom's remark and comparison are questionable, but even Aronowitz and Giroux, who are highly critical of Bloom's work, acknowledge its force.

The virtue of Bloom's tirade, despite its reactionary content, is to

remind us of what has been lost in the drive for rationalization, for the supremacy of science over philosophy, history over eternal essences. . . . In
effect, the historical legacy of technicization has been to turn universities
into training institutions, which creates few spaces for intellectuals. . . .
What must be accepted in Bloom's discourse is that anti-intellectualism in
American education is rampant, influencing even those whose intentions
are actually opposed to closing the doors to genuine learning. We know
that the environment in most universities is inimical to broadly based,
philosophically informed scholarship and dialogue concerning burning
questions of politics and culture. In a few places, liberal and radical intellectuals are building micro-institutions (centres, institutes, programs)
within the universities as outposts that attempt to resist the larger trends
toward instrumentalized curricula.

(Aronowitz and Giroux, 1988, pp. 178-9)

In their early days, a significant number of distance education institutions,
with their novel mandates and alternative methods, took liberal and radical
issues to heart in a way that the conventional universities might not have expected. But the more recent open learning institutions seem to have no stom-
ach for this at all! The transformation of universities into training institutions
and the parallel shift to instrumentalised curricula is described by Bloom
forthrightly when he speaks of the fudging of the distinction between liberal
and technical education (Bloom, 1987, p. 59). He refers to the highly trained
computer specialist who has learnt nothing about morals, philosophy or religion (ibid., p. 59). The task at hand is massively compounded when, having
taken to heart the limitations to which Bloom refers, the limitations of his
own scholarship surface. For, as Nussbaum argues, Bloom displays an ignorance of philosophical approaches from other cultures (cited by Aronowitz
and Giroux, 1988, p. 194).

The point is that if, as scholars and graduates, we are so limited in our
knowledge, and if these limitations reduce the effectiveness of our learning,
our speech and our writing, then how much more must this be the case with
students who are just beginning, and in such circumstances does it really
make sense for us to begin by trusting their abilities?

Differing student orientations to course materials and relativism

A student who attends my lectures on the sociology of work whose interest is
in the application of ideas to their role as a personnel manager in order to
gain a promotion is likely to hear something different from the student who
has an interest in understanding the place of work in contemporary society in
order to play a part in creating a better society. The fact that the latter is becoming an oddity in the contemporary university, and the former is becoming
the norm, is of considerable concern.

The following extract from David Lodge's novel, *Nice Work*, cited by

Bernice Martin (1992), makes a similar point about radically different readings far more eloquently and provides a route into a contemporary debate within sociology which informs my critique in this chapter of the rhetoric of open learning:

> A typical instance was the furious argument they had about the Silk Cut advertisement. . . . Every few miles, it seemed, they passed the same huge poster on roadside hoardings, a photographic depiction of a rippling expanse of purple silk, as if the material had been slashed with a razor. There were no words on the advertisement, except the Government Health Warning about smoking. This ubiquitous image, flashing past at regular intervals, both irritated and intrigued Robyn, and she began to do her semiotic stuff on the deep structure hidden beneath its bland surface.
>
> It was in the first instance a kind of riddle. That is to say, in order to decode it, you had to know there was a brand of cigarettes called Silk Cut. The poster was the iconic representation of a missing name, like rebus. But the icon was also a metaphor. The shimmering silk, with its voluptuous curves and sensuous texture, obviously symbolised the female body, and the elliptical slit, foregrounded by a lighter colour showing through, was still more obviously a vagina. The advert thus appealed to both the sensual and the sadistic impulses, the desire to mutilate as well as to penetrate the female body.
>
> Vic Willcox spluttered with outraged derision as she expounded this interpretation. He smoked a different brand, himself, but it was as if he felt his whole philosophy of life was threatened by Robyn's analysis of the advert. 'You must have a twisted mind to see all that in a perfectly harmless bit of cloth,' he said.
>
> (Lodge, cited by Martin, 1992, p. 111)

The difference between the business and intellectual middle classes is clearly illustrated here, and the relationship between the two is of major importance as we move into a period within which it might seem that knowledge and information are taking an ever more powerful hold.

This passage also illustrates that providing access is more than allowing something to be seen. Access is contingent upon the skills and interests of the viewer/learner, and if that poster was not fully transparent then how much more opaque are most scholarly works. For example, those of Bloom and of his opponents Aronowitz and Giroux are themselves firmly grounded in a body of complex and profound scholarship that needs to be grasped before anything beyond a superficial understanding can be obtained.

'[P]lacing learner rather than provider at the core of educational practice' (Field, 1994, p. 7) accurately describes the intent of the message conveyed by those promoting open learning. However, it is evident that such a version of the educational enterprise omits something vitally important when it is compared to Bloom's view of the teacher dedicated to a liberal education who 'must constantly try to look toward the goal of human completeness and

back at the nature of his students here and now, ever seeking to understand the former and to assess the capacity of the latter to approach it'
(Bloom, 1987, p. 19).

This provides a useful rejoinder to some aspects of the rhetoric about open
learning. Much of the rhetoric concerns understanding and assisting students, but little concerns the goal of human completeness. If the latter objective is lost, and teachers and institutions simply rely upon what students think
they need – upon the marketplace – then these teachers and institutions are
indeed in an arbitrary situation (Bloom, 1987, p. 19). The dangers of this
arbitrariness are projected by the following remarks from Bloom, even for
those uncertain about notions such as 'soul'.

> As it now stands, students have powerful images of what a perfect body is
> and pursue it incessantly. But deprived of literary guidance, they no longer
> have any image of a perfect soul, hence do not long to have one. They do
> not even imagine that there is such a thing.
>
> (Ibid., p. 67)

The decision not to engage in debate about what we want to teach and
learn, about what we want to be, is a concomitant of the open learning notion
that people can study whatever they want. It is also consistent with the idea
of the teacher as an enabler, rather than as having disciplinary expertise to
pass on. The teacher, as enabler, is only helping the students do what they
choose; the enabler does not have to engage in the difficult task of deciding
what ought to be taught: what ought to be learnt. This reflects the dominance
of a form of relativism that Bloom relates to openness and of which he is so
very critical:

> Openness – and the relativism that makes it the only plausible stance in the
> face of various claims to truth and various ways of life and kinds of
> human beings – is the great insight of our times. The true believer is the
> real danger. The study of history and culture teaches that all the world was
> mad in the past; men always thought they were right, and that led to wars,
> persecutions, slavery, xenophobia, racism, chauvinism. The point is not to
> correct the mistakes and really be right; rather it is not to think you are
> right at all.
>
> (Bloom, 1987, p. 26)

Bloom is not commending the study of culture or history as the source of
knowledge. Rather cultures are for him the caves out of which we must seek
to move if we are to obtain true knowledge. Of course, his opponents take a
different view. They see him as ethnocentric; as commending a vision of that
which lies beyond the cave that is merely the culture or tradition he wishes to
conserve and convey. As Apple says:

> we never act in a vacuum. The very realization that education is deeply im-
> plicated in the politics of culture makes this clear. After all, the decision to

define some groups' knowledge as worthwhile to pass on to future generations while other groups' culture and history hardly see the light of day says something extremely important about who has power in society.

(Apple, 1990, p. viii)

Siding with Bloom or with his opponents is not the issue here, rather it is acknowledging the quagmire upon which educational tasks and institutions are founded. Students should be made aware that scholarly activity is an uncertain, demanding, unending and exhausting process. Is this the message conveyed by the advocates of open learning?

ACADEMICS AS PROLETARIANS, PROFESSIONALS OR INTELLECTUALS

At this point we return to the contradictions and confusions revealed by the disruptions and dislocations that are occurring in the current period; the matter of the interests that underpin university activity; and the issue of the apparent shift of power and influence away from the academic profession.

Jakupec and Nicoll oppose that shift of power away from academics exemplified by the Open Learning Agency of Australia. They place their trust in the idea of academics as professionals (Jakupec and Nicoll, 1994c, p. 230). I want to conclude with a brief consideration of academics as proletarians, professionals and/or as intellectuals in the light of recent debate concerning new class theory and the hidden technocracy.

The essence of the new class theory is that, in a society in which knowledge industries/service industries have been growing rapidly, a significant increase in the number of service-related professions and professionals generates a burgeoning sector of the middle class; a sector which would not necessarily share the interests of the business-based middle class (the growth in the number of academics for example). The traditional view from the left was that this group would still serve the interests of business. However, more recently, in the light of events in the late 1960s, some saw this sector of society as possibly a new vanguard for radical change. The right, not surprisingly, viewed this prospect somewhat differently.

Kellner and Berger argue that the new technocracy has begun to have an important influence upon the methods of the more traditional business middle class such that an apparently 'softer' form of capitalism is in ascendancy. The corollary of this has been an increasingly less critical stance being taken by the new professionals as they are effectively co-opted (Kellner and Berger, 1992, pp. 1–23). What I am suggesting is that the provision of open learning may reflect a similar convergence.

Halsey (1992, p. 270) argues that: 'The attack on academic autonomy, or as we have described it the demand from the state that intellectual labour be proletarianized, has been conspicuously aggressive in the past decade.' He describes this process in more detail in a manner that is worth quoting in full:

At all events, it appears that one important aspect of adaptation to expansion is indeed the gradual proletarianization of the academic professions – an erosion of their relative class and status advantages as the system of higher education is propelled towards wider admission of those who survive beyond compulsory schooling. In the transformation there are many casualties. The traditional guild of autonomous fellows is driven to the margins of the academic system, albeit at the top of the pyramid of institutional prestige. Managerialism gradually comes to dominate collegiate co-operation in the organization of both teaching and research. Explicit vocationalism displaces implicit vocational preparation – the Victorian distinction between training and education – as degree courses are adapted to the changing division of labour in the graduate market. Research endeavours are increasingly applied to the requirements of government or industrial demand. The don becomes increasingly a salaried or even a piece-work labourer in the service of an expanding middle class of administrators and technologists.

(Ibid., pp. 136–7)

Much that Halsey says rings true and acts as a warning to those who might too readily place trust in the role of the academic as independent autonomous professional. Features of the specific subset of higher education related to open learning do highlight issues for the system as a whole, and raise questions about the wisdom of relying upon such an already increasingly domesticated profession (Campion and Renner, 1995) to provide a perspective independent of the processes of social and economic power (Jakupec and Nicoll, 1994c, p. 230). Regaining a professional foothold, as commended by Jakupec and Nicoll, will only be enough if the profession defines itself as having a mission that at least calls into question its various relationships to social and economic power. Indeed, if we consider contemporary dominant notions of the professional, we can see that the distinction between proletarian and professional is only one of degree. For example, when analysing the Richard Brookes Western entitled, *The Professionals*, Robbins homes in on two key characteristics.

Their [the professionals'] proficiency is for sale, and it is the buyer/employer [and we might add the stakeholder] who provides the task or goal. No pregiven goals or motives of their own are pertinent other than making a living.

They are professionals in that each is a highly competent specialist in some skill necessary to their joint operation.

(Robbins, 1993, p. 29)

Earlier I raised questions about too readily trusting students and in this section I am raising questions about too readily trusting academics. The argument that academic work is being proletarianised or that academics are professionals in the sense outlined immediately above clearly raises questions about treating academics as the repository or source of independent viewpoints. However, the role of the academic as professional has also come under scrutiny from another direction, through considerations of the relationship between notions of the professional and of the intellectual. Said (1994) speaks of professionalism in the following way:

> By professionalism I mean thinking of your work as an intellectual as something you do for a living, between the hours of nine and five with one eye on the clock and another cocked at what is considered to be proper, professional behavior – not rocking the boat, not straying outside the accepted paradigms or limits, making yourself marketable and above all presentable, hence uncontroversial and unpolitical and 'objective'.
>
> (Said, 1994, p. 55)

He contrasts this with what he refers to as the intellectual as amateur:

> someone who considers that to be a thinking and concerned member of a society one is entitled to raise moral issues at the heart of even the most technical and professionalized activity as it involves one's country, its power, its mode of interacting with its citizens as well as with other societies.
>
> (Ibid., p. 61)

Said appears to ask an enormous amount of intellectuals when he writes that

> However much intellectuals pretend that their representations are of higher things or ultimate values, morality begins with their activity in this secular world of ours – where it takes place, whose interests it serves, how it jibes with a consistent and universalist ethic, how it discriminates between power and justice, what it reveals of one's choices and priorities.
>
> (Ibid., p. 89)

Said reminds us that scholarship in certain circumstances requires sacrifice, this is why contemporary talk of open learning as a form of access that makes no reference to commitment is so unsettling, so disturbing and seems so superficial.

Robbins's position is far less readily summarised for it is far more nuanced than Said's above. However, his critique of Hofstadfter provides us with insight into a view which opposes that proposed in the extracts from Said's lectures. According to Robbins,

> Richard Hofstadfter defines the intellectual, once again, against the professional: 'The heart of the matter – to borrow a distinction made by Max Weber about politics – is that the professional man lives *off* ideas, not *for* them. His professional role, his professional skills, do not make him an intellectual. He is a mental worker, a technician. He may *happen* to be an intellectual as well, but if he is, it is because he brings to his profession a

distinctive feature about ideas which is not required by his job. . . . At home he may happen to be an intellectual, but at his job he is a hired menial technician who uses his mind for externally determined ends.'

By locating the intellectual in the home, Hofstadfter says more about the genderedness of the concept than he apparently means to, and thus also says more than he means to about the professionalism to which he opposes it.

(Robbins, 1993, p. 9)

Robbins then mounts a critique of this view of the separation of the home from the workplace, arguing against a radical disjunction between the role of the professional and that of the intellectual:

Let us be clear. There is no 'home' in this sense, no place where thought can be free of all material encumbrance and social entanglement, and it is time to stop trying to return there again and again. And by the same token, there is also no 'work' in Hofstadfter's sense . . . we must look closely at those supposed spaces of tyranny, like the professional workplace, which have been seen as antithetical to the intellectual. No principle of gender justice can allow the intellectual to be defined within this antithesis. Not disembodied freedom, but diverse embodiedness and incomplete servitudes have to become the common sense view of intellectual work.

(Ibid., p. 10)

What Robbins says of the home needs also to be said of the university. Then what is being said here about individual academics as proletarians, professionals and/or intellectuals begins to reveal something about what we should be debating when we consider the core defining features of the institutions within which we work. We need to work to ensure that in the process of opening education we do not allow the material encumbrances and societal entanglements within which universities necessarily operate to be masked. Furthermore, if we heed Bloom's recommendation concerning the Socratic dialogues referred to at the beginning, these matters are essential when debating the nature of open learning.

ACKNOWLEDGEMENT

I am very grateful to Terry Evans and Daryl Nation for all of their prodding and pushing in relation to this chapter and I wish I had been able to summon up the ability to make better use of it.

13 Educational futures

Globalisation, educational technology and lifelong learning

Terry Evans and Daryl Nation

A reader who has followed this book from the beginning will have completed a journey, not only via various points on the globe, but also through various educational sectors and approaches. *Opening Education* is the theme which links each of these points, but diversity is a theme in itself. Arguably, if educators, trainers, policy-makers and administrators are pursuing paths of opening their educational endeavours, they are likely to be diversifying in some way. Hence, it is not surprising that the preceding chapters have both a unity towards openness and yet a diversity in terms of practical and policy outcomes. However, the diversity is not random, indeed there are other common threads which one could draw. Few if any chapters avoid the mention of technology, especially new computer and communications technologies. Contemporary discourses of open and distance education policy and practice seem impossible without the lexicon of the new technologies.

At the heart of the preceding chapters is a concern for educational policy and practice: what educators plan and do. The economic agenda is never far from view, either in the sense of the 'costs of delivery' or in the sense of future 'capital accumulation'. The difficulties for analyses of education's economic productivity, or of education's economic costs, are significant, if not insurmountable. One cannot help feeling that the valuing of education for its cultural and humanitarian worth remains an underlying concern for most people, even if their concern is less powerfully articulated than those of the economic kind. Most of the chapters in this book have concerns for the economic, cultural and humanitarian, although the balances vary. It is important to make these themes part of the debates about opening education, especially as this *opening* is identifiable not only in global instances, but also as part of globalisation processes. Globalisation itself is often discussed in economic terms – the 'global economy', the 'global marketplace' – whereas its real significance, we would argue, rests in its cultural and humanitarian consequences. To close the book we would like to take up the matter of opening education in the context of globalisation, technology and lifelong education.

GLOBALISATION AND OPENING EDUCATION

Several of the chapters of this book illustrate how educational practices are being reformed and developed in ways that have international – even global – roots and implications. Many recent educational innovations that aspire to forms of open education are reflexively connected to innovations elsewhere in the world. Such innovations are connected, not just to innovations in education, but to changes, developments or innovations in other aspects of life. Changes in computer and communications technologies, and changes to the nature of work, are ones with which educational innovation and reform are most often reflexively connected in recent times.

These connections are reflexive because education does not merely respond to other changes, but also often effects and affects those changes itself. More broadly, reflexivity is a fundamental element of globalisation which relies as much on the sophistication of modern language, culture and education as it does on modern communications technologies and economic systems. It is worth dwelling on the concepts of globalisation and reflexivity here in order not only to demonstrate the centrality of education to these features, but also to indicate how contemporary changes to educational practices can be seen as part of global life.

As has been the case in some of our previous writing, the work of the social theorist Anthony Giddens provides a powerful analysis with which to work. Some of Giddens's recent publications have dealt with matters of the changing personal, social and political conditions in late modernity, a major aspect of which is globalisation (Giddens, 1991a, b, 1994; Jarvis, 1993). One of us (Evans) has made use of this work in relation to analyses of contemporary open and distance education and here we shall push the analysis further to help illustrate the global features of the current moves to opening education. Our intention is also to show that the previous chapters have connections between them, not just of an educational kind, but also in terms of personal, social and economic influences. Many of these connections can be identified in current government and institutional policy relating to education, which reflect both global and local concerns.

Giddens (1994, p. 7) makes the point that the core of globalisation is what can be called 'time–space compression'. Time–space compression occurs through modern communications and transport systems. These systems provide for virtually instantaneous communications – voice, vision and data – and for high-speed transportation – people and products – around the globe. In terms of global economic systems – which are often seen, incorrectly, as being globalisation itself – the time–space compression of communications and transportation has created the conditions whereby money, goods and even prospective goods – 'futures' – can be traded globally. This economic trading has almost replaced money 'changing hands' in its paper form, with electronic funds-transfers occurring for everything from the petrol purchase at the pump, through to trading in 'barrels' of crude oil with OPEC.

Distance education, in particular, has always been concerned with issues of time and space; as the term itself suggests, its educational practices have principally been designed to cope with distances, that is to enable learners to study in their own places – at home or work away from the campus 'headquarters' of the educational institution in which they are enrolled. Distance education has also been concerned with time too, in the sense that the learners have more opportunities and responsibilities to set their own learning schedule than in conventional education, within the broad constraints of their institution's timetable. Evans (1989) has explored these time–geographic features of distance education in more detail. Here we will consider the notion that, whilst time–space compression can be seen as the core of globalisation, it is the social and cultural capacities springing from this compression that create the conditions of globalisation to which open and distance education interrelate.

As Giddens makes clear, globalisation concerns

> the transformation of local, and even personal, contexts of social experience. Our day-to-day activities are increasingly influenced by events happening on the other side of the world. Conversely, local lifestyle habits have become globally consequential.
>
> (Giddens, 1994, p. 5)

A key point made by Giddens, which has considerable significance for open and distance education, is that the 'intensified reflexivity' of globalisation creates the conditions for 'a world of clever people'. He argues that

> individuals more or less have to engage with the wider world if they are to survive in it. Information produced by specialists (including scientific knowledge) can no longer be wholly confined to specific groups, but becomes routinely interpreted and acted on by lay individuals in the course of everyday actions.
>
> (Ibid., p. 7)

Giddens's claim that globalisation necessitates a world populated by 'clever people' refers to a global population comprising individuals who are able to read, understand, analyse and, where appropriate, act knowledgeably on the information they can obtain and, indeed, require, 'to engage with the wider world'. Not only does this say something about the need for high levels of education for the population, but it implies that the curricula involved need to reflect both global and local needs. We can also infer that, due to the reflexive, and therefore dynamic, nature of globalisation, people need to engage in life-long education in order to participate fully in social life. The importance of opening education to this challenge may be self-evident, but it is worth emphasising in this context.

Future forms of open education are likely to be facilitated by the processes of globalisation in terms of curricula and educational technology. We shall pursue the latter in the next section in more detail; however, it is worth stating that forms of international collaboration, joint course development, materials sharing, etc., are not only features of globalisation in themselves but also generally contribute to what might be called global curricula to the extent that they reflect global (as well as local) interest and knowledge. Globalisation, through its forms of communication and through what is communicated – especially in education, news and 'infotainment' – not only creates the conditions of a global present (that is, the immediate and current), but it also (re)creates a global past (that is, the cultural base). Therefore, globalisation also concerns the development of what might be called a locally or individually interpreted globalised culture. No longer does/can education teach principally about the local; it must engage with global information, issues and concerns. The further opening of education to the global, especially through the use of new forms of educational technology, seems inevitable.

OPENING THE CLASSROOM THROUGH TECHNOLOGY

In his manifesto for *The Emerging Worldwide Electronic University*, Parker Rossman pursues the theme articulated by James Hall (Chapter 2) and Andrew Robinson (Chapter 3) from a global perspective. Rossman is concerned that educators generally have not engaged positively with the new communications technologies that are driving global business and government. He concludes:

> We have come to the end of an era in which colleges can be 'bounded by a wall with a narrow gate' that keeps out all but a few who can afford high costs, when all students are kept 'in one place at one time', sharing finite resources and faculty and when they leave their education stops. But will universities join to plan the new era or leave it to others?
>
> (Rossman, 1992, p. 143)

His book is valuable for its reviews of an extensive range of cases, research reports and theoretical discussions relating to the use of computer networks in teaching. It assumes and asserts that universities and their teaching staff will resist these changes, but there is little analysis of why this pedagogical conservatism should persist. He dismisses 'traditional distance education' as part of a correspondence era which has now been superseded by electronic technologies (ibid., pp. 5–12). His dismissal comes without any detailed review of the substantial body of work in the field and is based almost exclusively on North American experience.

Rossman's failure to recognise the practical, research and theoretical work produced by the distance education community is as much a problem for the distance educators as it is for the validity of his own analysis. The work most germane to his project is that dealing with the development of various media – including, and especially, print – by distance educators. Bates (1991), Garrison (1985) and Nipper (1989) have traced the emergence of 'three generations' of educational technology and demonstrated how the various media have been used in an interrelated manner (Evans and Nation, 1993b, pp. 202–4). Rossman seems to regard the non-electronic technologies as part of what must become a bygone era. In fact, it is necessary to explain how the educational technologies that have been successively conventionalised in distance education can be part of a transition to the use of the new technologies elsewhere in education. Those in distance education who have made the earlier transition have some important lessons to teach.

Many within the distance education community have realised the potential for applying techniques developed within their own sphere to campus-based education (Evans and Nation, 1993a, pp. 1–27; 1993b, pp. 209–14). While views are far from uniform within the distance education community about how these developments could and should occur, the concluding comments by Ian Mugridge and James Maraj at a symposium convened by the Commonwealth of Learning and University Grants Commission of India reflect a prevailing international consensus:

> there may come a point at which there is no longer any significant division between distance and conventional education, when university education – as indeed that at other levels too – will be conducted by different means at different times and places according to the requirements of different groups of students and the resources available to different institutions. This trend is reinforced by what seems to be a worldwide tendency towards the enrolment of growing numbers of mature and part-time students and towards a growing use of various types of educational technology. Increasingly, the serving of the former and the use of the latter are coming to be seen as legitimate activities for all institutions rather than merely for the open universities that pioneered the more advanced kinds of distance education.
>
> (Mugridge and Maraj, 1992, p. 154)

This, in other words, is essentially the same judgement as Rossman's conclusion. It also reflects the theme of Hall's discussion, in which he illustrates his case with an extensive practical analysis of developments within his own university.

In their recent book, *In Search of the Virtual Class*, John Tiffin and Lalita Rajasingham (1995) offer a comprehensive discussion of the possibilities of employing the new communications and computer technologies in education at all levels. Their analysis is based on extensive practical experience in broadcasting and education, in almost all corners of the earth. It employs a theoretical framework which synthesises post-McLuhan communication studies, accounts of the 'information society' following in the wake of Daniel Bell, learning theories – especially those influenced by Lev Vygotsky – educational history, computing and futures studies. They have also tested many of their ideas in research work in schools, universities and workplaces.

Tiffin and Rajasingham's fundamental purpose is to present models of education that would be possible by the beginning of the twenty-first century. They advocate the creation of 'the virtual class' which will have its technological basis in 'cyberspace' rather than in a classroom on a campus. The technical basis for an effective virtual class is emerging, but is not yet established as part of the infrastructure of even the most advanced societies. This does not prevent the authors offering detailed blueprints of the hardware – and the software and ideas required to make it effective – needed to shift learning from the classroom into other educational spaces, the home and the workplace. They are careful to recognise that earlier attempts to reform education through the use of communications technologies have had very limited success. The postal system was the basis for correspondence education for those unable to attend a school. Film and radio promised much in the 1940s and 1950s and then settled on the instructional periphery. Likewise for television in the 1960 and 1970s and computers in the 1980s (Tiffin and Rajasingham,1995, p. 87).

Their approach is founded upon a deep respect for the classroom as a fundamental context for teaching and learning. Expressed in terms of their own communications theory, the classroom has the following advantages:

> It is a broadband, multisensory, multi-media communication system. It is possible to have a symbiotic relation between human memory and artificial memories and to turn quickly to knowledge that is in written form ... there are support and control systems and designs that are based on experience. What may also explain its survival is the way the classroom is integrated with the education systems of the home and the workplace. It works not just because it is an effective communications system for instruction, but because it is a keystone of society.
>
> (Ibid., p. 70)

Tiffin and Rajasingham express the conventional judgement about distance education: it has been essentially correspondence education, a 'second-class education tied to notions of deprivation; good enough for people on the periphery of society' (ibid., p. 89). The weakness of correspondence education is its 'lack of interactivity', the extensive time delay in communication between teachers and students. They concede that occasionally, 'correspondence courses achieve standards in clarity of exposition, organisation of content and instructional design which would be exceptional in classrooms' (ibid., p. 89). Distance educators are now adopting telecommunications technologies to improve their interaction and they are 'more aware of technological changes' than their classroom-based colleagues. Indeed, 'they are being transformed into telelearning systems' (ibid., p. 89).

Many of the chapters in this book demonstrate that these judgements are made on the basis of scant consideration of practical work by distance educators. Also, Tiffin and Rajasingham have chosen to ignore a vast body of easily accessible published research and theoretical work relating to distance education. Indeed, their review of correspondence education rests on one reference to Otto Peters. We would argue that there is much to learn from the literature of distance education, as other educators seek to open their practices beyond the campus classroom, using new computer and communication technologies.

SOME LESSONS FROM DISTANCE EDUCATION

Students, teachers and administrators involved in distance education have always had to face up to the practicalities of teaching and learning being located away from the campus. From their inception in the nineteenth century, the various forms of distance education have been regarded as alternatives to the 'real education' provided in schools, colleges and universities. A very important aspect of all forms of distance education has been the importance of the home as the primary site for students' learning. Teaching has also occurred in the home in the sense that it has been incorporated in the teaching materials provided to students. In another important sense the teaching has also been campus-based, given that the teachers have generally been gathered together at a central site to produce the teaching materials and to provide complementary teaching to their far-flung students. Distance education, therefore, uses space very differently to campus-based education: teachers and students do not need to be co-present for teaching and learning to occur. In recognising this, it is important to understand that all learning does not take place in the presence of teachers in campus-based education. Students in primary and secondary schools pursue their studies outside of the classroom as 'homework' and in libraries or other resource centres. University students are expected to undertake significant amounts of private study. This may occur in libraries or other study areas on campus or in their own residences on or off the campus (Nation, 1995, pp. 26–8).

As we move towards the twenty-first century there are the prospects of the home and the workplace becoming more significant as sites of education. This is not to suggest the sudden demise of the massive systems of education that commenced their development in the nineteenth century and have continued to grow throughout the twentieth century but, rather, to recognise that economic, political and social changes are occurring that encourage the growth of alternatives to campus-based education. It is now established that the computing, broadcasting, film, publishing, music, theatre and telecommunications industries have now merged organisationally and technologically. There is a 'knowledge' or 'information' industry which produces, distributes and sells ideas and communications services. It is a global industry. The industry regards education as one of its most important markets. This is a simple extension of the roles achieved in education by book, journal and magazine publishing and audio and video production by the 1980s: the provision of much of the basic information required by students through direct sales or via lending agencies. There are profound implications for education in the likely changes in the means by which knowledge is going to be distributed. Printed sources will remain very important because of their flexibility and cost advantages but various formats, based on digital technologies, are becoming ever more important on the 'distribution side'. This is likely to progress most rapidly in the domain of the library.

Rob Walker (1993) has explored these changes from an educational perspective on the basis of Nicholas Negroponte's theory of the convergence between broadcasting, computing and print publishing (Brand, 1988, p. 10). For Walker, the convergence is between computing, education, the media and publishing (Walker, 1993, p. 19). The crucial aspect of the combination, for Walker, is the fact that information can be provided in recorded rather than broadcast form. Of course, strictly speaking this principle relates to the audiovisual media. Print media have been a very effective form of information storage for centuries and a very cost-effective method since the end of the nineteenth century. Walker envisages the possibilities of learners having access to teaching materials in multiple media whereby the 'educational model is the student as editor' and within which students 'have to create a text which makes sense to them' (ibid., p. 29). Nevertheless, while Walker seeks forms of distance education that allow students to work at home and in the workplace without feeling alienated from their teachers and fellow students, sophisticated recorded media do not facilitate effective and chronic communication with their potential partners in learning. The telephone is a partial solution. Electronic mail and other forms of computer-based communication will be more effective ones. Even their advocates such as Tiffin and Rajasingham and Bill Gates (1995) are careful to point out that they may be daily realities in the cutting edges of business and education, but they will only move into the domestic sphere on the back of the entertainment industry.

Just as the location of teaching and learning is likely to change so is the timeframe within which they occur. We do not have the opportunity to provide an extensive discussion of all the ramifications of these changes and have chosen to focus next on an analysis of theories and policies associated with the terms 'lifelong education' and 'educational technology'.

OPENING EDUCATION TO THE KNOWLEDGE AND INFORMATION FUTURES

These specialised discussions are premised upon theories of societal change that understand 'knowledge' or 'information' as central forces. Four decades of scholarship within and between a variety of disciplines has reached this consensus, at the most general level. There is much less agreement on the detail of the explanations. These issues have been important for public intellectuals and the works of Barry Jones and Peter Drucker have been influential in these debates. For Drucker the 'post-capitalist society' is based upon a knowledge economy and is moving towards a 'knowledge society'. Knowledge is the most 'basic economic resource', Drucker argues, following the germinal ideas of Fritz Machlup and Daniel Bell (Bell, 1973; Drucker, 1993, p. 8; Jones, 1995, pp. 175–8; Machlup, 1962, 1980). The means of production, as conceived by conventional economics – capital, labour and natural resources – are very important, but it is knowledge that transforms them into technologies and, thus, knowledge which is fundamental (Drucker, 1993, pp. 6–9, 19–24).

In the early eighteenth century, Drucker contends, a 'radical change in the *meaning of knowledge*' occurred. Until then 'technological knowledge' did not exist. Knowledge, hitherto, was the sole province of scholars who rigorously pursued wisdom either for self-enlightenment or to exercise intellectual leadership. Acquiring and maintaining knowledge was not about 'doing', 'utility' or engaging in production. Those engaged in utilitarian pursuits acquired skills; they learned on the job and learned only about the job. The knowledge revolution occurred when the techniques of scholarship – rigorous collection, analysis and distribution of knowledge – were applied to the skilled occupations (Drucker, 1993, pp. 24–44). In short, technical education created the means for technological innovation.

Successful firms are those which emphasise research and development and the training of their workers. Such firms employ 'knowledge workers' who 'possess a substantial amount of formal knowledge, formal education, and the capacity for continuous learning' (ibid., p. 73). Fundamental to this is the cultivation of extreme specialisation in education and training. For Drucker it is the emergence of a professional class of managers who have provided the leadership and organisational forms that have fostered these developments. This began with the harnessing of F. W. Taylor's scientific management and has continued with the 'quality movement'. McIlroy and Walker (Chapter 11) have discussed how these ideas have influenced university administration recently and their potential for creating improved efficiency in distance education.

Drucker is ambivalent about the importance of general or liberal education. He concedes that an undergraduate degree is the accepted minimum qualification for knowledge workers, but claims that most graduates complain about the irrelevance of their degrees to their work and lives generally, yet endorse a liberal education for the rising generation. He has abandoned the belief that liberal education can unite the specialists and advocates, lamely, that the specialists should strive to understand each other (Drucker, 1993, pp. 216–17).

The educational manifesto for the knowledge society has '*process knowledge* – something schools have rarely tried to teach', at its centre, '[i]n the knowledge society, subjects may matter less than students' capacity to continue learning and their motivation to do so. Post-capitalist society requires lifelong learning' (ibid., p. 201). Educational institutions will no longer hold a monopoly on education and training, they will become partners with firms to make provisions in the workplace and in the school (ibid., pp. 206–7). Drucker advocates an 'educational system' that is 'open-ended', allowing people 'to enter its stages at any age' (ibid., p. 205). In this regard, he mentions Britain's Open University as one of the beginnings of these developments but he fails to recognise anywhere that teaching and learning can occur outside classrooms. As is evident from this book, and from our previous argument, it is very difficult to imagine opening education to the sorts of possibilities Drucker envisages without 'going the distance' and making connections to distance education. However, education, including forms of open and distance education, are no longer the only 'engines' of the knowledge industry, so there is not only a need to step beyond the classroom, but even beyond all forms of contemporary education, to glimpse the future.

The most profound implications of the knowledge industry for education are related to its increasingly dominant role in the economy. The industries based upon the production and distribution of information are becoming the major source of well-paid employment. They will be of fundamental importance in servicing those industries that have employed technologies to produce goods with a minimum of highly skilled labour.

Jones is concerned fundamentally with the relationship between employment and technological change. It is through successive innovations in technology that humans, organised in societies, have been able to deal more effectively with their needs for survival by freeing more and more of themselves progressively from manual labour and moving them to mental labour. Based upon a thorough review of production and employment statistics Jones concludes:

> Just as agriculture declined as a major employer in the nineteenth century to enable expansion in manufacturing to occur, as manufacturing declined as a major employer in the twentieth century to enable expansion in services to occur, it now seems inevitable that market-based service employment will decline rapidly – in exactly the same way, and for exactly the same reasons – due to the introduction of miniaturised, sophisticated, low-cost technology. We seem likely to pass through a post-service revolution into a post-service society which could be a golden age of leisure and personal development based on the co-operative use of resources. . . . But if we do not choose this option, and if things are allowed to drift, economic power will become even more unequally divided than it is now, resources will be the subject of a bitter struggle between the strong and the weak, and prolonged, massive unemployment will traumatise society.
>
> (Jones, 1995, pp. 5–6)

A very important aspect of Jones's analysis deals with the use of time, within and without the labour force (ibid., pp. 14, 77–80, 118–24, 153–6, 160–4, 203–13). An important means of reducing the numbers of people in employment has been the reduction in time of the normal working week, working year and working lifetime. The working week in developed countries declined from 80 to 60 hours during the nineteenth century and from 60 to 40 in the first half of the twentieth century. Internationally the 40-hour week remains the norm, with some white-collar occupations working 35 to 36 hours a week. In certain occupations, especially in economic booms, it is conventional for workers to work longer hours of paid or unpaid overtime. The rapid rise of part-time work is also a *de facto* means of shortening the normal working week. The working year is determined by the length of weekends, the number of public holidays and the amount of recreation and sick leave. In Australia the working year is about 230 days, it is slightly longer in Asia and North America and a little shorter in Europe. It seems to have stabilised at these levels.

The most substantial reductions in working time have stemmed from the reduction of the working lifetime. The norm was once fifty years and there is evidence of a movement towards thirty-five years. In the nineteenth and twentieth centuries the major contributions to this reduction came from the statutory abolition of juvenile labour and the steady rise of mass education. Another contributing factor was the removal of married women from the workforce, often by statutory means, from the late nineteenth century until the first economic impact of the resurgence of women's movement in the 1960s. In 1964, the ratio of male to female workers in Australia was 71:29; thirty years later it was 58:42 (Jones, 1995, p. 122). A large proportion of the increasing numbers of women in paid work have been engaged in part-time jobs. In recent years there has also been an increase in part-time work for men; this often occurs in the wake of a 'redundancy package' taken voluntarily or compulsorily in late middle age.

In industrialised countries participation in schooling until the age of 16 is now universal. Participation beyond that age varies internationally. In Europe, Japan and North America it is almost 100 per cent and it is moving towards this in many others (Jones, 1995, pp. 153–4). Participation in post-secondary education is also rising. In Canada and the United States, 55 and 60 per cent respectively of the 20- to 24-year age group are involved. Most industrialised countries have about 30 per cent of this age group participating. The rise in the participation rate since the 1960s has been substantial. For example, in Canada it has risen from a base of 16 per cent, and in France it rose from 7 to 30 per cent. In Japan the shift was from 9 to 29 per cent. Indeed, the United States was the only country where rates rose from a relatively high base – 32 per cent in 1960 (ibid., p. 159).

The social structural implications of these changes in the pattern of employment in post-industrial societies and their education systems are very interesting when brought into sharp relief. Adults between the ages of 24 and 55 are expected to bear the burden of paid work and they support the rising generation occupied in education as a preliminary to working life and an 'older generation' who are retiring from work earlier and living longer. Adding structural stress to this social system is the ever-increasing need for workers in full-time employment to maintain and expand their knowledge base to keep pace with rapid changes in their working life. Individuals, organisations and whole societies are faced chronically with the need to restructure the time allocated to family life, leisure, citizenship, education and work. Dealing with this, in a planned, semi-planned or unplanned fashion on a daily or weekly basis, is no longer effective; the emphasis must shift to a time-frame based on the whole of life, with regular reviews on annual, weekly and daily bases.

In attempting to come to grips with these issues Jones has constructed a model that identifies 'five educational revolutions' which have occurred since the late nineteenth century, with their basis in the industrialising societies of 'the West' (Jones,1995, p. 150). It commences with *Universal primary education, 1870–1900*, in which the emphasis was placed upon basic literacy and numeracy and discipline attuned to the timetable of the factory system. *Universal secondary education, 1945–90* took longer to establish and attempted both to increase access to tertiary education and to provide a more substantial foundation in literacy, numeracy, general, scientific and vocationally useful knowledge for all. The third phase is still under way, *Universal tertiary education, 1970–2010*. This revolution saw the end of the university as an elite institution and the constant struggle to resolve the balance between academic and vocational education, while expanding opportunities for widespread partici-pation. We have just entered, Jones believes, an era of *Lifelong education, 1990–2030*. 'Labour market changes will be increasingly dynamic and educa-tion can no longer be static', personal development will become very import-ant and 'education must be a whole-of-life experience' (ibid., p. 151). The fifth revolution does not have a specific timeframe and is titled grandly, *The global dimension: 'lifelong education for all' in the Third World*. Essentially, this is a UNESCO plan to bring culturally and economically appropriated aspects of the four revolutions in the West or the 'North' to the 'South'.

PROSPECTS FOR LIFELONG LEARNING

In the late 1960s educational theorists and policy-makers concerned with the development of education systems internationally began to turn their atten-tion to 'lifelong education' (CERI, 1973; Faure *et al.*, 1972). These thinkers argued for structural reform rather than further expansion of the systems which, in developed countries, were already providing for most of the eligible age group at the primary and junior secondary stages of education and moving towards mass provision in the senior secondary and post-secondary stages. Their emphasis was upon the educational needs of the 16–19 age group, especially those who were not intending to enter university and required an education as a preparation to entering the workforce. While they recognised that further expansion of post-compulsory education would be costly, the difficulties of financing expansion were not the major concern. They argued that a full-time education until 18 or 21 years of age could no longer be regarded as a preparation for life. Basic knowledge was increasing and changing at such a rapid rate that even a schooling based on 'the concept of "learning to learn"' would be unable to provide young people with the capacities to maintain an understanding of it without further intensive education (CERI, 1973, pp. 9–10).

The first wave of theorists and policy-makers concerned with lifelong learning and lifelong education succeeded in getting the terms, and the issues associated with them, on policy, theoretical and research agendas. However, there is no evidence of the adoption of their terms and ideas as central matters in the restructuring of education systems. At the broadest level, the expansion of higher education to mass systems in most developed countries throughout the 1980s and 1990s supports this view. The 18–21 age group has been incorporated substantially into full-time post-secondary education, with a minority in long- and short-term training schemes and a small remainder making up a large proportion of the unemployed labour force. A second wave of thinkers have been revisiting lifelong learning and lifelong education in recent years, and advocate using the terms and associated ideas as fundamental tenets in systemic reform.

Before reviewing some examples from the second wave it is important to give some attention to the germinal document of the first wave, *Learning To Be*, which was produced for UNESCO in 1972 by the International Commission on the Development of Education led by Edgar Faure. In thinking about the future, the commission advocated two fundamental concepts around which educational reform should occur: *lifelong education* and *the learning society*:

> If all that has to be learned must be continually re-invented and renewed, then teaching becomes education and, more and more, learning. If learning involves all of one's life, in the sense of both time-span and diversity, and all of society, including its social and economic as well as its educational resources, then we must go even further than the necessary overhaul of 'educational systems' until we reach the stage of a learning society.
>
> (Faure *et al.*, 1972, p. xxxiii)

The report placed great emphasis on opening up the structures of education systems, breaking down the barriers between types of education and encouraging teaching and learning outside schools and other educational institutions, especially in the economy. The commission believed there was the potential for great transformative power in new theories and practices of pedagogy, which stressed the active participation of learners, and 'new educational technologies' based on the audiovisual broadcast and recorded media and computers (ibid., pp. 105–44).

A quarter of a century later, there is no doubt that lifelong education, lifelong learning and educational technology have entered the discourse of policy and practice in many spheres of education. As we have seen already, it will take some time yet for these germinal ideas to develop. Now that these ideas are about to take their place in the wider world, it is instructive to return to their intellectual origins. This is not to suggest that all validity resides in classical beginnings or that concepts and theories are not refined by critical debate and research. To the contrary, it is to press a case for valuing such scholarly work. But why does it take a Drucker to shape these ideas into a message that 'business' and 'government' can understand? Indeed, it is both ironic and instructive that the Hawke Labor Government in Australia closed the Commission for the Future which had brought these ideas to the attention of the 'chattering classes', when simultaneously this same government was incorporating similar ideas into education policy in a quest to make Australia the 'clever country'. Jones had been a key figure in creating and promoting the Commission for the Future. Alex Butler's (1989) report to the Commission, *Lifelong Education Revisited: Australia as a Learning Society*, is a model of comprehensive critical scholarship and comprehensible policy advice.

The second wave of proponents has taken a keen interest in the prospects for using the 'new technologies' in lifelong education. As Robinson (Chapter 3) demonstrates for Europe, lifelong education has certainly emerged from the scholarly closet and hit the policy agenda. Likewise for Australia, where Philip Candy (1991), with an academic tome under one arm, has piloted lifelong learning very effectively on to the policy agenda for higher education (Candy *et al.*, 1994). It has to be recognised, however, that Candy and his committee were less than enthusiastic about the centrality of 'open learning and alternative delivery mechanisms' in achieving effective lifelong learning. Indeed, they deliberately ignored any detailed consideration of these matters. The 'lecture/discussion/seminar', they concluded, are still central but the new technologies are making 'inexorable encroachments'. From this viewpoint, educational technologies will have to be able to provide for the effective interaction amongst students and teachers necessary to foster 'a critical spirit' before they can effectively sustain lifelong education (ibid., pp. 148–9). Among others, we have been urging the distance education community to accept these challenges (Evans and Nation, 1989a, b, 1992). Many within the field have accepted this challenge positively, not the least of whom is Ross Paul (Paul, 1990a, pp. 89–90). There is impressive evidence from others that this is possible, as demonstrated by the recent work of two stalwarts of the second wave of lifelong learning, Arthur Cropley and Christopher Knapper. Knapper and Cropley (1991) have examined research and practice in university distance education and conclude that this field provides the most effective methodological basis for teaching and learning that occurs at home and in the workplaces – the primary sites of lifelong learners. The challenge now is to convince the sceptics that those who carry the stain of correspondence education can contribute theoretically and practically to the forms of lifelong education emerging in a global knowledge society.

CONCLUDING COMMENT

We contend above that many educational innovations are reflexively connected with changes, developments or innovations in other aspects of life. In some of our earlier work we argued for 'critical reflection' on the part of distance educators in terms of their theory and practice (Evans and Nation, 1989a). We would encourage a continuation of this professional reflexivity in the light of the policies and practices discussed in this book. Our earlier work was focused more on practitioners adopting a critical stance to their practices, especially in terms of what we saw as an emerging 'instructional industrialism' in distance education, which eschewed notions of dialogue in teaching and learning. This problem has not receded, but arguably can now be recast in terms of the globalisation of education, especially through the use and critical understanding of new computer and communications technologies. Indeed, this recasting can be seen in terms of the professional reflexivity of educators being informed by, and acting upon, the global educational context.

An important aspect of the challenge for future educational policies and practices is concerned with a deep engagement with technology. Such engagement needs to go beyond mistakenly viewing technologies as 'tools', especially when this is accompanied by a view of technology as a neutral entity – a product of 'objective' science. As we have argued elsewhere (Evans and Nation, 1993b, d), employing an educational technology is the art, science and craft of using a particular tool for educational purposes. Adopting this stance, it is important that practitioners and policy-makers are seen as people who actively shape technologies for their own educational purposes (and, indeed, in their own broader interests). Hence, the emerging globalised and globalising educational practices, which draw heavily on new computer and communications technologies, need to be understood as human and social constructions which have educational as well as broader political, social and economic and – sometimes – religious purposes.

The complexity of future educational endeavours points to a need for dialogue between researchers, policy-makers and practitioners, and across the various sectors, traditional disciplines and national contexts of education. It is all too easy to be consumed by one's own specific educational practice, in its particular context, and to ignore the potential contributions that could be made to, and from, other educational contexts. The irony here is that while the speed of change in computer and communications technologies is held to be rapid and accelerating, in education itself there is an apparently slow pace in change at the institutional, bureaucratic and practical levels. This is not a preface to a simplistic argument about the reluctance of educators to change, but rather an observation about the tensions that exist between education's purposes to preserve and sustain important traditions as well as to prepare people to construct their futures.

References

Aabenhus, O. and Kenworthy, B. 1993 *Development of Distance Education for 'Education for All'*, unpublished report to UNESCO, Paris.

Aabenhus, O. and Waast, S. 1994 *Capacity Building for Distance Education in Mongolia*, unpublished report to UNESCO, Paris.

Abe, D. and Wheelwright, T. 1989 *The Third Wave: Australia and Asian Capitalism*, Sutherland, NSW, Left Book Club Co-operative.

ACDP (Australian Committee of Directors and Principals in Advanced Education) 1988 *ACDP Response to 'Higher Education – A Policy Discussion Paper'*, Canberra, ACDP.

ACTU (Australian Council of Trade Unions) 1988 *Response to Federal Government Higher Education Policy Discussion Paper*, Melbourne, ACTU.

AIU (Association of Indian Universities) 1995 *University Institutions in India*, New Delhi, AIU.

Alaska Department of Education 1985 *SRA Survey of Basic Skills, Alaska Statewide Assessment Spring 1985*, Juneau, Alaska Department of Education.

—— 1986 *Results from 1981 CAT (For CCS)*, Juneau, Alaska Department of Education.

Alberta Advanced Education and Career Development 1995 *Vision for Change: A Concept Paper for the Development of a Virtual Learning System*, Edmonton, Alberta Education.

Alberta Education 1988 *A Vision for the Future Role of the Alberta Correspondence School – A Discussion Paper*, Edmonton, Alberta Education.

—— 1989 *1989/90 School Grants Manual*, Edmonton, Alberta Education.

—— 1995 *Technology Integration in Education – Discussion Paper*, Edmonton, Alberta Education.

Aldcroft, D. H. 1992 *Education, Training and Economic Performance 1944–1990*, Manchester, Manchester University Press.

Altbach, P. G. 1993 'The dilemma of change in Indian higher education', *Higher Education*, 26, 1, pp. 3–20.

Andersen Consulting 1995 *The Information Highway – Gallup Canada 1995 Survey – What Canadians Think about the Information Highway*, Ottawa, Andersen Consulting.

Andresen, L. and Nightingale, P. 1993 'Openness, distance and learner autonomy – turning an idea into reality in postgraduate professional education', *Media, Technology and Human Resource Development*, 6, 1, pp. 33–40.

Apple, M. W. 1990 *Ideology and the Curriculum*, New York, Routledge.

Aronowitz, S. and Giroux, H. A. 1988 'Schooling, culture and literacy in the age of Broken Dreams: a review of Bloom and Hirsch', *Harvard Educational Review*, 58, 2, pp. 172–94.

Ashby, E. 1966 *Universities, British, Indian, African*, Cambridge, Mass., Harvard University Press.

Atkinson, R. and McBeath, C. (eds) 1991 *Open Learning and New Technology, Australian Society for Educational Technology Conference Proceedings*, Perth, Australian Society for Educational Technology.

Australian Labor Party 1986 *Platform Resolutions and Rules*, Canberra, ALP National Secretariat.

AVCC (Australian Vice-Chancellors' Committee) 1988 *Excellence and Efficiency: The Vice-Chancellors' Response to the Green Paper*, Canberra, AVCC.

—— 1989 *Community Attitudes to Universities in Australia: A Qualitative Research Report*, Canberra, AVCC.

Baker, K. 1987 *Higher Education: Meeting the Challenge* ('The White Paper'), London, Her Majesty's Stationery Office.

Baldwin, G. 1994 'The student as customer: the discourse of "quality" in higher education', *Journal for Higher Education Management*, 9, 2, pp. 131–9.

Baldwin, P. 1991 *Higher Education: Quality and Diversity in the 1990s*. Policy statement by the Hon. Peter Baldwin, MP, Minister for Higher Education and Employment Services, Canberra, Australian Government Publishing Service.

Bangemann, M. 1994 *Europe and the Global Information Society – Recommendations to the European Council* (Bangemann Group Report), May, Brusssels, European Union.

Barache, J. 1988 'Total quality policy in distance education as a general process of innovation', *Epistolodidaktika*, 1, pp. 11–29.

Bates, T. 1991 'Third generation distance education', *Research in Distance Education*, 3, 2, pp. 10–15.

—— 1994 'Hello technology! Goodbye, distance teaching institutions', *Open Praxis*, 2, pp. 5–7.

BCA (Business Council of Australia) 1986 *Report on Education*, Melbourne, BCA.

—— 1988 *A Response to the White Paper on Higher Education*, Melbourne, BCA.

Bell, D. 1973 *The Coming of Post-Industrial Society: A Venture in Social Forecasting*, New York, Basic Books.

Bellow, S. 1987 'Foreword', in Bloom, A. *The Closing of the American Mind: How Higher Education has Failed Democracy and Impoverished the Souls of Today's Students*, New York, Simon and Schuster, pp. 11–18.

Bloom, A. 1987 *The Closing of the American Mind: How Higher Education has Failed Democracy and Impoverished the Souls of Today's Students*, New York, Simon & Schuster.

—— 1990 *Giants and Dwarfs*, New York, Simon & Schuster.

Bolton, G. 1986 'The opportunities of distance', *Distance Education*, 7, 1, pp. 5–22.

Boone, W. and Keough, E. 1994 'The challenge of providing equality of educational opportunities for secondary students in small schools in rural Newfoundland and coastal Labrador', *CADE/ACED Résumés des Communications/Abstracts*, Vancouver, Canadian Association for Distance Education, p. 16.

Botsman, P. 1988 'Post-binary arrangements and diversity of provision', in Harman, G. and Meek, L. (eds) *Australian Higher Education Reconstructed?*, Armidale, NSW, University of New England, pp. 35–48.

Bradbery, P. 1991 'The process is the content.' Paper presented at the 10th Biennial Forum, Australian and South Pacific External Studies Association, Charles Sturt University, Bathurst.

Brand, S. 1988 *The Media Lab: Inventing the Future at MIT*, New York, Penguin.

Brower, M. J. 1994 'The paradigm shifts required to apply TQM and teams in higher education', in Costin, H. I. (ed.) *Readings in Total Quality Management*, Fort Worth, Dryden Press, pp. 485–97.

Burge, L. 1988 'Beyond andragogy: some explorations for distance learning design', *Journal of Distance Education*, 3, 2, pp. 5–23.

Butler, A. 1989 *Lifelong Education Revisited: Australia as a Learning Society*, Carlton South, Commission for the Future.

Callan, P. M. 1994 'The gauntlet for multicampus systems', *AGB Trusteeship*, May–June, p. 17.

Campion, M. 1991 'Open learning: schooling and retooling society or deschooling and societal retooling?', in Atkinson, R. and McBeath, C. (eds) *Open Learning and New Technology, Australian Society for Educational Technology Conference Proceedings*, Perth, Australian Society for Educational Technology, pp. 65–75.

—— 1996 'The learning cult: reflections from Australia', *International Journal of University Adult Education*, 35, 1.

Campion, M. and Guiton, P. 1991 'Economic instrumentalism and the transformation of integration in Australian external studies', *Open Learning*, 6, 2, pp. 12–20.

Campion, M. and Kelly, M. 1988 'Integration of external studies and campus-based education in Australian higher education: the myth and the promise', *Distance Education*, 9, 2, pp. 171–201.

Campion, M. and Renner, W. 1995 'Goal setting, domestication and academia: the beginnings of an analysis', in Smyth, J. (ed.) *Academic Work*, Buckingham, The Society for Research into Higher Education and Open University Press, pp. 74–83.

Canadian Radio-Television and Telecommunications Commission 1995 *Competition and Culture on Canada's Information Highway: Managing the Realities of Transition*, Ottawa, Canadian Radio-Television and Telecommunications Commission.

Candy, P. C. 1991 *Self-Direction in Lifelong Learning: A Comprehensive Guide to Theory and Practice*, San Francisco, Jossey-Bass.

Candy, P. C., Crebert, G. and O'Leary, J. 1994 *Developing Lifelong Learners Through Undergraduate Education*, Canberra, Australian Government Publishing Service.

Carr, R. 1990 'Open learning: an imprecise term', *International Council for Distance Education Bulletin*, 22 (January), pp. 47–50.

Castro, A. 1993 'Distance education in Mongolia,' unpublished report to Australian International Development Assistance Bureau (AIDAB), Canberra.

CERI (Centre for Educational Research and Innovation) 1973 *Recurrent Education: A Strategy for Lifelong Learning*, Paris, Organisation for Economic Cooperation and Development.

Clark, B. and Haughey, M. 1990 *Evaluation of Year 1: Distance Learning Project North*, Edmonton, Alberta Education.

CMEC (Council of Ministers of Education, Canada) 1994 *Distance Education and Open Learning. A Report*, Ottawa, Council of Ministers of Education.

Coate, L. E. 1990 'TQM at Oregon State University', *Journal for Quality and Participation*, December, pp. 90–101.

Consensus Saskatchewan 1990 *Leading the Way: A Blueprint for Saskatchewan. A Report of the Distance Education Program Review Committee*, Regina, SK, Consensus Saskatchewan.

Corporate Higher-Education Forum 1990 *To Be Our Best: Learning for the Future*, Montreal, Corporate Higher-Education Forum.

Croft, M. 1993 'The Contact North project: collaborative project management in Ontario', in Moran, L. and Mugridge, I. (eds) *Collaboration in Distance Education: International Case Studies*, London and New York, Routledge, pp. 132–50.

Crosby, P. B. 1979 *Quality is Free*, New York, McGraw-Hill.

CTEC (Commonwealth Tertiary Education Commission) 1986 *Review of Efficiency and Effectiveness in Higher Education*, Canberra, Australian Government Publishing Service.

—— 1987a *Selected Higher Education Statistics*, Canberra, CTEC.

—— 1987b *Report for 1988–90 Triennium*, Canberra, CTEC.

Dale, B. G., Lascelles, D. M. and Plunkett, J. J. 1990 'The process of total quality management', in Dale, B. G. and Plunkett, J. J. (eds) *Managing Quality*, London, Philip Allan, pp. 3–18.

Dawkins, J. S. 1987a *Higher Education: A Policy Discussion Paper* ('The Green Paper'), Canberra, Australian Government Publishing Service.

—— 1987b *Budget '87 Information*, Canberra, Media Release – Department of Employment, Education and Training.

—— 1988 *Higher Education: A Policy Statement* ('The White Paper'), Canberra, Australian Government Publishing Service.

DEC (Distance Education Council) 1995 *Open Universities in India: Academic Programmes 1995*, New Delhi, DEC.

DEET–HEC (Department of Employment Education and Training–Higher Education Council) 1989 *The Report of the Joint Department of Employment, Education and Training/Higher Education Council Assessment Team on the Designation of Distance Education Centres for Australia*, Canberra, DEET–HEC.

Deming, W. E. 1986 *Out of the Crisis*, Cambridge, Mass., Massachusetts Institute of Technology, Center for Advanced Engineering Study.

Department of Communications, Canada 1983 *Educational Utilization of Telidon Delivered by Satellite, Sept. 1982/83. Report on the Northern Ontario Distance Education Project (NODE)*, Ottawa, Department of Communications.

Deshpande, P. M. 1994 'Quality enhancement activity at dual-mode distance education institutions in India: learning from each other', *Media and Technology for Human Resource Development*, 6, 2, pp. 119–24.

Dodds, T., Jenkins, J., Perraton, H. and Young, M. 1980 *Distance Teaching for the Third World: The Lion and the Clockwork Mouse; Incorporating a Directory of Distance Teaching Projects*, London, Routledge & Kegan Paul.

Drucker, P. F. 1993 *Post-Capitalist Society*, New York, HarperCollins.

Duger, H. 1993 'Non-formal education system in Mongolia', Government of Mongolia, Ministry of Science and Education (unpublished paper).

Duke, C. 1992 *The Learning University: Towards a New Paradigm*, Buckingham, The Society for Research in Higher Education and Open University Press.

Eaton, J. S. 1991 *The Unfinished Agenda: Higher Education in the 1980s*, New York, Macmillan.

Economic Council of Canada 1992 *A Lot to Learn – Education and Training in Canada*, Ottawa, Canada Communication Group.

EdCIL (Educational Consultants India Ltd) 1985 *Indira Gandhi National Open University Project Report*, New Delhi, Educational Consultants India Ltd.

Education and Manpower Branch 1995 *Legislative Council Brief: The Non-Local Higher and Professional Education (Regulation) Bill*, 18 October 1995.

European Commission 1993 *Growth, Competitiveness and Employment: The Challenge and Ways Forward into the Twenty-First Century*, Brussels, European Commission.

European Round Table of Industrialists 1995 *Education for Europeans: Towards the Learning Society*, a report by the European Round Table of Industrialists, Brussels.

European Union 1992 *The Treaty on European Union* (Maastricht Treaty), Luxembourg, Office for Official Publications of the European Communities.

Evans, T. D. 1989 'Taking place: the social construction of place, time and space and the (re)making of distances in distance education', *Distance Education*, 10, 2, pp. 170–83.

—— 1995a 'Globalisation, post-Fordism and open and distance education', *Distance Education*, 16, 2, pp. 256–69.

—— 1995b 'Matters of modernity, late modernity and self-identity in distance education', *European Journal of Psychology of Education*, 10, 2, pp. 169–80.

—— 1995c 'Thinking globalisation: issues for open and distance educators in Australia and the South Pacific.' Paper presented at the Open and Distance Learning Association Conference, Port Vila, Vanuatu.

Evans, T. D. and Nation, D. E. 1989a 'Critical reflections in distance education', in Evans, T. D. and Nation, D. E. (eds) *Critical Reflections on Distance Education*, London, Falmer Press, pp. 237–52.

—— 1989b 'Dialogue in practice, research and theory in distance education', *Open Learning*, 4, 2, pp. 37–43.

—— 1992 'Theorizing open and distance education', *Open Learning*, 7, 2, pp. 3–13.

—— 1993a 'Adapting classroom technologies for distance education: telematics in Victoria', in Numan, T. (ed.) *Distance Education Futures: The Proceedings of the Australian and South Pacific External Studies Association Biennial Forum*, Adelaide, University of South Australia.

—— 1993b 'Educational technologies: reforming open and distance education', in Evans, T. D. and Nation, D. E. (eds) *Reforming Open and Distance Education*, London, Kogan Page, pp. 196–214.

—— (eds) 1993c *Reforming Open and Distance Education,* London, Kogan Page.

—— 1993d 'Distance education, educational technology and open learning: converging futures and closer integration with conventional education', in Numan, T. (ed.) *Distance Education Futures: The Proceedings of the Australian and South Pacific External Studies Association Biennial Forum*, Adelaide, University of South Australia.

Faure, E., Herrera, F., Kaddoura, A.-R., Lopes, H., Petrovsky, A. V., Rahnema, M. and Ward, F. C. 1972 *Learning To Be: The World of Education Today and Tomorrow*, Paris, United Nations Educational, Scientific and Cultural Organisation.

Feigenbaum, A.V. 1983 *Total Quality Control*, New York, McGraw-Hill.

Field, J .1994 'Open learning and consumer culture', *Open Learning*, 9, 2 (June), pp. 3–11.

Finegold, D., Metarland, L. and Richardson, W. 1993 'Introduction', in Finegold, D., Metarland, L. and Richardson, W. (eds) *Something Borrowed, Something Learned? The Transatlantic Market in Education and Training Reform*, Washington, Brookings Institution, pp. 1–12.

Fiske, E. B. 1992 *Smart Schools, Smart Kids*, New York, Touchstone.

Fournier, L. and MacKinnon, K. 1994 *Educational Opportunities on Canada's Information Highway: The Use and Deployment of Communications and Information Technologies in Education*, Ottawa, Communications Development Directorate, Industry Canada.

Fox, S. 1989 'The production and distribution of knowledge through open and distance education', *Educational Training and Technology International*, 26, 3, pp. 269–80.

Friedman, M. 1962 *Capitalism and Freedom*, Chicago, University of Chicago Press.

Friedman, M. and Friedman, R. 1984 *The Tyranny of the Status Quo*, San Diego, Harcourt Brace Jovanovich.

Gardner, H. 1991 *The Unschooled Mind*, London, Fontana.

Garg, S., Vijayshree and Panda, S. 1992 'A preliminary study of student workload for IGNOU physics elective courses', *Indian Journal of Open Learning*, 1, 2, pp. 19–25.

Garrison, D. R. 1985 'Three generations of technological innovation in distance education', *Distance Education*, 6, 2, pp. 235–41.

Gates, B., with Myhrvold, N. and Rinearson, P. 1995 *The Road Ahead*, New York, Penguin.

Giddens, A. 1991a *The Consequences of Modernity*, Cambridge, Polity Press.

—— 1991b *Modernity and Self-Identity: Self and Society in the Late Modern Age*, Cambridge, Polity Press.

—— 1994 *Beyond Left and Right: The Future of Radical Politics*, Cambridge, Polity Press.

Gilmore, I. 1992 *Dancing with Dogma: Britain under Thatcherism*, London, Simon & Schuster.

Glines, D. 1995 *Creating Educational Futures*, Michigan, McNaughton & Gunn.

GOI (Government of India) 1960 *Third Five Year Plan 1961–66*, New Delhi, Planning Commission.

—— 1962 *Report of the Expert Committee on Correspondence Courses*, New Delhi, Ministry of Education.

—— 1968 *National Policy on Education*, New Delhi, Ministry of Education.

Green, D. G. 1987 *The New Right: Counter-Revolution in Political, Economic and Social Thought*, Brighton, Sussex, Wheatsheaf Books.

Grinyer, M. and Goldsmith, H. 1995 'The role of benchmarking in re-engineering', *Management Services*, October, pp. 18–19.

Gummesson, E. 1991 'Service quality: a holistic view', in Brown, S. W., Gummesson, E., Edvardsson, B. and Gustavsson, B. (eds) *Service Quality: Multidisciplinary and Multinational Perspectives*, Lexington, Lexington Books, pp. 3–22.

Guri, S. 1987 'Quality control in distance learning', *Open Learning*, 2, 2, pp. 16–21.

Guy, R. 1991 'Distance education and the developing world', in Evans, T. D. and King, B. (eds) *Beyond the Text: Contemporary Writing on Distance Education*, Geelong, Deakin University Press, pp. 162–3.

Halsey, A. H. 1992 *Decline of Donnish Dominion: The British Academic Professions in the Twentieth Century*, Oxford, Clarendon Press.

Harris, D. 1987 *Openness and Closure in Distance Education*, London, Falmer Press.

Hayek, F. A. 1967 *Studies in Philosophy, Politics and Economics*, London, Routledge & Kegan Paul.

—— 1978 *New Studies in Philosophy, Politics, Economics and the History of Ideas*, Chicago, University of Chicago Press.

Hewitt Research Foundation 1985 'North Dakota trial results pending', *Parent Educator and Family Report*, 3, 2, p. 5.

—— 1986 'Study of homeschoolers taken to court', *Parent Educator and Family Report*, 4, 1, p. 2.

HKCAA (Hong Kong Council for Academic Accreditation) 1994a 'Higher education 1991–2001: an interim report. Response from the HKCAA' (unpublished).

—— 1994b *Academic Programmes Guide 1994–1995*, Hong Kong, HKCAA.

Holt, J. 1982 *Teach Your Own*, Brightlingsea, Lighthouse Books.

—— 1991 *Learning All the Time*, Ticknall, Education Now Books.

Hornick, J. 1993 'Science instruction of home schooled teenagers', *Home School Researcher*, 9, 1, pp. 1–10.

IGNOU (Indira Gandhi National Open University) 1995 *Indira Gandhi National Open University: A Profile*, New Delhi, IGNOU.

Industry Canada 1994 *The Canadian Information Highway*, Ottawa, Industry Canada.

Information Highway Advisory Council 1995 *The Challenge of the Information Highway*, Ottawa, Industry Canada.

Irving, J. 1987 'Public perceptions of education: some comments on standards.' Paper presented at the 1st Joint Conference, Australian Association for Research in Education/New Zealand Association for Research in Education, University of Canterbury, Christchurch.

Jakupec, V. 1991 'Esoteric and exoteric concepts of quality in distance education.' Paper presented at the 10th Biennial Forum, Australian and South Pacific External Studies Association, Charles Sturt University, Bathurst.

—— 1993 *Das Fernstudium in Australien*, Geelong, Deakin University Press.

Jakupec, V. and Nicoll, K. 1994a 'Crises in distance education', *Higher Education Review*, 26, 2, pp. 17–32.

—— 1994b 'Legitimising policy analysis as research in Australian distance education', in Evans, T. D. and Murphy, D. (eds) *Research in Distance Education 3*, Geelong, Deakin University Press, pp. 180–92.

——— 1994c 'Open learning: politics or pedagogy', *Distance Education*, 15, 2, pp. 217–33.

Jarratt, A. 1985 *Report of the Steering Committee for Efficiency Studies in Universities*, London, Committee of Vice-Chancellors and Principals of Universities in the UK.

Jarvis, P. 1993 *Theoretical Principles of Distance Education*, London, Routledge.

Johnson, R. 1983 *The Provision of External Studies in Australian Higher Education*, Canberra, Commonwealth Tertiary Education Commission.

——— 1990 *Open Learning, Policy and Practice. Commissioned Report No. 4*, Canberra, National Board of Employment, Education and Training, Australian Government Publishing Service.

Jones, B. 1995 *Sleepers Wake! Technology and the Future of Work*, revised edition, Melbourne, Oxford University Press.

Joseph, K. 1985 *The Development of Higher Education into the 1990s*, London, HMSO.

Juran, J. M. 1989 *Juran on Leadership for Quality: An Executive Handbook*, New York, Free Press.

Karmel, P. (Chair) 1975 *Open Tertiary Education in Australia*, Canberra, Australian Government Publishing Service.

Kellner, H. and Berger, P. 1992 'Lifestyle engineering: some theoretical reflections', in Kellner, H. and Heuberger, F. W. (eds) *Hidden Technocrats: The New Class and New Capitalism*, New Brunswick, Transaction Publishers, pp. 1–23.

Kelly, M. and Smith, P. 1987 'Introduction', in Smith, P. and Kelly, M. (eds) *Distance Education and the Mainstream: Convergence in Education*, London, Croom Helm.

Kenworthy, B. R. and Russell, N. 1995 'Old technology–new solutions: educational radio for development in Mongolia', in Nouwens, F. (ed.) *Distance Education: Crossing Frontiers: Papers for the 12th Biennial Forum of the Open and Distance Learning Association of Australia*, Rockhampton, Central Queensland University, pp. 214–23.

King, B. 1989 'Educational development and the DECs.' Paper presented at the Australian and South Pacific External Studies Association Forum, Churchill, Gippsland Institute of Advanced Education.

Knapper, C. K. and Cropley, A. J. 1991 *Lifelong Learning and Higher Education*, second edition, London, Kogan Page.

Knowles, J. G. 1993 'Homeschooling and socialisation', Michigan, University of Michigan School of Education (press release).

Koul, B. N. 1994 'A case for collaborative "research and development" in distance education', *Media, Technology and Human Resource Development*, 6, 1, pp. 7–13.

——— 1995 'Trends, directions and needs: a view from developing countries', in Lockwood, F. (ed.) *Open and Distance Learning Today*, London, Routledge, pp. 23–31.

Lamontaigne, L. and Tobin, L. (eds) 1994 'Organizing distance between secondary schools – a contact North/Nord perspective', *CADE/ACED Résumés des Communications/Abstracts*, Vancouver, Canadian Association for Distance Education.

Le Monde de l'Education 1993, 205 (June), p. 41.

Lee, N. and Lam, A. 1993 'Overseas educational programmes in Hong Kong: competition or consortia', *Open Learning*, 8, 2, pp. 12–17.

Lewis, R. 1988 'The open school', in Paine, N. (ed.) *Open Learning in Transition: An Agenda for Action*, Cambridge, National Extension College.

——— 1989 'What is "quality" in corporate open learning and how do we measure it?', *Open Learning*, 7, 3, pp. 9–13.

Lewis, R. G. and Smith, D. H. 1994 *Total Quality in Higher Education*, Florida, St Lucie.

Lisewski, B. 1994 'The open learning pilot project at the Liverpool Business School', *Open Learning*, 9, 2, pp. 12–22.

Livingstone, K. 1988 'Recent commissioned reports on tertiary distance education in Australia: context and critique', *Distance Education*, 9, 1, pp. 17–28.

McGreal, R. 1994 'TeleEducation New Brunswick on the electronic information highway', *CADE/ACED Résumés des Communications/Abstracts*, Vancouver, Canadian Association for Distance Education, p. 40.

McGreal, R. and Violette, G. 1993 'Implementing distance education programmes in secondary schools', *Selected Readings, CADE '92 ACED*, Vancouver, Commonwealth of Learning & CADE/ACED, pp. 201–8.

Machlup, F. 1962 *The Production and Distribution of Knowledge in the United States*, Princeton, Princeton University Press.

—— 1980 *Knowledge: Its Creation, Distribution and Economic Significance*, Princeton, Princeton University Press.

McIlroy, A. and Walker, R. 1992 'Student and staff perceptions of quality in distance education: an investigation.' Paper presented at the 2nd Joint Conference, Australian Association for Research in Education/New Zealand Association for Research in Education, Deakin University, Geelong, November.

—— 1993 'Total quality management: some implications for the management of distance education', *Distance Education*, 14, 1, pp. 40–54.

Mahony, D. 1990 'The demise of the university in a nation of universities: effects of current changes in higher education', *Higher Education*, 19, 4, pp. 455–72.

Manitoba Education and Training 1993a *Annual Report*, Winnipeg, Manitoba Education and Training.

—— 1993b *Task Force on Distance Education and Technology*, Winnipeg, Manitoba Education and Training.

Marchant, G. 1993 'Home schoolers on-line', *Home School Researcher*, 9, 2, pp. 1–9.

Marginson, S. 1993 *Education and Public Policy in Australia*, Melbourne, Cambridge University Press.

Martin, B. 1992 'Symbolic knowledge and market forces at the frontiers of postmodernism: qualitative market researchers', in Kellner, H. and Heuberger, F. W. (eds) *Hidden Technocrats: The New Class and New Capitalism*, New Brunswick, Transaction Publishers, pp. 111–56.

Mason, R. and Kaye, A. (eds) 1989 *Mindweave*, Oxford, Pergamon Press.

Mazumdar, T. 1994 'India: government and higher education', in Neave, G. and van Vught, F. A. (eds) *Government and Higher Education Relationships Across Three Continents: The Winds of Change*, Oxford, Elsevier Science Ltd, pp. 128–49.

Mederos, C. R. 1985 'Radio ECCA: distance education for adults in Spain', *International Council for Distance Education Bulletin*, 8, pp. 37–42.

Meighan, R. 1984 'Home-based educators and education authorities: the attempt to maintain a mythology', *Educational Studies*, 10, 3, pp. 273–86.

—— 1988 *Flexischooling*, Ticknall, Education Now Books.

—— (ed.) 1992 *Learning from Home-Based Education*, Ticknall, Education Now Books.

—— 1993 *Theory and Practice of Regressive Education*, Nottingham, Educational Heretics Press.

—— 1995 *The Freethinkers' Pocket Directory to the Educational Universe*, Nottingham, Educational Heretics Press

Menon, M. B. and Joshi, V. 1990 'Distance education in India: a critical review', *Media and Technology for Human Resource Development*, 2, 3, pp. 135–45.

Menon, S. B. 1989–90 'A nation-wide distance education system', *Journal of Higher Education*, 15, pp. 41–53.

Mentor Role Committee 1994 *The Mentor Role at Empire State College*, Saratoga Springs, SUNY/ESC.

Mills, R. and Paul, R. H. 1993 'Putting the student first: management for quality in distance education', in Evans, T. D. and Nation, D. E. (eds) *Reforming Open and Distance Education*, London, Kogan Page, pp. 113–29.

Morgan, A. R. 1993 *Improving Your Students' Learning: Reflections on the Experience of Study*, London, Kogan Page.

Morris, P., McClelland, J. A. G. and Yeung, Y. M. 1994 'Higher education in Hong Kong: the context of and rationale for rapid expansion', *Higher Education*, 27, pp. 125–40.

Mugridge, I. and Maraj, J. A. 1992 'Distance education in single and dual mode institutions', in Mugridge, I. (ed.) *Perspectives on Distance Education: Distance Education in Single and Dual Mode Institutions*, Vancouver, Commonwealth of Learning.

Murgatroyd, S. 1993 'The house of quality: using QFD for instructional design in distance education', *American Journal of Distance Education*, 7, 2, pp. 34–54.

Naidu, C. G. 1993 'Some economic aspects of conventional and distance education systems in India.' Paper presented to Asian Association of Open Universities International Conference, Hong Kong.

Nation, D. E. 1990 'Open learning and the misuse of language: some comments on the Rumble–Lewis debate', *Open Learning*, 5, 2, pp. 40–2.

—— 1995 'Learning beyond classrooms', in Nation, D. E. (ed.) *Becoming an Independent Learner*, Churchill, Monash University, pp. 23–46.

NBEET (National Board of Employment, Education and Training) 1992 *Changing Patterns of Teaching and Learning: The Use and Potential of Distance Education Materials and Methods in Australian Higher Education*, Canberra, Australian Government Publishing Service.

NCERT (National Council for Educational Research and Training) 1966 *Education and National Development*, New Delhi, NCERT.

NDEC (National Distance Education Conference) 1989a *Agenda Papers: First NDEC Meeting, Paper No. 1*, Canberra, Department of Employment, Education and Training.

—— 1989b *Agenda Papers: First NDEC Meeting, Paper No. 2*, Canberra, Department of Employment, Education and Training.

New Brunswick Department of Education 1993 *Annual Report of the Department of Education*, Fredericton, New Brunswick Department of Education.

Nicholson, A. 1989 '"Quality of Service." Identification of the issues vital to providing a quality service.' Paper presented at the 33rd Annual Conference, European Organisation for Quality.

Nipper, S. 1989 'Third generation distance learning and computer conferencing', in Mason, R. and Kaye, A. (eds) *Mindweave*, Oxford, Pergamon Press, pp. 63–73.

Nova Scotia Education 1992 *Annual Report of the Department of Education for the Year Ending March 31, 1992*, Halifax, Nova Scotia Education.

Nunan, T. 1988 'Distance education, from margins to mainstream', *Unicorn*, 14, 1, pp. 3–9.

—— 1991a 'Responding to Dawkins' revolution – the case of distance education in higher education', *Unicorn*, 17, 3, pp. 17–26.

—— 1991b 'University academics' perceptions of quality in distance education.' Paper presented to the 10th Biennial Forum, Australian and South Pacific External Studies Association, Charles Sturt University, Bathurst.

Nunan, T. and Calvert, J. 1991 'Investigating quality and standards in distance education – an interpretation of issues.' Paper presented to the 10th Biennial Forum, Australian and South Pacific External Studies Association, Charles Sturt University, Bathurst.

OECD (Organisation for Economic Co-operation and Development) 1983 *Policies for Higher Education in the 1980s*, Paris, OECD.

—— 1985 *Education in Modern Society*, Paris, OECD.

—— 1986 *Education and Effective Economic Performance: A Preliminary Analysis*, Paris, OECD.

—— 1987 *Universities Under Scrutiny*, Paris, OECD.

Ontario Royal Commission on Learning 1994 *For the Love of Learning. Report of the Royal Commission on Learning*, Ottawa, Queen's Printer.

Panda, S.K. 1992 'Distance educational research in India: stock-taking, concerns and prospects', *Distance Education*, 13, 2, pp. 309–26.

—— 1995 'Research and development in open and distance education', in Singh, B. (ed.) *New Horizons in Distance Education*, New Delhi, Uppal, pp. 211–21.

—— (ed.) in press *Open and Distance Learning in India*, New Delhi, Sage.

Paul, R. H. 1990a *Open Learning, Open Management: Leadership and Integrity in Distance Education*, London, Kogan Page.

—— 1990b 'Towards a new measure of success: developing independent learners', *Open Learning*, 5, 1, pp. 31–8.

Perraton, H. (ed.) 1982 *Alternative Routes to Formal Education: Distance Teaching for School Equivalency*, Baltimore, Johns Hopkins University Press.

Pillai, C. R. and Naidu, C. G. 1991 *Cost Analysis of Distance Education: IGNOU (Indira Gandhi National Open University)*, New Delhi, IGNOU.

Piper, D. W. 1993 *Quality Management in Universities*, Canberra, Department of Employment, Education and Training.

Powar, K. B. 1994a 'The changing role of universities with focus on India.' Paper presented at the International Conference on the Open University System and Development, Nasik, India.

—— 1994b 'Higher education in India: historical perspectives, present status and outlook for the future.' Paper presented at the Indo-French Seminar on Higher Education, Paris.

Powar, K. B. and Panda, S. K. 1995 'Quality assurance in distance higher education', in Singh, B. (ed.) *New Horizons in Distance Education*, New Delhi, Uppal, pp. 175–88.

Prince Edward Island Department of Education and Human Resources 1993 *Annual Report for 1992/3*, Charlottetown, Prince Edward Island Department of Education and Human Resources.

Prosperity Initiative 1991 *Prosperity Through Competitiveness*, Ottawa, Steering Committee for the Prosperity Initiative.

—— 1992 *Inventing Our Future: An Action Plan for Canada's Prosperity*, Ottawa, Steering Committee for the Prosperity Initiative.

Pusey, M. 1991 *Economic Rationalism in Canberra*, Cambridge, Cambridge University Press.

Ramsey, G. A. 1989 *Report of the Task Force on Amalgamations in Higher Education*, Canberra, Australian Government Publishing Service.

Rathore, H. C. S. 1993 *Management of Distance Education in India*, New Delhi, Asish.

Ray, B. D. 1991 *A Nationwide Study of Home Education: Family Characteristics, Legal Matters and Student Achievement*, Seattle, National Education Research Institute.

Reddy, G. R. 1989 'The Indira Gandhi National Open University – case study', in Smith, K. (ed.) *Developments in Distance Education in Asia: An Analysis of Five Case Studies*, Paris, UNESCO and ICDE, pp. 111–27.

Reeves, M. 1988 *The Crisis in Higher Education*, Milton Keynes, Open University Press.

Reidlinger, D. and Weir, H. 1995 *The Information Highway and Canadian Education: Discussion of Issues and Policy Recommendations*, Vancouver, Ottawa and St John's, Canadian Educational Network Coalition, SchoolNet Advisory Board and Stentor Alliance.

Report of the Mentor Role Committee 1994 *The Mentor Role at Empire State College*, Saratoga Springs, State University of New York/Empire State College.

Restall, L., Bain, E. and Froese, C. 1987 'Taking the distance out of distance education. A regionalized approach', *DE by Design. Symposium Papers '87*, Edmonton, ACS, pp. 1–13.

Robbins, B. 1993 *Secular Vocations: Intellectuals, Professionalism, Culture*, London, Verso Press.

Roberts, J. M. 1995 'Towards excellence in distance education: national initiatives in the Canadian policy environment', in Koble, M. A. (ed.) *Towards Excellence in Distance Education – A Research Agenda: Research Conference Discussion Papers*, University Park, PA, The American Center for the Study of Distance Education, pp. 486–95.

Roberts, J. M. and Keough, E. (eds) 1995 *Why the Information Highway? Lessons from Open and Distance Learning*, Toronto, Trifolium.

Rosander, A. C. 1989 *The Quest for Quality in Services*, New York, Quality Resources.

Rossman, P. 1992 *The Emerging Worldwide Electronic University: Information Age Global Higher Education*, Westport, Greenwood Press.

Rumble, G. 1989 '"Open learning", "distance learning", and the misuse of language', *Open Learning*, 4, 2, pp 28–36.

Russell, B. 1916 *Principles of Social Reconstruction*, London, Unwin.

Russell, N. and Waast, S. 1994 *Non-Formal Distance Education for the Gobi Women's Project*, Paris, UNESCO (unpublished report).

Said, E. W. 1994 *Representations of the Intellectuals: The 1993 Reith Lectures*, London, Vintage.

Saskatchewan Education 1991 *Distance Education in Saskatchewan: Discussion Paper*, Regina, Saskatchewan Education.

—— 1992a *No Distance is Too Great: Report of the Minister's Advisory Committee on K-12 Distance Education*, Regina, Saskatchewan Education.

—— 1992b *Response to the Distance Education Discussion Paper*, Regina, Saskatchewan Education.

Saskatchewan Education, Training and Employment 1995 *Connections to a World of Learning: Saskatchewan's Multimedia Learning Strategy*, Regina, Saskatchewan Education, Training and Employment.

SCES (Standing Committee on External Studies) 1987 *External Studies in the 1988–90 Triennium*, published as Appendix 5 in Commonwealth Tertiary Education Commission *Report for 1988–90 Triennium*, vol 1, part 2, Canberra, Australian Government Publishing Service.

Schluchter, W. 1981 *The Rise of Western Rationalism: Max Weber's Developmental History*, Berkeley, University of California Press.

SCN (Saskatchewan Communications Network) 1995 *Annual Report 94/5*, Saskatoon, SCN.

Scurr, C. 1990 'Management services and total quality management', *Management Services*, July, pp. 16–18.

Sewart, D. 1983 'Distance teaching: a contradiction in terms?', in Sewart, D., Keegan, D. and Holmberg, B. (eds) *Distance Education: International Perspectives*, London, Croom Helm, pp. 46–62.

—— 1993 'Student support system in distance education', *Open Learning*, 8, 3, pp. 3–12.

Shavelson, R. J., Baxter, G. T. and Pine, J. 1992 'Political rhetoric and measurement reality', *Educational Researcher*, May, pp. 22–7.

Shyers, L. 1992 'A comparison of social adjustment between home and traditionally schooled students', *Home School Researcher*, 8, 3, pp. 1–8.

Singh, B. (ed.) 1995 *New Horizons in Distance Education*, New Delhi, Uppal.

Singh, B., Mullick, S. and Chaudhary, N. 1994 *Correspondence/Distance Education in India: An In-depth Study Covering the Year 1989–90*, New Delhi, IGNOU.

Sizer, J. 1986, 'Efficiency and scholarship: uncomfortable or compatible bedfellows?', *Higher Education Review*, 18, 2, pp. 45–54.

Smedley, T. 1992 'Socialisation of home school children', *Home School Researcher*, 8, 3, pp. 9–16.

Smith, D. 1993 *Parent-Generated Home Study in Canada*, New Brunswick, The Francombe Place.

Spanbauer, S. 1992 *A Quality System for Education*, Wisconsin, ASQC Quality Press Publications.

Stahmer, A., Bourdeau, J. and Zuckernick, A. 1992 *Technologies and Lifelong Learning*, vols 1 and 2, Ottawa, Steering Group on Prosperity.

Statistics Canada 1994 *Household Facilities by Income and Other Characteristics, 1993, Catalogue 13-218*, Ottawa, Statistics Canada.

Stoesz, D. and Karger, H. J. 1993 'Deconstructing welfare: the Reagan legacy and the welfare state', *Social Work*, 38, 5, pp. 619–28.

Sweet, R. 1989 'A new economics of education', *Unicorn*, 15, 3, pp. 11–25.

Thomas, A. 1994 'The quality of learning experienced by children who are educated at home.' Paper presented at the British Psychological Society Annual Conference, Brighton.

Thomas, N. A. and McDonell, D. J. 1995 'The role(s) of technology in minority group distance learning', in Roberts, J. M. and Keough, E. (eds) *Why the Information Highway? Lessons from Open and Distance Learning*, Toronto, Trifolium, pp. 185–99.

Tiffin, J. and Rajasingham, L. 1995 *In Search of the Virtual Class: Education in an Information Age*, London, Routledge.

Tilak, J. B. G. 1991 'Privatisation of higher education', *Prospects*, 21, 2, pp. 227–39.

—— 1993 'Financing higher education in India: principles, practice and policy issues', *Higher Education*, 6, 1, pp. 43–67.

Timmers, S., Bentley, M., Davies, C. and Yen, P. 1992 'Developing distance education business course for Hong Kong: a search for quality', *Quality in Distance Education: ASPESA Forum 91*, Bathurst, Charles Sturt University, pp. 482–92.

Townsend, P. L. and Gebhardt, J. E. 1986 *Commit to Quality*, New York, John Wiley.

UGC (University Grants Commission) 1972 *UGC Bulletin*, October 15, New Delhi, UGC.

—— 1993 *Upgradation of Correspondence Course Institutes to the Distance Education Mode*, New Delhi, UGC.

—— 1994 *Accreditation and Assessment Council: System and Modus Operandi*, New Delhi, UGC.

UGC (University Grants Committee) 1987 *Report to the Secretary of State on Universities' Response to the Jarratt Report*, London, UGC.

University of Queensland 1988 *Directory of Tertiary Courses in Australia: 1989*, St Lucia, Brisbane, School of External Studies and Continuing Education, The University of Queensland.

UPGC (University and Polytechnics Grants Commission) 1993, *Higher Education 1991–2001: An Interim Report*, Hong Kong, University and Polytechnics Grants Commission.

van Vught, F. A. 1993 'Towards a general model of quality assessment in higher education.' Paper presented at the 1st Biennial Conference and General Conference of the International Network of Quality Assurance Agencies in Higher Education (INQAAHE), Montreal, Canada.

Verstegen, D. A. 1990 'Fiscal policy in the Reagan administration', *Educational Evaluation and Policy Analysis*, 12, 4, pp. 355–73.

Viljoen, J., Holt, D. and Petzall, S. 1990 'Quality management in an MBA programme by distance education.' Paper presented at the Annual Conference, Australia and New Zealand Association of Management Educators, Palmerston North.

Walker, R. 1993 'Open learning and the media: transformation of education in times of change', in Evans, T. D. and Nation, D. E. (eds) *Reforming Open and Distance Education*, London, Kogan Page, pp. 15–35.

Walker, R. J. and Cull, M. 1994 'Eyeball to eyeball: team teaching distance students in the face to face mode.' Proceedings of 'Windows on the future', ICDE/DEANZ Conference, Wellington, New Zealand, May 1994.

Wei, R. and Tong, Y. 1994 *Radio and Television Universities: The Mainstream of China's Adult and Distance Higher Education*, Nanking, Yilin Press.

Wells, G. 1986 *The Meaning Makers: Children Learning Language and Using Language to Learn* , London, Hodder & Stoughton.

Wiggins, G. 1992 'Creating tests worth taking', *Educational Leadership*, May, pp. 26–33.

Worcester, K. 1989 'Ten years of Thatcherism', *World Policy Journal*, 5, 2, pp. 607–21.

Wran, N. 1988 *Report of the Committee on Higher Education Funding*, Canberra, Government of Australia.

Yadav, M. S. and Panda, S. K. 1995 'Distance education system in India: an appraisal of its effectiveness and feasibility.' Paper presented to the ICDE conference, Birmingham.

Index